THE CHAPEL IS ON FIRE

THE CHAPEL
IS ON FIRE

Recollections of Growing Up

Michael Levey

Jonathan Cape
London

Published by Jonathan Cape 2000

2 4 6 8 10 9 7 5 3 1

Copyright © Michael Levey 2000

Michael Levey has asserted his right under the Copyright, Designs
and Patents Act 1988 to be identified as the author of this work

First published in Great Britain in 2000 by
Jonathan Cape
Random House, 20 Vauxhall Bridge Road,
London SW1V 2SA

Random House Australia (Pty) Limited
20 Alfred Street, Milsons Point, Sydney,
New South Wales 2061, Australia

Random House New Zealand Limited
18 Poland Road, Glenfield,
Auckland 10, New Zealand

Random House (Pty) Limited
Endulini, 5A Jubilee Road, Parktown 2193, South Africa

The Random House Group Limited Reg. No. 954009

A CIP catalogue record for this book
is available from the British Library

ISBN 0–224–05156–3

Papers used by The Random House Group Limited are natural,
recyclable products made from wood grown in sustainable forests;
the manufacturing processes conform to the environmental
regulations of the country of origin

Typeset by Palimpsest Book Production Limited,
Polmont, Stirlingshire

Printed and bound in Great Britain by
Biddles Ltd, Guildford and King's Lynn

For

EMILY AND ROLAND

from their admiring, ever-loving G'pa

Contents

Foreword

All memoirs purport to tell the truth, and in that mine are no
different. Nowadays, however, we recognise the full force of
'jesting' Pilate's question: What is truth?

I was a prince in my childhood – but also a pauper.

As the steam slowly cleared from the bathroom mirror,
and by the time I could take a bath unassisted, I saw
reflected an Indian prince, simply clad in towelling cloak
and turban, the whiteness of which accentuated his sallow
skin and bright brown eyes. No, I would respond to any
knock or murmured enquiry from my mother outside the
door: No, I am not finished.

Only some years afterwards, and then without the aid of
mirrors, did I fall into the gutter. A tipsy, brawling couple
in Marseilles had bred me, beaten and abused me. I became
a skinny orphan who begged and wheedled to survive at all
in a squalid dockland environment.

Sooner or later – largely later – I had reluctantly to doff
the rags of the *gamin* and the robes of the prince. There was,
for one thing, the fact of my birth certificate. It named my
British parents, gave my father's occupation as Civil Servant,
Air Ministry, and showed that I was born on 8 June 1927 at
90, Kenilworth Avenue, Wimbledon, London, SW.

Before smiling too much at the tepid, safe reality, you
have to remember that 90, Kenilworth Avenue, Wimbledon,
more snug than smug in suburban south London, was new
to me on that summer day. I may have hesitated about
entering it. For a desperate few moments it was thought I

was born dead – as my mother never forgot, although she never mentioned the fact to me. But I lived. And when my consciousness awoke, and I began to use – of all my senses – the sense of sight, supreme to me, I thought it looked a brave new world, continuously exciting, continuously offering something beautiful or stimulating to enjoy. Already my imagination was at work; and only by its activity do I know that I am yet alive – enjoyably alive.

Many a contemporary book stated to be autobiographical strikes me as deficient, neglectful or forgetful, for whatever reason, in any realisation of the author's childhood. To protest that it was just 'ordinary' is patently a cop-out – perhaps a cover-up. Of course, there are, more often than is usually admitted, children who are dull. As adults they will be even duller, whatever exploits, frequently of a simple, physical kind, they claim, to give them interest. This is not a disquisition on dullness, but in my experience dull children, and certainly dull adults, are generally male. In the old-fashioned all-male school lie if not the origins then the fostering of what might be called dulling down. And in the exclusively all-male adult circle, the club or the society, it is preserved. There can hardly be a greater sign of immaturity than the need to belong to a group – the need so often exhibited by Anglo-Saxon men. Like the boor, the bore is generally masculine in gender.

I believe that there is nothing inherently 'ordinary' in the often prolonged process of growing from a child into an adult. In any case, I never felt my individuality to be other than extraordinary, in so far as I could judge the norm. From early on, I felt too that my personal circumstances had aspects of the unusual, for all the outward conformity my parents seemed anxious to display. I was very young when I first accompanied them to church on a Sunday morning. More vivid to me than any ceremony itself was the walk through empty streets. While most of our suburb or town slept, we would be on our way to Mass.

The actual walk I now see as significant of much else. It

was essential, especially to my father, that we attended Mass unfailingly. But the act should be as unobtrusive as possible. We were home in time to share the domestic Sunday routine of our neighbours: the roast joint at lunch, the lawn-mowing and weeding, all the pleasurably slow tempo of the single day of rest, as it wound down to tea and supper. Nothing should indicate that we had been out. Nothing showed in the downstairs rooms of our house that we were Roman Catholics. We held no family religious ritual except a brief, nearly gabbled grace at main meals. Nobody could have guessed how seriously my father fasted and abstained during Lent – nor how hard a penance that was for a man who loved his food, never smoked, or drank alcohol, but had a passion for sweets and sweet things. Close friends of his were seldom Roman Catholics, and some of them probably never knew of his profound yet unostentatious faith.

Religion as such was not discussed at home – any more than was sex. Yet the practical aspects of our faith were sharply and ubiquitously present. The location of the nearest Catholic church was a key matter when we went on holiday or moved house. The prerequisite of any school I might attend was that it must be Catholic. From the day of my baptism, which doubtless followed closely on my birth, I was enrolled as a member of the Roman Catholic Church. Thence it followed, regardless of discussion, let alone disagreement, that my creed was fixed for life and that any woman I married would be Roman Catholic, or at least would accept 'instruction' in that faith, and that any children of ours would be indoctrinated from infancy, exactly as I had been.

It no more occurred to my father, I understand now, that these things would not happen, subject to God's dispensation, than that he would go to the Air Ministry without wearing a white shirt and a dark suit. Presumably, it had been bred in him as the product of the large family of an Irish Roman Catholic father, though his English mother remained a practising member of the Church of England.

In that Church my own mother was also, vaguely, brought up. Her conversion to Catholicism was brought about by marriage to my father – a fact I was not aware of as a child.

Adulthood and, above all, parenthood forced me into reasoning for myself. Quite apart from my own beliefs, I could not and would not enrol any infant in a faith which it could discard, when it began to reason, only by risking pain and guilt and trauma. At once I experienced what such traumas are like. Nobody could describe what ensued as 'ordinary' or uneventful.

Lying largely beyond this book is a dénouement. It is less about how I lost my faith, and declined to have my daughter baptised, than about how I lost my father. Faith faded painlessly, like an insubstantial pageant, leaving no rack behind. Pain and shock accompanied the emotional estrangement between me and a man who had for so long appeared to be the perfect father: loving, generous, wise, perpetually good-tempered, and also outstandingly gifted mentally and physically. Always, he had been my bulwark, my benefactor, my idol. Though the evidence was there, I had failed to realise that where religion was concerned, his feet were not of clay but of iron – and so was his mind. He was unyielding, merciless almost, in the pressure he put upon me to bend to his wishes. Perhaps the Church of Rome is always proud of such adherence. I was bitterly disillusioned, and so of course was he. Buffeted and gravely weakened, some natural affection yet survived between us but it dwindled into being distant, constrained and too patently polite.

Years after his death, my mother made an unexpected, unprompted remark which I have never forgotten. To her he had been simply the ideal husband, loved – forever and rightly – for his myriad marvellous qualities. Speaking of attitudes to religion, she suddenly said, 'You know, I always thought all your aunts, and even your father, inclined to be intolerant.'

Foreword

None of my relations has any responsibility for my written recollections. Nor shall I be so bold or so foolish as to claim that my version is true – though it is true to my memory. I have not made a point of checking every fact, and once or twice I have preferred to change a name.

There are, however, three cousins of mine to whom I am affectionately indebted: Diana Levey first stimulated my interest in our Levey (O'Shaughnessy) heredity, kindly sharing with me her own discoveries about it; John Francis Levey has been notably generous in communicating his extensive research into the family, and he also very kindly undertook some research into my mother's family; Bernard Hoole has been part of my life from earliest childhood, and he has discussed numerous shared memories, correcting some of mine with characteristic acuteness. I appreciated his encouragement of this project, and I hope he will not object to his appearance in these pages.

I am very grateful to several friends who kindly listened to me and encouraged me from the first to put down some childhood memories on paper, and I must single out with particular gratitude Professor Christopher White, who generously read and helpfully commented on this book. I am also deeply indebted to Dan Franklin at Cape for his friendly faith in it.

My thanks go too to Caryl Yendell at Louth Secretarial Services, for kind interest as well as for expert coping with a messy manuscript.

MICHAEL LEVEY
Louth, Lincolnshire, 1999

Prologue:

God is Not Mocked

We were rehearsing scenes from *The Taming of the Shrew* on that Sunday evening at school, and as Katharina I was getting ready to slap the face of Wilson II as Petruchio when another boy burst into the room.

'Oh, sir, sir,' he exclaimed, almost colliding in his excitement with the tall, bony figure of our producer, who was also the ex-Headmaster. 'The chapel is on fire.'

After a moment of general disbelief and immobility, we all rushed to the windows. The Second World War was still on. It was inevitable that we should remember the drill of switching off the lights before opening the shutters in the black-panelled 'Black Room', blacker yet as a result.

There was no doubt about it. We could see at once, across the lawn and through the trees beyond, a fierce glow in the sky. Soon we were all dashing up the dark path to the walled kitchen-garden where stood the handsome, white-washed barn that was the chapel, its timbered roof a blazing mass of flame and sparks. For masters as for boys there was nothing to do but gaze, fascinated by the flaring spectacle, and await the arrival of the fire-brigade from some miles away, in Reading. It was slow or the roof burnt fast – or both. By morning the chapel was a sodden, smouldering ruin.

How on earth, everyone kept asking excitedly, could it have happened? There was no question of enemy action. It must have been a candle, the sanctuary oil-lamp, an electrical fault, even some careless cigarette in the vicinity.

I had my own suspicions, though I did not voice them

openly. And the matter was never finally settled. In any case, it was clearly an accident. I could agree about that. Even were I somehow involved, I had never intended to set fire to the chapel. I was devout, in my fashion, addicted to pious practices and certainly attached to appearing prominently as one of the chief servers during the celebration of sung Mass most Sunday mornings.

I think it was the Bursar, poking around among the charred rubble on the following Monday, who unearthed what resembled some *art nouveau* meteorite: a stream-lined slab of melted silver, which had been the fragile, filigree, thurible, the pepper-pot-shaped vessel holding charcoal and incense, which I, the thurifer, swung on its thin silver chains as I emerged from or exited to the sacristy.

Off-stage, as it were, we were always playing with fire. In addition to the thurifer were the two younger boys who served as acolytes. They carried giant, gilded candle-holders whose candles must be alight when the three of us re-entered the chancel as the choir began singing the *Sanctus*, signalling the most solemn portion of the Mass.

Because the chapel had originally been a barn, there was little space, no more than a narrow passage-way, between the chapel as such and the sacristy. It was there that we waited for our cue, chatted quietly and tended the various flames. As well as keeping an eye on the two acolytes, my task was to ensure that the charcoal in the thurible remained adequately hot through steady swinging. It had to be glowing satisfactorily when the trio of us swept back, for much business centred on the thurible.

Up on the altar steps, I raised the pierced top of it and proffered it to the priest celebrating Mass, who was usually the Headmaster. Gravely and gracefully, he would scatter some grains of incense over the charcoal. Absorbed as he was in the whole ritual of the Mass, he could yet indicate, by the slightest lift of a thin eyebrow, that the charcoal burned inadequately. When he swung the thurible towards the tabernacle, he expected gratifyingly fat clouds of incense to emerge.

Once Mass was over, and he had reverently folded away his vestments, the Headmaster resumed his secular role. He might want to have 'a word' with me, about the charcoal or about chatter he had detected, penetrating from the passage during Mass, before he left me to my last task: cleaning the dark, sticky interior of the thurible with a spent matchstick or two, after tipping the dead charcoal onto the soil outside the sacristy door.

That door opened directly on to the kitchen-garden of the old house which formed the school's main building. On sunny Sunday mornings, during the service, I liked to lounge at the doorway, in cassock and surplice (called by us a cotta), gossiping lazily with the two acolytes, giving an occasional swing to the thurible and trying not to forget our next entrance.

Everything seemed to induce reverie. Whiffs of incense were in the warm air, and the choir might be heard singing, invisible but near at hand. I looked out on the beds of lettuce and the neglected though still fruitful cages of raspberries, the yellow variety as well as the red. Against the brick wall of the chapel grew a peach tree, flowering in spring with delicate sprays of pink blossom. Its fruits were green and hairy, never becoming quite edible enough even for schoolboys in wartime.

More like an adult than a child in this, I found such tranquil moments made it only too easy to ignore the fact that a war was on, had been on for several years and showed no sign of coming to an end. From the day of its declaration, I had hated it. The siren wailing on that first Sunday morning symbolised my feelings. I anticipated disruption to my life and to that of my parents. Our settled existence, I thought, would never again be the same; and I was right.

Hardest of all to believe, as I lolled at the sacristy door and gazed at the familiar garden, was that the war would ever catch me up in it directly. I knew of its impact. I had been briefly in London during several air-raids. Older cousins of mine – female as well as male – were in the Forces. Boys I had known as seniors at school had disappeared, only to return on a visit in the glory of officers' uniform. When one of them won the MC, the Headmaster had it displayed in the Hall, on a piece of velvet. I failed, privately, to be thrilled, or inspired by anything except distaste, though inevitably I joined in the act of semi-adoration.

Wilson II, the Petruchio to my Katharina, was no longer strictly that, since his elder brother had left, to join the Navy. Wilson II's turn was coming, and he would be commissioned into a Rifle regiment. And then, astonishingly, my turn approached, without the war ending. I could scarcely believe the Headmaster was advising me about exactly which smart regiment to be commissioned into and about obtaining an interview in London. Had the country really been reduced to the point when it needed me to fight for it?

I could face anything except the future. Anyway, I should never have conceived the bizarre reality, however extravagant my imagination. The Army was to be fertile in situations improbable and absurd. I doubt if most novelists would dare devise the incident in which I next raised my hand to the one-time Petruchio, myself no longer the angry Shrew.

I was a mere rifleman, walking to my hut in a huge camp in the wilds of Wiltshire. Coming towards me was a Lieutenant, and my hand was up in salute before I realised that I was saluting Wilson II.

'Wake up,' one of the acolytes might have to hiss at me, jogging me out of reverie: 'We're on again.'

'Don't be cheeky,' I would probably reply, even before realising what he was telling me.

The giving – and the taking – of cheek, or 'lip', was part of everyday school routine. It had about it something of oriental etiquette, and without it we would have felt deprived. Younger boys were constantly accused of being cheeky to older ones, who might themselves cheek a master. To be cheeked implied you held a position. Indeed, as a prefect in a school of meagre numbers, in wartime conditions, the chief privilege was receiving cheek and rebuking it.

What was immediately important was for the thurifer to regain command. Flanked by my acolytes, as I thought of them, I had to re-appear from the sacristy speedily yet without betraying haste. For one thing, if we moved too fast, the acolytes' candles tended to blow out in the draught. More important was the consciousness that my big moment had arrived. Ritual demanded that the thurifer, unusually, turn his back on the priest, and on the Blessed Sacrament, and descend to the altar rails, looking towards the congregation. Po-faced, barely seeing in my determination not to catch any grinning boy's features, I had gravely to cense – left, right and centre – the assembled worshippers, who had risen for this act.

Normally, I felt not just quietly dignified but almost disembodied, superior in some spiritual way to the mundane world. But on that particular Sunday morning, I was already somewhat preoccupied, more than once recalling that I had accidentally given the thurible a considerable knock against the passage wall. Some charcoal might have fallen out, but my concern had been for the thurible itself, fortunately undented.

As a typically leisurely school Sunday unfolded, with the pleasant looming of the evening's rehearsal, I forgot to think about the incident – until we were so dramatically interrupted. And then it came back as I watched the chapel burn. I had an uneasy, queasy sense that this might somehow be my fault.

I needed to unburden myself, and I chose first the good-natured Chaplain. He thought it all so unlikely that I think I next told the Bursar, who was even more dismissive. He could not see how a piece of charcoal could have caused a fire that started in the roof, and only in the evening. In my obscure feeling of guilt, I failed to grasp that my recollections were not very welcome or very convenient. The important fact was that an accident had occurred. That was perfectly true. I could – and did – cease to think of myself as an unwitting arsonist.

Besides, the holidays were fast approaching. End of term was conventionally hailed as wonderfully liberating, but too much had changed, not least in physical circumstances, for me to feel any thrill. I certainly had no intention of confiding in either of my parents about the destruction of the chapel, and I anticipated long, empty days, deprived of the bustle and companionship of school, reading and walking by myself in the safe but odiously complacent environment of wartime Harrogate.

While not entirely clear about what a passage of arms was, I engaged in one with the Headmaster over the matter of war-work during the holidays. Several boys were going, joyfully, it seemed, to a farming-camp. Others were 'doing their bit' in different directions. What was I intending to do? The answer was brood – the natural state perhaps of any teenager. So desperate was I to avoid the farming-camp that I got my father to write something about my being unsuited to the labour. I explained unconvincingly to the Headmaster that once in Harrogate I should seek some part-time work. He had never cared for me. He said little, but I knew, in the way pupils do, that he was already meditating how to phrase his unfavourable comments in my next report.

Had I been writing such a report, I should have explained how deep was the damage inflicted on me by the war. Without any bombing, my home had gone. A comfortable suburban house and an intriguingly beautiful garden, giving an illusion of greater space than it possessed, ceased to be my home virtually as war broke out. My father's ministry, soon to be renamed more urgently the Ministry of Aircraft Production, was evacuated to Harrogate. Our furniture was stored, along with most of the items I prized as part of my personal existence.

At first it was supposed that the war would be over speedily. My parents had to find lodgings in Harrogate, itself contributing to the war effort by making the influx of strangers from the south feel as unwelcome as possible. My mother had to carry the burden of shopping and cooking in alien, awkward circumstances, and also bear most of the awkward social burden that inevitably arose from forced proximity.

As the war dragged on, so did we move on, from one house to another, living on sufferance, though we paid, in houses not built for sharing by two families. Whatever the problems, my presence during the school holidays compounded them. An extra bedroom had to be sought for me, but fitting me in emotionally was even harder. I was increasingly discontented at school and ill at ease in what passed for home. Each house might have been dubbed Elsinore; and in each I played the moodiest of Hamlets.

In time, the very journey to Harrogate, anyway lengthy from school in rural Berkshire, lost whatever interest it had originally had. Stopping over in wartime London became less attractive to me. Trains were delayed or diverted because of air-raids, and they seemed to grow more grimy and crowded on each journey.

However frequently I tried not to contemplate my future, it began to thrust itself forcibly upon me. There had never seemed much reality to the military games at school, when we dressed up in uniforms so antiquated that they included puttees and paraded as the Junior Training Corps (previously more ambitiously named the Officers' Training Corps). And, naturally, we smoked at school in a slightly aimless way as well as swearing now and then, rather consciously.

But I was unprepared for the assault of actuality when real soldiers, 'men' looking little older than myself, invaded the train and took over the carriage. For a while I saw them as merely the accompaniment to all wartime travelling. I shrank into my book and my corner, and on one journey early in the war, at the end of a summer term, my chief fear was that my straw boater, prominent on the rack, would be noticed. It seemed to flaunt my remoteness from the world of khaki forage caps and tin helmets which sealed the bulging kitbags that every man in his thick battle-dress had lugged on to the train and piled in the corridor.

Never had Harrogate seemed a more desirable destination. It was a relief to see my mother waiting anxiously on the platform, and she was unusually delighted by the sight of me in my boater. We walked out of the station talking cheerfully. A sneaky gust of wind caught the boater's brim and sent it bowling down the pavement: greetings from Harrogate.

More complex were my emotions on the journeys back, via London, to Berkshire. When I thought of the steadily approaching alternative of the Army, I suddenly had fits of affection for school. As the train swung into dingy Wakefield or Retford, the charm of the school's country-side surroundings overwhelmed me, regardless of my cool assessment of it as an institution. I might believe myself too old for the system, but I felt too young for the Army. I wished away the din and pressure of the huge boots tramping indifferently over my feet and over the butterfly fragility of my unfocused vision.

Like it or not, I was drawn, half-fascinated, into the coarse tent of fug immediately pitched by the soldiers invading my carriage. Sweat and smoke and blanco were not smells new to me. On JTC parades we all wore boots. But these boots were somehow bigger and blacker, and more threatening – and the smoke was stifling and the swearing so repetitive that in five minutes it no longer registered. From the first cheerful shout for an effing fag from among those sprawled, exhausted figures, to the demand to shut the effing window (its unwashed glass dimly labelled 'No Smoking'), they had established a compulsive, sharper, superior reality.

Only a few months more of war and I would no longer be making this journey. Instead, I began to descry, I should be in command of such men. Perhaps, too, I might return to school in uniform, to be welcomed by the Headmaster and to swank around, in a modest way, when the hour came for chapel.

The next time my mother met me at Harrogate station, I felt inwardly – if only momentarily – altered.

'How was the journey?' she asked, rather apprehensively.

'Effing awful,' I nearly replied.

My mother looked, for the first time, altered herself, thinner and more tired. I saw what I already knew: that the very existence of the war weighed on her by its duration. Hers was a tedious routine, with little to vary the round of shopping and the coping with rationing. My companionship was a doubtful aid, once the novelty of being 'home' had diminished. Not only did my father have important, interesting and highly topical work to engage him, but his whole temperament instinctively led him to make light of problems. The war would soon be over. We would return south. We might live on the Sussex coast. Meanwhile, he hid any fatigue he felt and was delighted that Harrogate offered one outstanding recreation, its gallant and lively repertory theatre. More cautiously, my mother would agree to go, providing the play was 'good'.

Comedy rather than tragedy was anyway my father's preference. Wartime Harrogate amused him as much as did the spectacle of jostling, ambitious colleagues and minor office politics. The town was never more excited than when rumours spread, as they often did, of a major occurrence: the Princess Royal was coming in from nearby Harewood House, to do some shopping.

Just once did a small bomb fall, by mistake, on Harrogate. I had not been there on the occasion, but I asked my father about it and the damage. He repeated the quip circulating in the Ministry:

'A toothbrush was dislodged in one of the bathrooms at the Majestic.'

It was a prominent cliff of a building, the hotel occupied predominantly by the richer old ladies.

I am sure my parents dreaded the sheer length of the holidays as much as I did. Perhaps, privately, they wished I had gone to a farming-camp. My mother and I were poor at raising each other's spirits, try as she at least might. Shrewder in this than my father, she detected my mood of world-weariness and detachment. She frequently told me to remember that one's schooldays are the happiest days of one's life. I groaned in response. Still, I forbore to point out the remark's implications for her own life. As her sole happiness lay in being married to my father, and nothing could shake that happiness, her statement struck me as phoney – like much that was then current.

The holidays after the chapel fire I particularly dreaded. I knew that the Headmaster's report would be unfavourable, though only in extreme fantasy did I envisage him accusing me of impious arson. Even then, I was convinced, my father would smooth away my mother's fears for my future, and the disappointment and the shame. To me he would speak gravely yet forgivingly: I must have had some reason for what I did; he was convinced I was not wicked by nature; he knew I would never do anything similar again.

It might have been better, as far as my mother was concerned, had the Headmaster accused me of arson. When the report arrived, it proved the usual mixed bag under subjects: *Maths*: has difficulty grasping much beyond the rudiments; *English*: excellent but must apply himself more; *Geography*: appears listless in class. 'I can't understand it,' my mother said, not for the first time. 'Your father is so brilliant at mathematics, and always was.'

But it was the last sentence of the Headmaster's overall comment, in elegant, admirably clear calligraphy, that did the harm. 'Unfortunately,' he wrote, 'his manner has become of late somewhat supercilious.'

'Oh,' my mother gasped across the breakfast-table in our borrowed dining-cum-sitting-room. 'What an awful thing to write. What can you have done?'

'Modelled my manner on his,' I replied.

But she was not amused.

'I don't know,' she went on, 'what your father will think. It seems such a pity when you could be so nice if you wanted, and the school is so good. By the way, that butter has to last us for the month.'

'Well, I'm off to the library this morning,' I said.

It was another admirable amenity of Harrogate's, where I could moon away whole mornings and return to lunch laden with books. As I had to cross the Stray, the wide expanse of common, to reach the library, I could also claim to have taken exercise.

My father had left much earlier for the terrace of houses occupied by the Aircraft Ministry. On that evening, in what I thought of as a thoroughly Ibsenish atmosphere, and before we sat down to supper, my mother indicated I should hand him my report.

'Look,' I began desperately, feeling the tension had got to us all. 'I'm not being expelled.'

'No, but wait till you see what the Headmaster says about his behaviour,' my mother said. 'I'm terribly worried.'

My father read quickly, almost impatiently, and then he smiled.

'I don't think it's too bad. You did well in English, and in French. Even your Latin seems—'

'But they call him supercilious,' my mother interrupted.

'Is it a crime?' I angrily demanded. I meant to go on about the millions of people suffering in Europe, and our troops fighting, and . . .

'Let's have supper,' my father said. 'I'm starving.'

'Yes, of course.' My mother jumped up immediately. 'You must be. I'm afraid it's mainly Spam.'

'Doesn't matter, so long as it's food.'

And, as we moved a few feet to the table, I had a sensation less of being forgiven than of being *de trop*.

If a wool-work motto had adorned the walls, it would have read: We must make the best of it. My father did that effortlessly. My mother had to struggle with the ingrained pessimism of her temperament, but she would struggle when my father showed her the need, and in a true crisis she became calm and stoic. Theirs was a perfect marriage of optimism and pessimism. No wonder if its offspring's nature tended to be mercurial.

The reality of school-life is something the majority of children probably do not wish to talk about to their parents. The experience is coped with – for the most part – on their own. I think my parents recognised as much, and their few questions usually tended to be dutiful preliminaries to the holidays, just like my guarded replies. They had made sacrifices, that I understood very well, to send me to a 'good' boarding-school. My obligation seemed to be to leave intact their concept of the school, based on pre-war recollections of it apparently flourishing in a different location, and blended, more erroneously, with school as presented in *Goodbye, Mr Chips*. Only rarely did they visit the cinema, but that became a favourite film.

'Not altogether,' was as far as I felt I could go, when my mother asked whether it reminded me of my school-life. 'We're nothing like as big, for one thing, and – well, it's difficult to explain.'

Difficult to explain that we were in fact a handful of boys in a very small country house, supervised and taught by a succession of masters, of varied ability. Some academic standards were maintained by the Second Master, experienced, intelligent and unpopular. But the ethos of the school as spacious, civilised, distinguished, discriminating in choice of pupils, firm and yet urbane in fostering gentlemanly Catholicism, was the creation, or re-creation, of the Headmaster, who had once been the chaplain. In its way, his performance was as good as Robert Donat's. And he too had, at least during the war, a favourite film, *In Which We Serve*.

He spoke eloquently of it one morning at assembly, commending its inspiring message, and about bravery, piety and patriotism. He was anyway an effective speaker, and he was clearly stirred himself as he stirred us. I suspect his eye may have ranged, in imaginative long shot, over serried rows of boys, extending into hundreds, each with uplifted, attentive face: boys on the superb playing-fields and in their comfortable studies, boys setting out to fight in a just war, some possibly to die, replaced at school by fresh generations whom he would address down the years, to an increasing thunder of applause.

He deserved a far larger audience, and we might have benefited from realisation of his vision there and then. What I saw as the peculiarities of my education, and its defects, I tended to blame on the war, if not the school, and certainly as unconnected with my personality. It never occurred to me to reflect that the school's very smallness, and its general intimacy, probably suited me much better than would a bigger, grander one.

The Headmaster I viewed entirely through my own per-spective, conscious that he was widely cultured, almost excessively aesthetic, nervously energetic and – to me – unpredictable. It was not my job to write his report, so I missed the bravery of his vision and the loneliness of his position. Subsequently, I have wondered if his instinctive dislike of me arose from seeing in me distorted aspects of himself.

But my greatest grievance was with the war. After all, I had been just twelve when it broke out, and before then I had anticipated my teen years as an enjoyable, liberating period of being 'grown up', without any adult responsibilities. Rather vaguely, improbably, given my parents' lifestyle, I had envisaged those years as largely filled with parties and dances and girls. By the time I was sixteen, I felt the war had robbed me of all three, though of course I dared not complain. I was lucky, wasn't I, to be lonely in Harrogate and not in battle or in a concentration camp? Nobody needed to tell me that.

'Oh, God,' I shouted inwardly, as once more I crossed the windy Stray, to or from the library. 'What is going to happen to me?'

The Second Master at school had often spoken of my getting a scholarship and going to Oxford – indeed, he was to take me there on one enchanted summer's day visit. But first came the war and military service. God might intervene there yet, as I regularly prayed He would. I had been good – in my estimation – even if largely through lack of knowledge and initiative. And as I knelt in such an intense posture in the pew of the ugly church at Harrogate that my mother glanced at me apprehensively, I felt convinced that either God would do something dramatic or I would soon die.

As well as ejecting me from my own home, the war had contributed to the dissolving of another household I loved, that which had been my father's place of birth, in then respectable, semi-prosperous, secluded Brixton. Five of his seven spinster sisters continued to live there into the 1930s, and it was rich in magical associations for me as a child.

Christmas was the time there I remembered most vividly, but all or most of my visits seemed for long linked with festivities of some sort. A welcome shone out from the moment I pushed at the stiff, always stuck half-open, iron gate and saw above the front door the panel of glass with its old-fashioned gilt lettering that read: 'Homeleigh'.

Any Victorian pun in the word I totally missed. Its sound was too deeply embedded in my consciousness to register as other than evocative of traditional family life, and anyway the house was fascinatingly exotic in atmosphere compared with my own modern home. When my father referred to it and the 'Girls', I thought with no incongruity of my aunts, who seemed to have no specific age, though all were older than him. Even the drab, threadbare scrap of front garden, with its sparse, sooty shrubs, was delightfully different from our well-kept concrete and rose-beds. And often, before I reached up to the heavy knocker, a twitch of patterned lace curtain at the bay window told that our arrival had been noticed. The door opened. In the familiar, unchanging hall, already waiting to welcome us, stood a smiling aunt.

This had been my grandfather's house. 'Papa' (with the accent on the first syllable) was frequently spoken of among the sisters, and in no morbid way he seemed to live on, with my grandmother occupying a less dominant place in their minds. Huge framed photographs of them both hung as a pair in the dining-room, looking out serenely across the long mahogany table where we sat for all meals – including tea, itself a substantial, unhurried affair.

Wherever I looked – and there was always time for looking, especially while the numerous adults talked – intriguing objects caught my eye. But it was the general atmosphere that intrigued me most and which made the greatest difference from any other house I knew, or would know. Nor was this some childhood illusion. Much was due to the fact that the house was lit by gas.

Explicitly and consistently I disliked at home the moment when the curtains were drawn and the electric light was switched on, many times begging my mother to leave our room illuminated only by the fire. As with a good deal of my behaviour, she characterised it as eccentric, yet she was not immune to the charm created.

At 'Homeleigh', nearly naked gas jets flared on the stairs and in the passages: small fans of light that wavered constantly and which could make a shadowy adventure even out of going along the short corridor to the lavatory after nightfall. That location itself was concealed under a euphemism perhaps Edwardian, or earlier, which had its own splendid touch of satire, always being referred to as 'The Houses of Parliament'.

Downstairs, the gaslight was not so much hidden as adorned, with lace-like mantles around which were hung greenish-tinted globes of etched glass or bowls of pinky-yellow alabaster. A bloom spread softly through the rooms when the gas was lit, with its characteristic sighing hiss. Darkness was not banished but seemed to merge with the areas of light, and there was magic in the moment when the gas was first turned on.

At the approach of dusk, it was one of the privileges for children to be permitted to run into the hall, stretch up to the chain of the lantern hanging there and give a tug that – thanks to its minute pilot-light – brought instant illumination. All the more vividly could you see perched high on one wall the wooden cuckoo-clock, which I never knew to function, and below was the gong, suspended between a pair of antlers. Another privilege was being allowed to strike it – gently – before mealtimes. Within touching distance on the wall opposite hung a handsomely gleaming barometer, though it too seemed to have stopped working, however often you tapped its glass or twisted its brass knob. But I enjoyed reading again and again not the pressure and the temperature but the names printed on it of its manufacturers: Negretti & Zambra.

I felt sure that it had been bought by my grandfather, dead long before I was born. As for the cuckoo-clock, with its pendant weights resembling pine-cones, dangling uselessly, that had either been bought by him in Switzerland or, more probably, given to him by one of his several Swiss business partners and friends. Strange, I used to think, that nobody bothered to get it mended.

With the coming of the war, and my parents' removal to Harrogate, I began to stay at 'Homeleigh' for a night or two, to break the journey to and from school. By 1942 my welcome was none the less warm, though by June of that year only three aunts survived. Ironically, it was easier to find a spare bedroom for me as well as for my cousin, Bernard, who was at the same school. But the household was inexorably declining as an entity, under the pressure of financial difficulties, and age and weariness – and the war. Perhaps I imagined that the big mirror on the first landing was growing more tarnished, but it was true that the bell-push in the dining-room, to summon the maid, was broken. To get that repaired was pointless, since there had ceased to be a maid. And Julia, the old, much-loved cook and part-nurse, who had lived with the family from her teens, and had known my father as a baby, was soon to die.

So the house would be given up, its contents sold, and the three sisters would disperse. Virtually my last recollection of

'Homeleigh' is of being there, sitting silently in the dining-room with two aunts, on a gloomy, foggy afternoon. Perhaps memory has clouded the weather to match our mood.

A letter written by one of the aunts to another nephew, my much older cousin Haydn, serving in the Navy, had just been returned to her, with the intimation that he was missing at sea, presumed killed. I knew him only slightly but I knew the smiling, debonair photograph of him in uniform which stood on some side-table. Only gradually did I absorb what was happening – above all that this was news which had not yet reached his parents.

'We can only pray,' my aunts must have said, almost in unison. Pray I certainly did: for the soul departed, for his parents and his two sisters, for my grieving aunts, for the rest of the crew of his mine-sweeper and for myself. I was sad, embarrassed, puzzled. Prayer had been bred in me from my earliest years. I had never paused to question any of the beliefs which home and schools had combined to inculcate, and I did not do so then.

But what I was seeking through my prayers was, on this occasion, unclear. Every form of prayer I knew emphasised God's supreme goodness. He was in heaven, where we all prayed to join Him. Existence on earth was a preliminary to that desired, eternal state. Should we then be mourning the sudden and horrible death of a young man whose life-expectancy in normal times would have been far longer? My faith was not shaken, but I felt I had never understood the system of heaven and earth to which I was pledged.

There was one aspect of my religion which I could not speak to anyone of disliking but which had haunted me from very early childhood and had been put before me by the time I was four.

Charming was the message exuded by some prints after paintings by Margaret Tarrant which had been chosen, possibly by my mother, for the walls of my first bedroom. Children figured in them, along with animals like rabbits and lambs: a boy and girl worshipping at the cradle of the

Infant Christ, born in some wood; and a small boy kneeling in a vague landscape, illustrative of the verses beneath (from Coleridge):

> He prayeth best, who loveth best
> All things both great and small

I wanted to be that boy, surrounded by friendly animals, or in the wood with the other boy and his elder sister. Some visiting aunt would confirm the charm and suitability of my pictures, before she joined us for lunch, which could well be of rabbit. Or, as a treat, we might be having roast leg of lamb. Very likely, I had accompanied my mother to the butcher's when she selected the meat or asked the butcher to skin that particular rabbit. I never felt any discrepancy, and no more did my family. I loved animals – whether toy ones or living ones or ones killed for human beings to eat. I said my prayers and went on with my 'loving', and everyone was content.

In my room, over the bed, hung another image. I had not asked for it and – had I dared – I would have asked for its removal. It was a small, metal crucifix, whose surface I had sometimes experimentally explored with my tongue. Nobody entering my room commented upon its presence, though family visitors presumably noticed it approvingly. A miniature figure of a nearly naked man was pinned there, nailed with tiny, tin-tack nails to a cross. He was Jesus, the Son of God, and somehow the same person as the Infant Christ, the baby boy worshipped by the children painted by Margaret Tarrant. I could not possibly – mercifully – have understood the suffering he had undergone, but I knew that his was a dead body exposed on the wall above me, visible each morning when I woke.

After the chapel fire at school, I continued to be the thurifer, though I now swung a less elegant, almost 'utility' thurible. And I went on accepting in much the same automatic,

unthinking manner God and the saints, and every manifestation around me of religion. God was all-seeing. If I
had not already been convinced of that, the sequel to the
fire seemed to prove it.

Among the gifts I had failed to inherit from my father
was that for sports and games – games of every kind, in
his case, with an outstanding ability in soccer. Team games
were ordeals for me. But I did not mind the comparative solit-
ariness of cross-country running, and took positive pleasure
from playing squash. We had a court, one conveniently close
to the main school house.

I suppose that the choice for the temporary chapel was
obvious, and it converted ingeniously, even to provision of
a choir-loft; but I felt God's intervention when I learnt that
the site chosen was the squash-court.

1

A Born-again Pagan

I have a clear recollection of being born – though it was some three years, I suppose, after the actual, physical event.

I was lying on a sofa one warm afternoon, alone in a quiet room. It was so quiet that I could hear a faint, lulling buzz which might have come from the sofa's interior, as I pressed my cheek against its hot, thick, almost dusty-smelling tapestry. I could sense it was imprinting its pattern on my skin, and if I bothered to open my eyes I saw close-up an intricate design of pinkish-mauve birds and foliage on a black background.

All was familiar. I knew that I was lying on the sofa in my home, lying there for my regular rest, in a room that faced the garden. My mother had as usual placed me there and told me to rest even if I could not sleep.

Asleep I may have been for a while on that afternoon, but suddenly I was awake, alert and excitingly conscious of being alive. I tingled with awareness, and it seemed best preserved by keeping my eyes shut, though I clutched the heavy, braided cushions as if to assert my vitality and the thrill of my own existence.

I was and am sure of exactly where I lay – in the drawing-room of our house in Wimbledon. I did not need to open my eyes to see high on the wallpaper, near the window looking on to the garden, a stain that remained partly visible after all attempts to remove it. I smiled when I thought of how it had happened, though I had been told that the incident was serious.

A Born-again Pagan

Two boys who lived next door – two extremely naughty boys – had been fooling around with a syringe filled with ink, and by accident had squirted some into our drawing-room. That was very bad. I understood that they were very sorry. Although I never saw the boys, I often heard them playing, and I used to wonder drowsily, perhaps hopefully, whether some afternoon a fresh jet of ink would shoot through the window.

I may have had with me, as I awoke to the immediacy of life, a toy rabbit, upright and unyielding, quite uncuddly yet dear to me for being blue. Never had I yearned for a teddy bear, and I would always feel ambivalent about lifelike toys – half alarmed by a fluffy chick, for instance, which clucked across the floor and laid eggs. My rabbit had no pet-name. I knew that real rabbits were not blue, any more than the birds in the garden were the colour of those on the fabric of the sofa. Those spiky, peacock-style birds, dipping their heads and spreading their tails in pairs amid the curling foliage, were the ones I preferred.

Until the discovery of self on that particular afternoon, I had led a floating, slightly unfocused life. I had no awareness of what I wore, and the floating sense of things was fostered by being wheeled to and from different places by pram, though even that item had no defined appearance as such to me. It was just a means of locomotion – my car, with my mother as chauffeuse. After it, walking was rather a bore.

I can recall being left outside the grocer's shop in my pram, amusing myself by trying to whirl a cardboard disc on a string, perhaps given to me by the grocer. In the window of his shop was a large, automatic doll, a fascinating yet dubious object which I gazed at hypnotised, as the girl raised tantalisingly to her lips and jerkily lowered a muffin-like biscuit.

It was as I sat outside the grocer's that my mother one bright day told me that if I watched carefully I would see a flash of light from the distant roof of the Crystal Palace. Watch as I did, I failed to detect the flash but I took in the words 'Crystal Palace' as though they had been a cool drink. It hardly mattered that I could not see it, for a palace of glass lodged in my mind, and it is glistening there still.

Most of the few other incidents in my existence pre-four are not true reminiscences but were told to me by my parents in my early childhood – and when told by my mother seemed to suggest a precocious, talented baby, who had grown progressively less amusing and less talented. I cannot remember the peaceful routine of going up to the pond on Wimbledon Common to feed the ducks or swans. I cannot recall the disturbing day I got hold of a pair of scissors and swiftly severed the stems of all the crocuses and daffodils in the garden. Even at the time I apparently offered no explanation.

However, I can remember noting as we passed the pointed shapes of the gables on the houses in our road, which I liked for their variety. I had distinct emotions and felt a *frisson* of fear when we encountered a woman acquaintance of my mother's, also wheeling a pram, with a boy in it who had hit his head badly, just above one eye. I could not help looking, though I wished I hadn't, at the iodine-coloured, encrusted lump which bulged on his forehead.

Sitting in the pram, I was able to give directions, and frequently I directed us to go down a certain road at the end of which was a toyshop. In that window the most prominent item was a pony, big enough to be ridden by me. My mother told me it was a rocking-horse, but that meant little. It was black, with gold-studded, scarlet harness, covered not with black paint but with some sort of black hide. I longed for the days when I could go to see the horse. At first I hardly realised it was for sale, and nothing else in the window attracted me. The window simply served to frame the one object. I don't think I ever asked to go into the shop, but my mother must have told my father of my obsession, and it would be typical if he, or she at his encouragement, went to enquire about the price. Anyhow, the information seeped into me that we could not afford it.

Up to that stage I had not been conscious of my father as a separate entity or as directly relevant to my daily life. Traditions of the period and a natural reluctance will have kept him out of any intimate involvement with me as a baby, though he will also have been affectionate and amused as I developed. Unlike many a father of that time, he was unafraid of and fond of small children; and they reciprocated his feelings.

Before I could show any disappointment about the rocking-horse, which I had never truly believed would become mine, my mother made a statement which I took as solemnly as she uttered it – one which would be repeated by her often enough in the years ahead, though lacking that first, thought-provoking impact:

'Your father' – and her use of that form told me how earnest she was – 'is not made of money.'

Taking the words literally, I looked at him again. He appeared solid enough and was obviously made of something. But not money. All the same, he or my mother told me that one day he would try to buy me, when I was older, a comparable horse.

Perhaps I showed a new realisation of his presence when – in an anecdote retailed to me in later childhood – I awoke in my parents' bedroom one early morning, feeling thirsty.

'Orange juice, please, Ma,' I was reported as requesting.

When she failed to stir, I varied my request: 'Orange juice, please, Da.'

That got a laugh and results.

Before that I had given my mother great hope that I might be clever – which she, too modestly, would call taking after my father – by an ingenious way of informing her of something I had glimpsed from my pram in shrubbery as we were passing. She stopped, to look vainly, while I babbled a word she could not identify. At last, in my desperation, I asked her to recite the nursery rhyme 'Miss Muffet'. When she reached the word 'spider', I triumphed. And the tale will certainly have been told, admiringly, that very evening to my father. I, of course, was not present to receive any admiration, and I heard of my moment of brilliance only when I was about nine – by which time my mother implied that I had singularly failed to sustain it.

I was certainly not conscious of the most dramatic event in our tranquil days at Wimbledon – when burglars broke into the house. My mother confronted them in the hall, crying out that they could take everything – provided they left the baby. This struck me as terribly funny as a boy, and my mother herself laughed in recollecting her words; I hardly realised that, while our burglars were content with some silverware, kidnapping of babies was a possibility and was then topical.

Even photographs of myself at Wimbledon prompt no memories. All I truly recall is the regular visit of the laundry-cart down the road, drawn by two heavy, handsome, brown and cream horses. Their actual names must have got twisted in childhood, as was so often to happen with me, because I came to believe they were called Bob and Maud, the names of an uncle and aunt who also lived in Wimbledon. Or was that muddle set off by my father, making a casual joke not intended for my ears?

In any case, we were leaving Wimbledon. We were going to live at the seaside, at a very healthy place, apparently for my benefit, where the mud and the air were 'good'. The word would reverberate in every possible context throughout my upbringing. I must, I was constantly adjured, be 'good'. Some specific foods were 'good' for me. Although my parents lived frugally, with little money to spare, they both felt it important that one or two items of wear should be 'good' – especially shoes.

I had no idea, and neither perhaps had my parents, of how, in moving away to the seaside, to Leigh-on-Sea, in Essex, we were embodying a trend of the new decade, the 1930s. I learnt that we were to have a house built for us, in which I should have my own bedroom. Everything, it seemed, was going to be new, which sounded exciting. Our house would be on an 'estate', a word which had its own novelty and excitement for me. On hundreds of such estates, had I known it, thousands of small houses similar to ours were being built, and the majority of their male owners were paying – like my father – not only financially but in terms of long journeys by bus and rail to and from London six days of the week (work ending officially at lunchtime on Saturday).

All that was unknown to me, though I felt the importance of the fact that we were moving because of me and my health. I had not been ill, and, though I might be thin, even weedy, I was not sickly. Perhaps I was 'delicate'? – another word with connotations of the period and which hid a multitude of reasons for being given obscure tonics and daily doses of cod-liver oil and malt.

More than once on an afternoon, as I rested on the sofa in the drawing-room, had I tried to recover the thrill of that moment when I first became conscious of my individuality. All the circumstances seemed the same, but nothing happened. I merely grew hot and damp and uneasy. The tapestry fabric was prickly, and lying there became tedious.

Anyway, we were off to Leigh-on-Sea. Signs of our move accumulated, as I saw vividly enough at my own level. Under the sideboard, whose beaded panelled doors and spindly legs I had liked to fondle, jugs and bowls and other china began to be stacked. It could all be looked at, but not touched. And then it was gone – and so were we.

When I awoke next, it seemed, I was staying at Miss Bartlett's, on the sea-front at Leigh. Our house was not yet finished, so we were 'in rooms' with her. No steam-train, as I might have expected, had brought us there but some friend's motor-car.

For my mother, the weekdays at Miss Bartlett's must have been wearisome. In the old, tree-lined streets of Leigh, with their trams or trolley-buses, there was little to occupy her and a small child. The beach was rich in smelly mud and seaweed, though not much else, and the tide looked strong and the waves grey. Miss Bartlett had a parlour overlooking the sea, where guests breakfasted. There my mother and I could perch precariously to pass the time, as an alternative to walking in the town.

I was happy enough, however. I was the sole child in the establishment. Black-clad, bustling, bespectacled Miss Bartlett smiled at me (her spectacles I found particularly reassuring, since my mother also wore spectacles). Equally friendly were some of the almost entirely male clientele. I think several were 'travellers', in a commercial sense, and one, Mr Harris, definitely travelled – in Mackintosh's toffees. I had never realised sweets came in such huge drums of tins as he had always at hand, and it was bewildering to me to see a lid come off and be invited to select one from the glittering array of brightly-wrapped, variously-shaped Quality Street toffees.

'Thank Mr Harris for your sweet,' my mother would say, while her tone conveyed the not-unfamiliar message of 'get a move on'.

It was impossible to explain that pleasure lay in the hesitation and the contemplation – more really than in any actual sweet.

Life at Miss Bartlett's introduced me to some complexities of adult existence, which seemed strangely hectic in its tempo compared to mine. That my father and the other men had to get a move on after breakfast I quite understood. Miss Bartlett and her maids also had to get a move on, with breakfast things to clear away and beds to be made. But why my mother and I were obeying the same compulsive rhythm I failed to follow – quite literally, as I trailed behind her. 'Dawdling', I learnt the process was called, and it was liable to cause grown-ups peculiar irritation.

Dawdling on the beach was permissible. If my mother was not much allured by popping seaweed bubbles, she joined willingly in searching for unusual pebbles and shells and pieces of glass which the sea had licked into milky lumps.

Dawdling on the pavement was a nuisance, regardless of

other people. But the pavement slabs themselves were often of different colours and split by interesting fissures, and finished off in slimmer sections where they met the kerb. As I walked everywhere – the pram or pushchair long banished – I naturally looked at the pavement, as indeed I was on occasion told I should. The kerb too had its importance, as a place to watch and to wait at.

'We shall be here all day, at this rate,' I heard my mother frequently observe to the general air, though the application was to me.

Perhaps I had just noticed the very bright green carpet of grass, spread under the fruit outside the greengrocer's shop, and longed to finger it. It was too brilliant and glossy to be real. I wondered, but I did not ask, where it could be obtained.

'Can we dawdle today?' was another question I wanted to put, when I learnt that this morning in June, as I went to the window and saw the sun flash blindingly on the sea and the seagulls swooping and shrieking, was my birthday.

I was told it was my fourth birthday, but I had no distinct recollection of previous ones. To me it felt like my first. In my excitement I would have rushed into breakfast with the news. Wouldn't Miss Bartlett like to know? And possibly Mr Harris?

Apparently not. A birthday was a private, family affair, and I was to walk into breakfast as quietly as usual. Still, no docility could conceal my joy in one of the presents my parents had given me: a miniature hurdy-gurdy, from which hung red ribbons with bells and pink plastic parrots. It came to symbolise my fourth birthday – and most later birthdays passed pleasantly yet far more prosaically. In the sunshine, on the steps of Miss Bartlett's, I flaunted this gaudy toy, delighting in it more perhaps than had been foreseen or was eventually thought quite suitable by my parents.

My fourth birthday was, I think, the occasion for initiating me into a regimen which combined brushing my teeth and saying my prayers. Both I carried out unhesitatingly and briefly. At that age I had not been to the dentist, and nor had I entered a church. My mother had given me the words for a simple prayer to God the Father, which I recited each evening, kneeling by my bed. God was someone invisible but overhead, up in heaven. She had also proposed that a cold bath each morning would do me good, and that too I more hesitatingly accepted.

Once or twice, we took the bus from Leigh proper, away from the sea and up to the newer, expanding part, with its fringe of shops and the burgeoning estate of Scottish street names, to inspect our house, nearing completion. Braemar Crescent curved away from older Stirling Avenue, itself reached from the wide stretch of Highlands Boulevard. In its miscellany of styles, the Crescent had quiet sociological interest, though its general architectural idiom was rooted in the blandest suburban Tudor.

Most of it was not merely new but raw, extending on to open fields. Gaps of land existed between some houses, and what would be our back garden was a chunk of uncultivated earth with an open fence around it. Where the front garden would be made, a cement-mixer stood, chugging and churning, and absorbing to watch. While my parents toured the interior of the house, I stared at the cement-mixer, its noise almost intrusive in the intense silence and emptiness investing the Crescent. Nobody appeared to live in any of the houses, old or new, though curtains neatly draped the windows, and over the low walls, often of concrete posts and chains, could be seen front gardens so ordered that their grass might have come from the greengrocer's and the flowers been glued into their beds.

It was a shock when one day I saw a boy. He was at my side, having crept up silently, attracted by the cement-mixer. About my own age, and with startlingly white fair hair, he stood there shyly and together we stared. In the end, he said that he lived just up the road and that his name was Trevor Morgan. I explained that we should soon be moving in. It seemed agreed that he and I would meet again.

One other person whom I met, or at least became aware of, was the stout, red-faced, talkative man who was the builder, Mr Doe. He seemed to grow fatter and redder with enthusiasm for our domestic future. He showed us the space available for a garage, despite the fact that we owned no car. He could easily alter the position of the staircase, which my father wished should not be visible on entering the house. He could fence in the garden completely, so we would be less exposed to our neighbours. And he had his own suggestions, such as improving the windows by some coloured glass. He thoughtfully took us to the show-home of his house, where I at once noticed in the hall a splendid, leaded window, of a galleon in full sail on waves of billowing blue and white.

But when we left, he looked rather deflated and sounded subdued.

'No stained glass at all?'

'None, thank you,' my father replied, and my mother nodded in agreement.

Yet I had deliberately nudged her on our arrival, to ensure that she saw the window.

On the bus back down into Leigh, I sat a seat away from my parents. The prospect of soon being in the new house had excited them to unusual animation in public. I could overhear that they were planning what should go in the garden, before reverting to our visit to Mr Doe's house. That had apparently amused them both. My mother's face must have relaxed from its normally slightly worried expression. She was smiling if not laughing at something said by my father, and then she exclaimed:

'And, oh, that window.'

My disappointment was modified when we did move in, for I found that Mr Doe had managed to slip a few loz-enges of palely-tinted glass into some windows downstairs. Nobody mentioned them, and over the years they seemed to fade or blend into the overall neutrality of the décor.

However, I was given not only my own bedroom but choice in its colour-scheme. Electric blue, magenta and rose madder were colours I had not yet discovered. Only slightly later at Braemar Crescent did I receive the first of so many paint-boxes, a great improvement on the paint-charts consulted by my parents – in variety and in intensity.

Green, I declared, was my favourite colour, and for long I had to stick to that choice within the home. Green was a colour I knew my mother approved of. She said it was 'soothing'. It was, too, the colour of nature in the sense of trees and grass, and of a natural world I now became aware of, flourishing surprisingly close to the Mr Doe-made one of our road.

With a bedroom of my own had come something much more important – virtually the key of the door to existence. It was as an individual that I moved through the pristine new house, savouring it as my environment, noting how its box-style rooms took shape, as did – more obviously – the raw chunk of land outside that would become a garden which I privately looked on as mine. And beyond was the newness of the road and its houses to study, as I stood by myself at our gate. I knew that only a few steps away – steps that I might take, with permission – were fields and hedgerows to explore. Cows were pastured there and a lark would rise or fall suddenly in the sky, and I kept thinking I should one day stumble on its nest.

If you walked further, as I did at weekends with my parents, you entered the woods that flanked the velvety green expanse of Belfairs golf course, an enchanted, little-trodden, bosky realm where grew massed ferns and blue-bells. Giant ants' nests were always under busy construction at the base of trees, and in lieu of finding birds' eggs I was happy enough to find lost golf balls.

I knew that this – all of this – was my life, opening on my senses each day, as I opened the curtains of my window. Dull and soon sun-bleached buff linen as they were, I had the power to draw or not draw them. I could scamper back to bed, survey my room, and then tunnel into the green eiderdown and munch on its crinkled corner like a caterpillar on a leaf, quite consciously reverting to babyhood because the morning was dark and already it was raining outside. Or the day was excitingly bright well before I was fully awake, and shafts of light tickled and teased me to do something daring, take off my pyjamas and rush to the bathroom, to encounter my father shaving.

Possibilities for each day seemed endless, and the implementing of them was largely left to me. That I was an only child was a fact I had – if not grasped – at least nearly got my fingers around. Looking at the larger Margaret Tarrant composition which hung on my wall – balancing on the bed to get a better view – I could gaze at the girl and her younger brother peering on tip-toe into the crib of the Infant Christ in an English woodland setting. The two children intrigued me most, just because there were two of them; that was more intriguing, then, than their difference of sex, though I registered that the girl *was* a girl and therefore wore a skirt.

In my room I was alone but never lonely. I could summon up a younger sibling, boy or girl, as the feeling took me. Instinctively, I knew that he or she would never exist in reality. And I had gained a sense that I and my parents, isolated though we seemed in Braemar Crescent, and in Leigh-on-Sea altogether, had behind us 'family' in the form of innumerable aunts and uncles and children, most of whom were to be met, sooner or later, in the family clearing house of 'Homeleigh'.

The promised green of my room, with a rich, foliaged green wallpaper and ghostly green lighting, which I had barely been able to articulate as my wants, faded to the actuality of some green linoleum on the floor and a fawn rug, with a narrow, half-apologetic inset of a different green, and an off-white wallpaper covered with minute dots and dashes of which a sprinkling were greenish, all lit by a clear bulb under a sensible, sallow, parchment shade. An old chest of drawers served for my few clothes – charmless garments I thought them: khaki shorts and Aertex shirts in white or egg-yolk yellow. They hardly differed in appearance from the spare blankets and sheets which filled the lower drawers of the chest.

Clothes and décor, however, were not ultimately a hindrance to the excitement of each day and the novelty of life. If I should not have chosen the beige and primrose environment which seemed to suit my parents, I found a lot to ponder on in their choice of framed reproductions, which passed as pictures, and stood out the more starkly for the neutrality of the walls and the visual poverty of the so-called ornaments. There were not many books to be seen, and those that filled one bookcase were chiefly factual, informative and illustrated. Books on birds and beasts I could at least open, to study their plates; and there was an atlas featuring the British Empire, with flags of all the nations. I had some books of my own, alphabet books from which I learnt by heart, without as yet quite reading, that 'Y is for Yugoslavia, only recently made.' And I had animal alphabet blocks which told me, and showed me, that 'I' stands for Ibex, a creature I became fond of for its very name and for its proud, eccentric look.

The prim and uncomfortably cold formal drawing-room was transfigured at weekends when my father was home, for placed there was the gramophone – probably the sole inanimate item he would have rescued from our blazing house. Music mattered to him. How passionately I only gradually understood, myself sometimes bored or puzzled by the singing and other sounds which filled the space, yet stirred too by intimations of still another world, an aural one, less accessible to me.

The room in the house which held most mystery for me was the 'spare' room, kept for visitors but doubling as a box-room, and only occasionally entered. My mother took me into it as though it was a repository of the past – hers in particular. Several trunks were piled there. One dominated the room by its sleek black bulk and high curved lid, buckled with wide, flapping straps of leather. It was old, out of fashion, I learnt, but kept by my mother partly for its associations.

'May I open it?' I would ask, even though I knew something of what it contained. 'Nothing of real interest,' my mother hastened always to say, unconvincingly.

We both took pleasure, without mentioning it, in the trunk's delicate, candy-striped interior and perhaps in the whiff of mothballs that exuded from it on opening. Inside, there was a tray which had to be lifted, and under that lay a miscellany of items, including a mouldering leather bag, with rusty lock.

'It's a Gladstone bag,' my mother told me.

Poor at making connections, I did not link the name with the person I heard of at meals, Mr Gladstone, a mythical, exemplary figure, who was notable for having chewed each mouthful of food twenty-four times (or was it forty-four?).

The Gladstone bag contained merely unremarkable cutlery, but in the depths of the trunk my mother made re-discoveries, and I shared her interest in examining an elaborate, tarnished, silver belt-buckle, given to her by some relation, and a casket carved out of scented wood which, it seemed, had been a present once from an admirer. The trunk itself was a sort of heirloom, perhaps belonging originally to her grandmother, and as we bent over its tissue-wrapped contents we were delving into layers of previous lives.

In some misty way my mother had, I realised, her own family, though most of the members she remembered affectionately were now dead. She had never known her mother, who died very young. Her grandparents had brought her up. Her father had re-married, and she had two half-sisters. And this other family, which was partly mine, lived far off in Yorkshire, mainly in the small village of Hutton Rudby, her birthplace. It seemed so very long ago – in the days before I was born – quite apart from the physical distance separating it from Braemar Crescent.

'You won't find Hutton Rudby on any map,' my mother remarked, in a contented tone.

When we went downstairs I would look again at the few pieces of discoloured creamy china, lightly flecked with zig-zag touches of lustre, blue and red, that were arranged on the shelf in the hall. They were in a different category from the modern ornaments in the rest of the house. They were valuable, at least to my mother, and they were of impressive age, beyond my computing. The one or two plates, a saucer and a bulbous milk jug were what remained of the set of wedding china on the marriage of my great-grandparents.

It was a terrible morning, never to be forgotten, when I was playing ball in the hall, because of the wet weather, and I saw it bounce against – of all objects – the milk jug, which smashed at once.

I was only too glad to obey my mother's sad, exasperated command to go and play outside and the pouring rain mingled with my tears. I longed to be soaked to the skin, to catch a dreadful cold and die. But the sun began to emerge and, probably in the afternoon, Trevor Morgan came round to play. Nevertheless, I knew I had done something awful, even if it was unintentional. I couldn't tell Trevor, and it never occurred to me to refer the matter to God.

Trevor represented yet another novel aspect of life. Before him I had never had a friend – never known you could have one. Ours was a friendship of convenience, strictly considered, because Braemar Crescent, with its discreet, almost invisible inhabitants, who yet contrived to keep their gardens trim and their windows gleaming, provided no other children.

It was as though procreation had been banished as rigorously as was the sun. Our side of the road faced east. And against the sun curtains were rapidly drawn, blinds lowered, awnings extended and the milk speedily removed from doorsteps. Motor-cars seldom disturbed the silence. It was safe for Trevor and me to meet on the pavement and to wander into the nearby fields or even as far as Belfairs woods, territory already familiar to him. All our mothers did warn us about was not talking to strangers and keeping away from any gipsies who might approach.

We obeyed these stipulations, but in Trevor's company I often enjoyed a feeling of undefined naughtiness. He was bolder and more adventurous: more the normal boy of the period, eager to go bird-nesting and to hide among the ferns beside the golf course in case we might pinch a stray golf ball while a game was in progress. Our fondness for the balls had a sort of semi-destructive surgical curiosity; we liked to cut them open and unwind their tightly-woven rubber innards until the moment when the rubber filaments began to unwind of their own accord and the central sac was revealed. It contained liquid lead, poison, we had been told, and that increased the thrill of the procedure.

We talked a good deal when we were together, without sharing confidences. Although I enjoyed escaping with him out into the fields, scrambling through hedgerows and watching absorbed as hundreds of ants toiled at the huge heap of some nest, before we deliberately disturbed it, I guessed that Trevor would have no sympathy for most of my indoor activities. And anyway I was shy of speaking of my inner preoccupations, my fondness for colouring and cutting out paper shapes at the dining-room table, not only of farm animals but, more privately, of fairy beings.

A picture on our walls, some illustrations in the books I owned, with tales my mother recited or read from them to me, had merged in my mind with the experience of being in the endless-seeming woods, where empty acorn cups suggested elves, and fairies might have flitted from the bluebell glade or perched on the pointed caps of the toadstools clustered at the mossy roots of the towering tree-trunks.

It was fun to plunge noisily into the bracken with Trevor and hear it crunch and to feel fronds of fern roughly brush my bare legs. It was pleasant to accompany my parents, more quietly, on weekend walks, when my father asked for total stillness as he tried to identify some bird in the hedgerow or among the trees, though I frequently failed to spot the individual bird and lacked my father's acute, appreciative ear for the different bird-calls.

For me the most intense pleasure, however, lay in contemplating the natural scene animated by beings bred in my imagination, and there I loved to linger.

'Oh,' my mother often exclaimed, shrewdly yet not unsympathetically. 'He's in a daydream much of the time.'

'But not all of it,' I could have retorted.

It was too much trouble to explain my disappointment at the prevalence of small dun-coloured birds, indistinguishable to me, after I had expected something showy from the mention of a 'whitethroat', and seen in one of my father's bird books that blue and chestnut plumage is the mark of the nut-hatch. By comparison, a tree-creeper – despite its antics – looked dull.

After all, it was not I who had invented that alternative world, devised for children, where frogs went a-wooing, cows jumped over the moon and a trio of bears lived in a cottage. Nor was I the first person to depict a fairy swinging daintily from a bluebell stalk. I had been instructed to believe in a God who lived in heaven yet was invisible to us. With equal faith, and more real fervour, I believed in the existence of fairyland.

Trevor remained my friend, although his behaviour was too robust to suggest he had any interest in fairies. Where he led, I was prepared to follow. I suspected that he knew more about life. He certainly knew that one day we would have to go to school, but the word had little significance for me; I had a feeling that somehow I should contrive not to go.

It was Trevor who began doodling in the back of a book of mine, with a crayon of mine, one afternoon, smiling slyly as he passed the drawing across the table. With a startled, shocked giggle, I saw he had drawn a penis. After a moment, I drew another. Then he seized the page to draw one more, before I tugged it away to add a second of my own, and our efforts grew frantic as we shrieked and scribbled, until in panic I shut the book. Nothing was said. I attempted to erase or disguise what we had drawn, and we never repeated the incident.

That happened at our house, which Trevor seemed rarely to enter. But I became familiar with his, one of a pair of drab, far from new bungalows at the top of the road, reminiscent to me of stranded but inhabited railway carriages, a not uncommon sight in Essex. A narrow, sunless stone passage connected the two bungalows, and we played sometimes in it, for what there was of garden was filled with growing vegetables.

At Trevor's everything struck me as intriguingly different from all that constituted my home. He had a grandmother, for one thing, and she lived in the other bungalow. I saw her sometimes: a very old woman she appeared, dressed in black, crossing between the two buildings. I knew Trevor was fond of her and he was fond too, almost to my surprise, of his much younger brother who would toddle occasionally into the passage.

Shyness came over me at the intrusion, as I saw it, of either person. And I experienced a quite new emotion, compounded as much of envy as embarrassment, when Trevor briefly broke off from some game of ours, to hoist up his brother's slipping shorts, murmuring good-humouredly. 'Yer trucks are coming down.'

If I could hardly expect to go home to find a baby brother, we might at least have had a cage of love-birds, as did the Morgans. There was charm in the plumage of those birds, whose powdery colours looked to have been achieved by scattering talc on them, and whose correct name, I must have been told by my mother, was 'budgerigar'.

In Mrs Morgan, Trevor's mother, I had for the first time a mother to compare with my own. Large and slightly untidy, with a florid complexion and wild fair hair, Mrs Morgan seemed always busy, but warmly kind and openly welcoming. I preferred a hunk of bread and jam handed out by her to Trevor and me, before she hastened to do something else, than the better-cut bread and butter at home, even though I felt disloyal in my preference. Once, my mother went, or came, to tea at the Morgans and the occasion was consciously special, with an air of the best of everything laid out. But I sat in an agony of constraint, wishing that something, anything, would break up the party.

Mr Morgan was there. Perhaps I had not explained to my mother that he was an inevitable, invalid presence, in a chair in the corner. He seldom spoke or moved. He had dark eyes and a dark moustache, all the darker in the pallor of his mournful face. He had been a miner in South Wales, I understood, had contracted some disease and had moved to Leigh-on-Sea for the air. All the implications of his condition I missed, as I did the strain underlying Mrs Morgan's brave cheerfulness. Nor did I realise that some of the differences I noticed at Trevor's were due to near-poverty.

My mother was glad I had a friend in Trevor, and she said that Mrs Morgan was nice. Yet it appeared that he and I would be going to different schools. When Mrs Morgan and my mother met in the street they might pause to chat, but something tore in the flimsy relationship on the morning I was there too and Mrs Morgan kindly told me in future to call her 'Auntie'. My mother mimed her instinctive reluctance, while I may actually have blurted out that I already had lots of real aunts.

Almost dizzy in my sense of all-round awkwardness, I gripped the handle of my mother's shopping basket. I could find no words for the experience, which continued to chafe like a blister for the whole day. Already in my life my mother had admonished me not to be shy, and already I thought she set a poor example herself. So adults were not exempt from such sensations: and, indeed, their world seemed one I had no eagerness to enter.

Back home in the drawing-room, I took comfort from gazing at the familiar, large framed picture of a man seated piping under a gnarled tree in a woodland glade. He wore a peacock feather in his cap and piped as though lost in reverie, oblivious of the robin perched on his boot and of the ethereal fairy forms who swirled around him. It was entitled 'The Piper of Dreams' and something about it had made it a favourite picture with both my parents. I never enquired, but I in turn was touched – permeated, rather – by its spell.

More than half a century would elapse before I learnt that the painter of 'The Piper of Dreams' was Estella Canziani, who exhibited the work at the Royal Academy in London in 1915, when she was twenty-eight. It returned to the Academy for the exhibition of Victorian Fairy Painting held in 1997–8, and the catalogue refers to the extreme popularity of (Medici Society) reproductions of the original watercolour – begun in the spring of 1914 – with British soldiers in the trenches during the First World War. Its wistful, peaceful, half-fanciful yet somehow not ludicrous rustic vision will have had poignant appeal to thousands of people who suddenly found themselves caught up in carnage of a kind and on a scale previously inconceivable.

Both my father and my mother were directly involved in what remained in their minds as the Great War. And I think now that 'The Piper of Dreams' (a boy, in fact) must have had more than charm or wistful significance for them. Terrible as the War had been, and my father carried an unextracted bullet in his body for the rest of his life, it was the event without which he and my mother would almost certainly never have met.

2

The Wounded Soldier and the Nurse

Saint-Omer was a name I often heard pronounced by my parents in my childhood, talking between themselves and making allusions I could not always follow. My mother in particular lingered over the syllables with unusual, caressing fondness. In the military hospital there, she had first met my father among the wounded.

And so Saint-Omer took on its own associations for me, regardless of where it was, or what it was, becoming one of those place-names, like Avalon, that had existence without precise location. It had long receded to the back of my mind, virtually vanished, when in a car speeding away from Calais towards the Belgian border, not many years ago, I suddenly saw a signpost indicating a right turn. There was the name in print before me: Saint-Omer.

Momentarily, I was tempted to make a detour, as I heard again my parents discussing a never-realised holiday we should take in France during the 1930s. It would be in part a revisiting of the Northern France they had known. And my mother's voice was once more audible to me, saying, 'I should love to go back to Saint-Omer.'

However, it acted on me as a warning: not to attempt to raise vicariously the memories that belonged to her. Besides, I should hardly have known what I was looking for in the modern town, bombed in two world wars, and with a history of being fought over bitterly in the many centuries since the otherwise obscure saint founded a monastery there. Despite the fact that Saint-Omer has a museum with some interesting paintings, I think I was wise to leave it as a place in my imagination.

Inextricably lodged there with it was my concept of the Great War, which seemed in our household to be kept subtly topical. Because of its happy outcome, in personal terms, I was not disturbed – as I might otherwise have been – by the thought of battles fought and people killed and wounded. Guns and mud and blood, and the senseless slaughter of it all, were remote from me. I envisaged battle as a sort of contest between two teams, and I saw it occurring, for some reason, in a big, corrugated-iron-roofed building a few streets away, which we frequently passed. There, I felt, though did not say aloud, must have been where the Great War took place. Gradually, I gained a clearer idea of it as having been fought out of England, and then as mainly in Flanders – somewhere I looked for vainly in the atlas. My error about the nearby building made me flush at the sight of it, after I learnt that it was the local Methodist Chapel.

Like gunsmoke, a reminder of the Great War – of every war – hung acridly in the light, bright atmosphere otherwise conveyed on entering our dining-room. Above the fireplace, unmissably, was a small picture, sombre in colour and patently sad in mood. A man in a long blue coat stood alone in a featureless, wasted landscape, his head bare and bowed, contemplating a rough mound of earth marked by a wooden cross. Along with a helmet, a few flowers, poppies perhaps, lay on the mound. Underneath were the words: '*Le Tombeau de son Fils*'.

At some stage quite early in childhood, I must have asked for an explanation of the composition of those words. I understood and yet of course I did not understand, despite the sadness. It may be that my parents had not anticipated questions about the picture, least of all from their son. I still do not know who painted the original and whether it had once enjoyed fame and popularity, possibly at the time of the Armistice. Nor do I know which of my parents chose it.

Perhaps it was a joint choice, but I suspect that my father, with his acute eyesight yet total blindness to the visual arts, was moved by its subject and interpreted its message as pacific.

He never spoke of his feelings about it – but then he never spoke of feelings, in the sense of profound emotions, at all. Nakedness of any kind, I would eventually realise, caused him agonising embarrassment, and nothing could be more embarrassing than naked emotion. Instinctive good manners and instinctive good humour played as a fountain in him, and served like spray to conceal the inner man. Cheerfulness carried him through most situations; for those beyond even his optimism, he preferred silence (and, doubtless, prayer). And in remaining silent about what he had witnessed and experienced during the War, he was entirely typical of those who had fought in it.

Only at odd moments did he make or quote some joking reference, arcane at first to me, which related to life in the trenches or in hospital. Such light-heartedness deceived me, for it was so much part of the father I knew and trusted, and I probably gained an impression of his days at the Front as passed in a delightful haze of playing football, joshing with comrades and whistling songs. I knew how amusing he could be and how tunefully he sang – often snatches of ever-evocative Army songs, like 'Tipperary', which had additional suitability for someone half-Irish. I grew familiar with a virtual catch-phrase used by both my mother and him, long before I could set it in context: 'Straightaway, Sister'. Indeed, it was only when poring over First World War copies of *Punch* at school, in my teens, that I fully appreciated the dragon stereotype of the then hospital ward sister.

It was my mother who told me – not about her war but about my father's. The essence of it was that he had been wonderfully brave, which was or would be no surprise. In his absence, she showed me his medals. Among them was the Military Medal 'for Bravery in the Field' and a clasp – of oak leaves, I think – for being mentioned in despatches.

From my mother I began to learn other things which told me about my father's character and about the adult world. He was 'a natural leader of men', which were not in fact her words but those of his commanding officer, in a post-war testimonial copied on a sheet of paper from my grandfather's London business address.

Yet my father had ended the War not as an officer but as a Company Sergeant-Major. For that reason he received only a medal, not the more prestigious Military Cross. Did my mother intimate already what I would come to recognise as the salt of keen satire in the spray of my father's humour? It was satire directed at the pretentious and the pompous, and at conventional social values. He disliked all that was represented by officers and by the officer-class as such, then and subsequently. More than once, therefore, he had declined a commission, happier to be of and with the ranks – as he would be, metaphorically, throughout his life. I like to think that his commanding officer perceived something of his true nature when to praise of his 'strong and magnetic personality' he added, 'he has much self-confidence and independence'. When finally my father sent me to a 'good' school, he was oblivious of or indifferent to the paradox that most of the boys there whose fathers had been in the First World War were the sons of officers.

I was innocent of snobbery at the age of five or six, unaware of any nuances of Army rank. But I should feel hurt by my father's scornful attitude some two years later, when it emerged by chance that a schoolfriend's father used his temporary wartime title of Captain in civilian life. I could see the man was conceited and possibly stupid – devoid of my father's boyish gaiety and unpretentiousness. Yet he was kind to me. He was tall and mildly swaggering, if not especially military, and privately I thought him rather suited by the title. But then I was beglamoured by this family of four, the Moxons, by the Russian mother and my friend Eric's older sister, Nadia, who was so beautiful, though Eric pointedly failed to notice it. I was learning the world's way and proved easily susceptible to the very aspirations my father ridiculed. Soon, I should be worried that my mother lacked both the style and the garment exemplified by Eric's mother wrapped luxuriously in her long fur coat. As I had failed to deduce the comparative poverty of the Morgans, so I failed to deduce the comparative prosperity of the Moxons.

Commissioned or not, my father had shown his bravery most by going to war in the first place, by enduring all that he did endure, believing presumably that it was his duty to fight, while by nature sensitive, fastidious, affectionate and utterly unaggressive. The first-class shot, the bombing instructor, the soldier wounded three times, loathed brutality and practised active goodness to everyone he met. What the War perhaps confirmed in him was a natural belief that all men are or should be equal in life – as they become on facing death.

Mere chance made the dining-room the place where my mother talked most freely about my father as a soldier. It was a domain I looked on very much as mine, once breakfast was over and he had set off on the arduous, never-complained-about journey from Braemar Crescent to the Air Ministry, via the dingiest of main-line London stations, Fenchurch Street. My mother went off too, to domestic chores, leaving me free to turn the room into various things, chiefly a shop, created out of the shady area under the table, draped in a blue chenille cloth that I arranged to keep out much of the light. With empty jam-jars, to be filled – carefully – by water tinted from my paint-box, the shop resembled my idea of a chemist's. Or it became a post-office, and any item of stationery my father might bring me from his Ministry, a few paperclips perhaps, or an old diary, I hoarded.

No injunction was needed to make me play quietly. I could pass days in that fashion – months even – absorbed by acquisition of a rubber date-stamp, before graduating to the thrill of using molten sealing wax for the envelopes that

I despatched and delivered around the table legs. I was still playing there when I began to notice I had grown too tall to fit comfortably under the table, and it was necessary to surface.

In doing so, I found myself facing the only other picture in the room, one I had long been familiar with, though it continued to fascinate me. Large, and heavily framed in black, it was a scene of blinding blizzard in some icy, desolate region, its tone more greyish-green than white. Dimly through the whirl of snowflakes a single, muffled figure was visible, staggering away from what was just discernible as an encampment.

Even before it was explained to me, the picture exercised its appeal. I associated it with my father – indeed, I may have thought when very young that he was that muffled figure. And there is a sense in which I was not mistaken. From the way my mother spoke of my father's character, I was able to perceive that unobtrusive bravery typified him, and it was Captain Oates's heroic but deliberately understated action on Scott's South Pole expedition which had caught his imagination. The picture happened to illustrate what he must have read about, like many people in England in 1912, or in the following year, when Scott's journal was published. Lamed by frostbite and conscious of handicapping his comrades on their return journey, Oates had chosen to walk undramatically out into the snow, to die.

It was not difficult to conceive my father behaving similarly, and in any such fantasy my mother for once encouraged me. She impressed upon me that he was an ideal father, if occasionally too indulgent, and that I must do my best to grow up like him. It was, she intimated, going to be a very hard task.

I looked at the muffled figure of Captain Oates, now I knew the story, and felt inspired. I loved to watch from the window when snowflakes were falling. I delighted in the idea of Jack Frost who breathed on the panes and ornamented the gutter with icicles. Only actually being out in the freezing cold, with the snow soaking through my gloves, my nose dripping and my fingers growing numb, tempered my enthusiasm. By the time I was planning possible careers, I had decided against that of Arctic or Antarctic explorer.

The reticence which I detected in my father, and as shared less compulsively by my mother, extended to their environment and even beyond. Loudness manifested in any manner caused him almost physical pain. Little in Braemar Crescent could offend him. Our immediate neighbours were an elderly, apparently childless couple and a youthful couple so far without children. Friendly distance, in spite of actual proximity, marked our relationship with them all, and in each of the three households, different as they were, quietness seemed the desideratum. An observer flying overhead might have been amused by the sight at weekends of three adjoining strips of garden being tended so dutifully but silently by their owners.

It was only the retired man, Mr Cull, with time to lavish daily on his gross, shaggy plants and vast, fleshy vegetables, who felt any urge for a chat. Up he popped like Mr Punch, rubicund and jovial, standing on a box to see over our high fence. Usually it was I whom he saw, and I became accustomed to his greeting – mimicked sometimes by my father – of 'Hullo, Mickey Mouse, and what are you a-doing of?'

'Well,' I might begin, 'today I'm having a funeral for a newt that's died.'

Mr Cull would laugh a lot, but then he laughed at virtually everything I said. Perhaps he could not see the dead newt lying in its matchbox coffin, surrounded by daisies, and quite possibly he had not heard exactly what I said. He popped up grinning and then he popped down again, with a snort of laughter.

I welcomed Mr Cull's appearance, as I would later welcome the indications I could piece together of a scandalous stir in the Crescent, centred on a showy-looking bungalow, named 'Dalmeny', lived in by a showy young wife and husband, Mr and Mrs Strutt. They had a baby and late-night parties – a then daring combination. On Saturday nights, noisy sports cars started to scream up and down the road. Mr Strutt himself drove one. The rumour ran that he was involved with unsavoury elements in Southend, a place notorious for that reason. Then, suddenly, there was silence at 'Dalmeny'. It became known that Mr Strutt was doing a short term in prison.

Down in the town of Leigh on a Saturday afternoon, the sea might be far out, and the odd dinghy lying upturned on the shore, but the tide of human existence was full in the streets, with noise and friendly jostling. People seemed excited by mere human contact with each other, as they milled at the entrance to Woolworth's or stood staring into shop windows. Regardless of season, there was rock on display and toy windmills, whose celluloid sails stirred in the faintest breeze. Something raffish in the air mingled with the pervasive smell of mud, emphasising the fact that this was a seaside town, one popular with 'trippers', day-trippers mainly, since Leigh was easily reached from London.

I would feel weary, trailing behind my parents and weaving among so many adult legs. I felt also how we belonged to no group. We, or at least my parents, signalled detachment from the scene, amused by it and often critical of its individual manifestations in dress or speech or behaviour.

If we entered a café for tea, it was almost invisibly. Nothing ought to attract attention to our table (barely even a waitress). Around us, families talked, and even fought, as they stacked their shopping bags and seated tired, recalcitrant children. A parent shouted and a baby wailed. I had never heard my parents' voices raised, and I knew how important it was to be quiet in public. It was no fleeting, tolerant glance that my father directed at the noisiest table near us. Indeed, I was surprised that it did not take immediate effect.

So we tended more and more to keep away from Leigh at the weekends. It was pleasanter – certainly, it was quieter

– in our garden, slowly coming into existence, and in the drawing-room whose French windows opened on to it. My father wanted a garden of flowers, not of vegetables (which anyway he happened not to eat), and had no love of toil for its own sake. Unlike our immediate neighbours, we employed a gardener, frankly for the boring tasks – just as we employed a handyman for those inside jobs, like putting up shelves, which my father detested. Had he boasted of anything about the house, it would have been that nothing you saw was his own work.

Perhaps what most marked us off, in unobtrusive fashion, were the weekend afternoons and early evenings passed in the drawing-room, over tea, listening to gramophone records. In these informal equivalents to concerts, my father was impresario as well as in the audience. My mother listened and shared most of his tastes, while I sat and fidgeted, frequently puzzled by words as well as by music, aware of lacking my father's natural ear. I looked rather than truly listened, absorbed more by the flimsy paper record-sleeves, some of which showed a flame-like spirit inspiring a fiery violin virtuoso. By chance, that image increased my chagrin. I knew that my father's father had been a serious amateur cellist, and his father – my great grandfather – Richard Michael Levey, had been a professional violinist and a well-known conductor and composer in Dublin. His two favourite composers were said to be those whose names he had given to my grandfather. Haydn Handel.

Some of my puzzlement was caused by the extreme variety of the programmes my father devised. Even I was susceptible to musical mood – if only rather in the manner of a dog scenting emotional tension in its human owners. I felt a cloud of desolation darken the primrose walls of the drawing-room whenever I heard Olczewska's deep brown voice lamenting loss, as she sang '*Che farò*' from Gluck's *Orfeo*. Even I stopped fidgeting at that; and indeed my first reaction could have been a primitive howl.

I was then unprepared for the subsequent Gilbert and

Sullivan patter-aria – or something acceptably cheeky from Arthur Askey, like 'The Bee Song' – to be followed by a much-loved Chopin nocturne or Massenet's popular 'Meditation' from *Thaïs*. A piece of virtuoso violin-playing by Heifetz, perhaps of his own composing, seemed to evoke family associations, and through the whole musical patchwork usually gleamed threads of green, with something Irish, whether 'The Rose of Tralee' or 'Phil the Fluter's Ball', to which we listened possessively, as if to a national anthem. I somehow intuited that such songs reinforced our racial difference from our neighbours. And although having no idea what a 'fluter' was, I smiled and shared a feeling that we too had had the gaiety, 'at Phil the Fluter's Ball'.

Had I realised it, these easy, relaxed occasions, in which music *was* the relaxation, provided a revealing portrait of my father. He was happy with the physical restriction of records in those days, which imposed a diet of excerpts. Central to his tastes was the human voice, though he was also fond of chamber music. Schubert was the composer who best satisfied his requirements, but plenty of opera figured among his preferences, with a special place for *Don Giovanni*. Wagner (one of my grandfather's favourite composers) was never heard. Nor did we listen to much conventionally 'religious' music. Nevertheless, I think that certain compositions and certain voices (Maggie Teyte's, Gigli's, John McCormack's) gave my father experiences as spiritual – of their kind – as those he experienced in church.

Tantalising wisps of melody floated like cobwebs around the house, well after the gramophone had been shut and the tea-things removed. I could sense if not hear occasional echoes of music we had played. Unaware that there was anything of parody about *Iolanthe*, I just accepted my father as the Queen of the Fairies, humming 'Oh, foolish fay . . .' But though I saw nothing incongruous when he – of all men – assumed the persona of the Duke in *Rigoletto*, I felt I was intruding on some private, elusive relationship, beyond my comprehension, as I entered the kitchen and heard his *sotto-voce* rendering, '*La donna è mobile* . . . *woman is fi-i-ckle*', while he helped my silent, smiling mother with the washing-up.

Of all roles, it was that of Company Sergeant-Major which appeared least to fit him – and the difficulty was reinforced when I joined the Army. Yet it would be the Army, forever educating me in its forceful, practical way, that brought home this very aspect of his abilities.

As a recently-commissioned young Second Lieutenant, with the duty of getting two platoons of men across London, before embarking for the Middle East, I mislaid a number in the passages of the Underground. With great discretion, my parents had come to see me off at Victoria. It was my father who went back to retrieve and round up the missing troops. He reported to me with the equivalent of, 'All present and correct'. I couldn't have borne the irony had he tacked on a 'Sir'.

When my father left school he had gone into a bank but resigned when his superiors would not give him time off for playing football matches. That, at least, was the immediate reason, but I doubt if the work had utilised a tithe of his mathematical skill and mathematical imagination. He entered the Air Ministry, thus becoming a civil servant – and few things were to irritate him more than the common assumption that all civil servants are timid, plodding, bureaucratic creatures, with no purpose but to paralyse the body politic.

On 11 July 1914 he became twenty-one. It was a significant occasion in those days, and that actual date now has a certain poignancy when I look at it inscribed on the case of the silver watch his father gave him, accompanied by the words: 'Papa, to Otto'. Breakfast that summer morning at 'Homeleigh' must have been – certainly should have been – particularly festive. The youngest of my grandfather's fifteen surviving children had reached his majority. He and his second wife, my father's mother, could congratulate themselves on a large and largely contented family. And Otto was popular, I think, with all his siblings.

Within a month, the Great War had broken out and my father enlisted in the Civil Service Rifles. I like to believe that he took his watch with him to the war. And perhaps also a football.

He definitely took a character keenly sensitive under its cheerful skin. It was probably in the Army that he learnt to dislike and conceal his fine first name, with its thoroughly Teutonic ring. Everything German was being hysterically stigmatised, and a Tommy called Otto might have been dubbed a spy. It was no moment to explain that he was named after a businessman friend of his father's who was Swiss. His other two names were Lemuel and Herbert, and both he understandably abhorred. Yet he was more fortunate in every way than his immediately older brother, a married man with two small sons, whom my grandfather had named Fritz – the archetypal name for the enemy. In 1917, at the age of twenty-seven, Fritz was killed. And late in the previous year, my grandmother had died. That she died while he was away at the Front never ceased to be a mournful event for my father.

Of course, he looks smiling, as well as youthful, in such photographs as exist of him home on leave, always in uniform: with my grandfather, himself looking dignified, benign and self-content; reading in a deck-chair; playing with a young niece; and standing between two uniformed comrade friends. Some of his Army friendships lasted most of his life, though his closest friend, perhaps from schooldays, was killed.

'Ah,' Senta, the sweetest of my seven maiden aunts, would sigh, 'Lovat was so good-looking, I was quite in love with him. If I had ever thought of marrying, I think I could have married him.'

Even without his first name, my father was saddled with that of Levey, which suggested Jewish if not precisely foreign origin, and he was sometimes greeted by men under him singing a period song about a second-hand clothes dealer 'Old Solomon Levi', which had the unabashed antisemitic flavour of references to Jews by Dickens and Trollope. He seems to have taken that good-humouredly (or taught himself to take it so), sure of his Christian creed and that Levey was merely an adopted name, his own grandfather being properly called O'Shaughnessy.

He delighted in telling a story of his wartime life, when he became involved in a drunken quarrel between two soldiers, one of whom was Irish. After the Irishman had threatened to knock the other man's block off, he calmed down and ended by claiming to recognise in my father a fellow-countryman, saying, 'I knew it from the first. Like meself, you're an O'.'

It was after being wounded for the third time, I think, that my father was taken to the military hospital at Saint-Omer, in 1917. Among the nurses who tended him was my mother.

Gladys Mary Milestone was her name. To me her surname has rooted, rugged, rustic associations, and the Milestone family is recorded from the eighteenth century as living and working in and around the village of Hutton Rudby in the North Riding of Yorkshire. They certainly were 'Far from the madding crowd's ignoble strife' (my mother was fond of Gray's 'Elegy Written in a Country Churchyard'), with occupations like shoemaker, gardener and joiner. Thomas Milestone, my mother's grandfather, was a gardener whose status may have improved by the time of her birth, for he seems to have become a factor at a grand local property, Skutterskelfe Hall, built by Salvin. He lived in a house called Folly Hill, perhaps on estate land, where my mother and her elder brother, Oswald, were to be brought up.

By the light of an oil-lamp, as it were, my mother gave me in my childhood glimpses into her own childhood which wavered between the vivid and the shadowy, with all the appeal of the different and the long-ago. Braemar Crescent was losing its closeness to the natural world, as more and more houses ate up the open ground, but the surrounding prosaic blocks of concrete and tiles melted when my mother talked of the snowy fields through which she and her beloved Auntie Martha used to walk to fetch the morning milk from a farm. In the spring they picked primroses by the banks of the river Leven, which runs under a bridge close to the church of Hutton, at some distance from the village on its hill, where the houses were divided, unnumbered, between North Side and South Side, and up the middle extends the long broad tongue of the Green.

Adventure was provided by incidents such as being chased by an angry bull as she and her aunt fetched home the milk, and pleasure by the peaches and pineapple which came occasionally from the Skutterskelfe glass-houses. Although she and her brother got on well, she seems to have been happiest just wandering in the countryside at any season or reading – poetry chiefly – in the parlour at Folly Hill.

'One day,' my mother would say, without conviction, 'I'll take you to Hutton, and you'll see it all for yourself.'

That would remind her of the first visit my father, her unofficial fiancé, made to the village. He thought she was joking when she told him – Otto – to ask at King's Cross for a ticket to the name of the nearest station, which happened to be called Potto.

I wonder how much my father saw on that visit – not of the deep, rich countryside, with its backdrop of the gentle Cleveland Hills, but of the facts of my mother's upbringing, which had marked her for life. There were things she rarely referred to, at least to me, and other things I presume she never knew.

Sadness impinged on both her parents. Her mother, a girl born Emma Hawes, illegitimately, to a Bathsheba Hawes in Norfolk, somehow met Thomas Milestone's son, Arthur, a joiner, and was living with him as his wife at Hutton in 1891. They had a small son, Oswald. In 1892 Gladys Mary, my mother, was born. Two years later Emma died, of tuberculosis, at the age of twenty-seven. Although Arthur's parents were growing elderly, the brother and sister were sent to live with them, looked after mainly by their unmarried daughter, Martha. Arthur seems to have moved back to Folly Hill for a period, but in 1898 he married the much younger Clara Bussey, with whom he would have two daughters and a separate household.

My mother would refer openly to never having known her mother, whose personality remains unknowable. About her father she was guarded, detached, possibly resentful. Surprisingly early in my childhood, and with uncharacteristic drama, she told me that he 'drank'. I have often wondered since whether the actual disclosure of this fact, which was accompanied by begging me never to 'drink' when I grew up, was prompted by news of his death. At any rate, he became to her a distant, if pitiable, figure, and I think she felt no bond between them. She may even have felt that he connected her with her mother's dying. And although she liked and kept in contact with her half-sisters as adults, she never forgot that her father – for whatever reason – did not take the two children of his first marriage to live with him and his second wife.

I know nothing of how my mother was educated. While fond of constantly assuring me about schooldays being the happiest days of your life, she was totally silent about hers, leaving me to ask myself now whether she had ever been to school. She was naturally intelligent, and in one area – English poetry – she educated herself. It was an extension of her affection for the English countryside, one unlikely to be shared by anybody in her immediate childhood environment.

Effectively an orphan, she lost her brother's company when he went out comparatively young to New Zeland (and only in old age were they reunited, visiting Hutton together). Dark, tall, thin, and intense, and aware of lacking prettiness, as she lacked self-confidence, she must have been the first to recognise that her future was uncertain and that she must cease as soon as possible to be a 'burden'. Some farmer or gardener would, no doubt, have been prepared to marry her, and she had learnt housewifely skills of the necessary kind, but she was shy with men. She wanted to be loved, and to love, though the prospect will have seemed remote to a personality imbued with a sense of unworthiness.

Duty, rather than any sense of vocation, probably guided her to take up nursing – almost the secular equivalent of taking the veil, and at the period nurses and nuns dressed very similarly. Socially humble though a nurse was, she yet performed a useful task. How great the national use could and would be can scarcely have been apparent when, around 1910, my mother went to train in a hospital at Stockton-on-Tees. The work proved to suit her. She was compassionate but practical, and whatever her nervous, self-deprecating manner, she was professionally calm. She made friendly acquaintances among the other nurses and may well have felt happier than in adolescence.

I doubt if anyone at Hutton had ever bothered to take a photograph of her, but there exist snapshots of her in nurse's uniform during the Great War. One of her standing with two senior-looking colleagues, all slightly smiling on a bright spring day, is annotated in her unexpectedly bold, firmly legible handwriting, 'In the snow, March 1917'. Another shows her in France, probably at Saint-Omer. A military hospital seems to be in the background. She looks shy and gaunt but cheerful, standing taller than the notably youthful convalescent Scots soldier beside her. She always remembered him as 'a nice boy called Jock'.

My father was first photographed as a baby, seated comfortably on his mother's lap, at the centre of the large family group which includes all his fourteen siblings. The next photograph I know of him shows an eager boy of about eight in a sailor suit, kneeling on a chair and playing chess with his father – beating him, according to my aunts. Obviously posed though the photograph is (by Brookman of East Dulwich Road), it is as accurate as it is charming. My father's ability at the game was precociously manifest, and my grandfather was proud enough to have it commemorated.

A huge gap existed between the environment in which my father was nurtured and that which had conditioned my mother. From the contrast between urban and rural, south London and north Yorkshire, the differences multiply until their two temperaments stand for two contrasting types: the easy-going, outwardly friendly, confident, Irish Roman Catholic, and the nervous, repressed, preoccupied Northerner, with a stoic rather than a Christian outlook on life.

Horrendous events, unleashed by individuals but rapidly out of their control, were responsible for bringing these two people into contact. And some of the horror lies in the by then commonplace nature of the contact, as thousands of wounded soldiers were tended by nurses professional and voluntary. Many of the men will have died, nevertheless, or been so mutilated that they might better have died.

It is mere luck that my father survived, while his brother was killed. It is mere luck that my mother happened to be a nurse in the hospital to which he was sent. After that I know nothing until a couple of post-war snapshots show the two of them together, very much an engaged pair, in somebody's suburban garden.

I have no difficulty in recognising them, and in many ways they would change little in the following forty years of married life. Neither of them ever suffered any serious illness. An unaffected sort of boyishness and buoyancy stayed with my father until the day of his very sudden death in his own home. Even in widowhood my mother's hair remained brown (just as had her grandfather's she said), and she was still thin and brisk, as well as brave, as a widow celebrating her eightieth birthday. But it is typical of their temperaments that my father should photograph easily – if here looking uncharacteristically serious – while my mother appears tense in the knowledge of being fatally un-photogenic.

The survival of photographs of them together, indeed of any later photographs of her, is rare. Ingrained self-deprecation led to her taking the scissors to most images of her. 'I only spoilt them,' she would explain, listing her physical deficiencies – from too long a nose to hair so thin that nothing could be done with it.

My father might reasonably have responded that, as the engagement photographs hint, he was growing plump and his hair was already receding. But, she would have countered, you look attractive; you are charming. Nobody could love her for her looks, and she was sure she had no charm.

It might have developed into a duet – though, of course, she would have pointed out that she lacked his tuneful voice. Her anti-narcissism began with loathing the name Gladys (and it is true that neither he nor anyone else cared for it; he often called her 'GML'). That he should dislike his name seemed to her perverse. Then, she had no taste or interest in clothes, and dressed largely on a camouflage principle in tones of brown. But it was his turn to counter: he disapproved of women who set out to be chic. He wanted a wife with a mind above clothes and fashion.

So I envisage a dialogue of courtship, in which she kept emphasising her defects, without ever denying her love of him. And he kept effortlessly reassuring her. Yes, his vast family would be delighted with her – and anyway it didn't matter what they thought, since he loved her. And as they went through this unconventional ritual, it must have become compellingly clear that their affinities outweighed all the superficial differences. Both had the same modest dream: of life as peaceful and stable, with a modicum of money, a small house, and a relationship of mutual affection.

Different though their ways might be, both of them were basically shy. Both were reticent in physical terms and display. Both believed implicitly in goodness and in the need to be good. His belief was built on the Catholic faith. Hers was more impersonal and Wordsworthian, derived from a sense of the good in nature. And he, I suspect, no less than she, might have wondered before they met whether the world conceivably had in it someone who could be a compatible, lifelong partner.

Lack of money would delay their marriage for several years. And, of course, she had to undergo 'instruction' in his faith from a priest, with the not very subtle pressure to convert to it, which she did. They were eventually married in his local Brixton church in 1924. But before the actual ceremony they must already have felt emotionally linked together for better for worse, for richer for poorer, in sickness and in health, until death should them part.

Never would they tire of each other's company over the three decades or so ahead. Half-teasingly but fondly, she saw in him always something of the good-looking, good-hearted, happy-go-lucky lad with Irish blood and a trace of cockney or south London accent. To him she was a tender, dependable, thrifty Yorkshire lass, needing to worry less about everything, though not even his temperament could change her ingrained, Northern pessimism, while he delighted in her occasional Northern vocabulary. They met with her nursing him, but for much of their lives together it was he who – figuratively – nursed her.

Their mutual love could only grow stronger as they came to know each other more profoundly. So contented was their union that it must have been a shock, however joyful on the surface, when they realised that they would no longer be a couple: they were to be joined by a little stranger.

3

The Little Stranger

In the winter after we had moved into our newly-built house in Braemar Crescent, my mother became ill with what was passed off as some form of flu. It was unlike her to admit to more than a cold, or to stay in bed for even a day, but this illness, probably nervous exhaustion, was prolonged to the point where we needed a temporary housekeeper.

My father turned to the Catholic church in Leigh, and from its congregation emerged a wee white-faced mouse of a woman who always wore a big black velvet hat. Miss Stewart was a Scots spinster, appropriately living in nearby Stirling Avenue. Possibly she had kept house before, so easily and discreetly did she take up the role with us. I barely noticed her presence as she crept up the stairs with a tray for my mother or timidly and sweetly smiled without speaking as we met in the hall.

I guessed that under his normal demeanour my father was concerned about my mother's illness, and I found it odd to go into their bedroom to say good-night to my mother lying there. But I enjoyed the sense of freedom during the day, confident that Miss Stewart would not interfere with my pastimes. Indeed, I rather wished that she could remain part of the household.

My parents, too, liked her, and trusted her, and perhaps had their own regrets when it came to her leaving. But my mother was almost recovered and was anxious to resume looking after the house, which Miss Stewart handed over in a state of unostentatious spruceness, with the larder prudently stocked and the housekeeping purse little depleted.

As quietly and demurely as she had arrived, she departed, embarrassed by thanks, reluctant to take any payment, delighted by a bunch of anemones. It had all been a pleasure, she implied, before slipping off with a final remark that my father came to tell me straightaway, laughing as he did so.

'What did she mean?' I asked, indignant yet also intrigued.

'Just what she said, I suppose,' he replied. He could catch her soft accent admirably and he repeated her observation: 'Isn't Michael foony?'

My mother's recuperation seemed accelerated as she also started to laugh.

'But what did she mean by calling me funny?' I asked, this time plaintively. 'I don't understand.'

It was no good, however, hoping for clarification. Repeating the question only caused an outbreak of renewed, complicit smiles.

Miss Stewart had left in a gentle cloud of goodwill. Yet at the doorstep she had dropped that last cryptic comment which irritated me like a stone in my sandal. And it hurt the more because I had believed her to be so mild and nice. Was it perhaps a joke? Maybe I had amused her by something I had said, though I could think of few exchanges between us.

I was certain that I had never allowed her a glance into the glinting passages of my imagination which led to the secret mental theatre where dramas were daily taking place. Conceivably, she might have seen an old shoe-box converted to give actuality to my ideas, based on the elaborate toy-theatre I had played with in the home of some of my cousins. It was possible, too, that she had noticed among the sprouting leaves of my mother's indoor crocus some strategically-placed paper fairies, but that was no business of hers – any more than was my assembly of translucent, jewel-like handles, amethyst, amber, emerald, of discarded toothbrushes.

When, as I was gradually inducted into regular attendance at Mass on Sunday mornings, I saw Miss Stewart across the church, praying demurely, I longed to volley questions at her. After all, who was she, with her chalk-white face submerged by an inky old bonnet, to pronounce on which of us was 'foony'?

She could scuttle away, with a fleeting smile of acknowledgment of us, to her nest of a house, with nothing to do but make herself a miniature cup of tea from a miniature tea-pot. I had not merely my ongoing occupations but the whole huge business of life to cope with. More and more people were appearing in it, and I had somehow to comprehend what they were meant to mean to me. And I had the specific responsibility of dealing with the two people who were my parents. Like God, they expected things of me: primarily to be good, of course, but other things as well, which were less explicit.

I had much to be thankful for, my mother said, and when I asked what, for example, she answered, 'A roof over your head.'

Now, I had never thought of that. The next time I lay on my bed I stared through the ceiling, and through the attic, to the roof. Whereas some houses had green tiles, ours had the more usual red ones. The roof was a sort of umbrella, permanently up. Presumably there were people who had no roof over their heads, and I ought to be sorry for them. But others had roofs of their own personal kind, and to me images of a wigwam, or a hut of leaves, occupied by a solitary person, possessed enormous allure. From my bed, it seemed not far to the idea of a native seated under his roof of a palm-tree, on an island floating in a tranquil sea. Even as I had the thought, I could sense the bedstead slipping its moorings and drifting out across the ocean.

Yet I was thankful to be fixed in Braemar Crescent, and thankful for the domestic noises which told me that my parents were alive and active. If I was lucky, my mother might even be taking the trouble to prepare a special, delicate dessert called something like 'floating-island pudding', although were the day Sunday I knew dessert would be my father's favourite, trifle. No one but my mother, he always said, had the skill to produce the perfect trifle. And she always replied that it was simple enough: crisp sponge, home-made custard, whipped cream and plenty of strawberry jam.

Mysteries existed even there, because my father never drank milk (only sweetened condensed milk) and was unable to eat fresh fruit of any kind. It was a strawberry, in fact, which figured in a rare revelation of his childhood. His father offered him a sovereign if he could eat a whole one. After a single bite, he had had to rush from the room.

At many a mealtime, I would encounter thickets of conversation suddenly sprung up between my parents, thickets which, it seemed, I was not intended to penetrate. And the steady flow of maxims from my mother included one meant pointedly for me: Speech is silver, but Silence is golden. Indifferent to its message, I welcomed that maxim for its balancing of the two precious metals. They presented themselves in association with my father, because he had two pocket watches. As well as his father's twenty-first birthday gift of the silver one, he owned a more beautiful one, a gold half-hunter, with a double case at the back which, when very young, I had enjoyed blowing on and making magically open; and I always enjoyed a sight of its minute, intricate, jewelled workings.

If I was frequently tempted to go off into a daydream, who – I asked myself – would not on those occasions when I was of the company but expected to be mute? The three of us had in front of us at table our plates and glasses, and our three individual napkin-rings, as well as the food for which we should be truly grateful. But some of the topics which arose were for only two people: not my concern; not, properly for my ears; or, most maddeningly of all, would not be intelligible to me until I was older.

Getting older seemed, if I interpreted my mother correctly, among the most pressing of my duties. Not that I ought to puzzle too fiercely about how to achieve the aim. At least, I was to stop making faces and frowning, because – according to her – that would make me an old man before I had grown up.

I could not help noticing that my father appeared altogether less bothered over the urgency of my growing up. To him, my activities were always of interest or amusement. A sight of my sploshy water-colours, supposedly of our house or the garden, impressed him, and he at once appreciated my need for a new, bigger paint-box. He was prepared to admire my paper cut-outs, whether they represented fairies or farm animals. And when he saw my efforts to construct a theatre, he was stirred to genuine enthusiasm. Love of the theatre generally, and of theatrical performances, ran in the blood. Most of his family liked going to a show, preferably one with music and not too solemn.

'But you're fond of a good show, too,' he might add, chivalrously eager to include the brooding figure of my mother, and looking up at her while he squatted on the floor, the better to examine my stage.

Her response became familiar: 'Well, I loved seeing *Lilac Time* with you.'

'And you loved *Chu-Chin-Chow*. And *Merrie England*.'

'I've glued some string on to this angel,' I would be quick to interpolate. 'So it can fly down from heaven.'

All three of us, he assured me, would one day go to a theatre and see a play. When he said it, I knew it would come to pass – as certainly as would his provision of a new paint-box, probably next week.

Partly, he was impressed by what I did because of its novelty to him. Neither he nor any of his siblings had aspired in their childhood to paint or draw. He was fully conscious of lacking any visual artistic knack – and, still more, any instrict.

Deeply embedded in his temperament, however, was a

response to the glamour of theatrical performance, of actors and musicians, and all that was involved in going to the theatre. It extended from serious plays to musical comedy, the pantomime and the less ribald of music-halls. Often, the performer stood out in his memory more than the production. He never forgot seeing Sarah Bernhardt, reduced by then to lying on a sofa, in a scene or speech from Rostand's *L'Aiglon*, when he was on leave in London during the Great War. And he spoke with equal enthusiasm, it seemed to me, of Dan Leno: a comedian who lived on in his memory as a genius, although he had in fact died (as I could not then know) when my father was aged only eleven.

In my muddled way, I used sometimes to wonder whether Dan Leno might not be a relation, so familiar was his name in our house. Seldom would I meet people elsewhere to whom he was even a name, while the sense of affinity with him was enhanced on learning that he was Irish by origin and in private life had owned a house not far from Brixton, in Balham. And gradually I became aware also that to his closest friends outside the family my father was addressed – for reasons unconnected with Leno – as 'Dan'. It was a biblically-derived joke, based on the tribes of Levi and Dan.

My attraction to the theatre might or might not be a matter of heredity, but since it was shared with my father, it could not be dismissed or denigrated by my mother, whatever she thought of its manifestations. Anyway, it was true that she herself was far from immune to the spell of theatre-going. And in Harrogate, during the Second World War, she frequently indicated to me, with subdued yet noticeable excitement, some prominent actor or actress from the local repertory company, seen by daylight shopping or having coffee. Of course, she would immediately compensate by emphasising that theirs was a terrible life: 'I hope you will never want to go on the stage.'

I am not sure she ever knew how many of her husband's family had, before I was born, ignored hopes of that kind. They might have been cited to demonstrate that in the tendency to be stage-struck I could not be accused – for once – of being eccentric. My grandfather, to take it no further back, had probably turned attraction into the safer path of theatre-going, going as far as Bayreuth to see Wagner's operas and commemorating his attachment by naming three of his daughters after Wagner heroines: Elsa, Senta and Eva. And in a tangle of brothers and half-brothers of his, mainly professional musicians, one was a performer so confident of his virtuosity that he appeared publicly in the character of 'Paganini's Ghost'.

Seeing my interest, my father was early prompted to touch on other performers in the family, without nostalgia, though on occasion with pride. He told me of his cousin Sivori (the unusual name stuck in my mind), 'The Musical Reciter', as he advertised himself when performing at the Steinway Hall: 'Popular Poems at the Piano'. It was reckoned a treat at 'Homeleigh' when Cousin Sivori ('Sivvy') came privately for a supper party and delivered some of his popular dramatic and humorous recitations with music.

There was another performer my father mentioned, in an anecdote that increasingly seemed ambiguous to me as I grew older. I never was bold enough to ask for elucidation. At first, I took it as a delightful joke, though it did not seem to amuse my mother. His father (my grandfather, Haydn Handel) had once walked past a fiddler playing in the street, before going back, or sending back one of his children, to put some money in the man's cap. And then it emerged – would you believe it? – that the fiddler was no other than his own brother. I laughed at the trick, and had no thought, when I first heard the story, that the fiddler might have been playing for pennies in the gutter through poverty.

Chatter freely as I might about my theatrical and other projects to my father, I felt there was a bar always on putting personal questions to him. Either he volunteered information about members of his family, and, more sparingly, about himself, or he showed indifference, distaste and unusual near-asperity under any attempt to interrogate him.

Just as I had to learn not to bump into people physically, so I had to learn the more subtle art of not coming up against them psychologically. The fact that he was my father, who loved me, as I him, gave me of itself no knowledge of his personality. Indeed, only slowly was I growing conscious that he possessed a personality and that he had not been placed on earth exclusively in the role of my male parent.

Possibly because of his rarity value, in the sense of being at home and available only for the one day in the week, I found he required much more study by me than did my mother, about whom I thought far less and whose attitudes were largely predictable. I loved her too, but about her loving me I was already more dubious, despite her unremitting care, her moments of tenderness and – perhaps paradoxically – her shrewdness in seeing into my mind. She and I were together so much at that pre-school period that familiarity bred in me not only blindness but indifference to shades in her personality. And if I put my father at the apex of our triangle, I was merely obeying her unspoken or – more likely – spoken wish.

When my father showed momentary impatience with me, or was tired of the subject, whatever it was, I had two alternatives: retreating into profound sulks, or advancing, accepting a change of mood and, where useful, a change of place. After a tactical break during which he might concentrate on the harder of the *Observer* crosswords or idly consider the chances of some fancied horse in a forthcoming race (one more among the sports he followed), I might return, refreshed, having mentally washed my face and improved my demeanour.

Like the household, the house exuded a firm, almost palpable harmony. There seemed nothing excessive, nothing obtrusive, about it. Everything had its own place in interiors neat and polished, and yet planned to be rooms in which ordinary people would live and relax. It could not possibly be called opulent, but still less threadbare. It was far from smart or modern, but not at all old-fashioned. It was plain and calm, and as balanced as its owners. If anything threatened to upset its atmosphere, it was I, liable to rush in and trip on the carpet, to bump into even familiar easy-chairs and to let a door slam behind me.

'You never look where you are going,' my mother would remark, in a tone already resigned.

I had no intention of contesting the point. But should I necessarily be expected always to know where – in the wider sense – I was going? The carpets and chairs were substantial enough, and they received little actual damage from me. What I was more liable to disturb, wilfully sometimes but often in innocence, truly by accident, was the framework of the relationship between my parents and myself. That piece of invisible furniture was everywhere, and the essence of its shape remained triangular. No fourth presence, not even that of a domestic animal, would ever alter the outlines or add an ornamental top-knot to the structure.

For me, it had many of the qualities of bamboo. It looked fragile and it was rickety, but it had its own resilience, as well as its tension. And if occasionally I knocked up against it quite deliberately, or gave it a good shake, I did so to learn more about its exact nature.

Certainly, it was no accident that I was most liable to upset something on a Sunday. About that traditional day of rest there frequently gathers in any household, regardless of any religious constraint, an air of restlessness. Our Sundays were kept severely domestic. Nobody visited us. Trevor Morgan and I never met on a Sunday. It was a day for families to be together. Our family was pared down to the basic trio, locked into an emotional and physical proximity that could appear imposed, as the hours elapsed, not for enjoyment but as a test of temper.

Long before I was born, my parents had constructed their relationship. And now, though the fact lay beyond my perception, they had constantly to make adjustments to it – add an extra bedroom, as it were, and more furniture –

in order to take account of the developing personality who was their son. He had his task too, in relation to them – a double task, since he must discern and define how he stood to each of them.

On any Sunday, in that controlled environment, I tended at some moment to retire upstairs, having – wittingly or not – unleashed a poltergeist. I left it frolicking about, a warning to my parents that they were no longer just a couple. My moods could make the whole house uneasy and drive them out into the garden, where to stumble over some toy of mine was to be given a new, painful reminder of my existence. On occasion, even adults could fail to look where they were going.

As the one who had precipitated the situation, I never doubted my responsibility. It was for me to descend and act as exorcist before our Sunday concluded, and down I would come, with a power of seeing through walls, fairly certain of where, and how, I should find each parent.

In that slack, unsatisfactory period of the day, when the afternoon had evaporated but evening scarcely begun, I felt I should be most welcome. It might be that I should discover my parents together, gazing hopefully at some patch of flower-bed where they had planted a favourite flower of my mother's, love-in-the-mist (a favourite of mine also, because of its fat, gooseberry-like seedpods). But it was more probable that they were inside, and apart, and I could weigh which of them I should approach.

In the kitchen, my mother would be preparing a cold supper, minus salad, very much for my father, who would happily eat cold roast potatoes left over from lunch. If she greeted me with a sad, abstracted expression, I realised that this was less censure of any previous conduct of mine than a signal that she was wearing, in her own familiar term, her 'thinking-cap'. I was past the stage of supposing that this could be seen, except from the way it wrinkled her forehead. She was planning the main meals for me and herself over the forthcoming week, and since she believed in meat as other people believe in metaphysics, it was a strain to vary our diet on a limited budget.

I could anticipate the pattern: cold joint on Monday, mince on Tuesday, liver on Wednesday ... And Friday beckoned joyfully, since it was the day on which we had to eat fish. Only Thursday's meal seemed insoluble, and she might well wail aloud, 'Oh, what are we to have on Thursday?', as though she saw herself reduced to beggar-woman status, clutching to her withered bosom her puny, starving infant.

I was incapable of making sensible suggestions of the kind any child could today: pasta, say, or cheese and bread. And, had I done so, they would have been dismissed as nearly shameful. Food that was cooked without trouble, or not cooked at all, did not rank as proper food.

Over any recent outburst of mine, my sighs, my sulks, my piece of bored or bad behaviour, I felt no special fear of her rebuke, for rebukes were as much part of the daily menu as the meals. I was inured to being, along with the food and the shopping and the laundry (which, I noticed, she always pronounced 'larndry'), one of her problems. She loved me, of course, but she had the duty of improving me. That, she implied, is what a mother's love consists of; and as I had then no direct experience of other mothers, I presumed it must be so.

Seldom did we have quarrels, and sometimes when we were alone together, she surprised me by a sudden confession (of how, for instance, she dreamt of going to India) or by an affectionate, sympathetic response to some request of mine. It was odd – she said it was odd – but she could understand why I asked to be allowed out in my oilskin mac and sou'wester to stand in the pouring rain. She, who saw colds coming on as soon as she saw damp grass, led me conspiratorially into the windy, soaking-wet garden where worms were wriggling ecstatically on the drenched Essex clay. Tacitly, we agreed that this was not an incident to relate to my father.

I had my mother to live with throughout six days of the week, which in itself explained why I probably chose on a Sunday to leave her undisturbed in the kitchen and instead push open the door of the drawing-room, in the hope of interrupting my father. Whatever he was doing, I could be sure he was not conventionally resting. If he had solved the crossword, and prepared it for submitting in the weekly competition, he was probably amusing himself with a mathematical problem of his own devising – and there no amount of love could let him suppose I shared his interest. But though exercising – in echo of a Gilbert and Sullivan song – 'of his brains', he quickly turned his attention to me, at once inferring that my coming was some form of apology. It sufficed, and words were not needed, which was both relief and frustration to me, eager to throw myself into his arms and be treated as a prodigal son. Yet I knew that any excessively emotional scene would only set up fresh currents of disturbance in the house, as well as being repugnant to him.

He never articulated the ideals that ought to guide me, but I was convinced he held them. I cannot remember his ever mentioning the existence of God. He had no list of grumbles about my daily conduct ('Ah, but he doesn't have to put up with you as I do,' my mother at her gloomiest would have declared). But I was attuned to any hint of his disapproval, and sometimes I felt savage denunciation would have shamed me less than his lightly-delivered verdict that I had behaved 'like a chump'. Willingly would I have abased myself on the carpet, moaning for forgiveness of my sins. Much harder to bear was the stinging sensation, breaking out all over, like nettle-rash, when he said that frankly I was in danger of becoming a pain in the neck.

After that, I could only run wildly into the garden, kicking at the first ball I happened to find at my feet and almost wanting to be punished for scuffing up what had become the lawn. I recalled the morning when men had arrived to lay it, unrolling before my fascinated sight each divot, curled in on itself, until they had created one huge, seamless rectangle of turf. On either side of it were long herbaceous borders, dug by my father, and at one corner, near the coal-shed, was a rockery, nominally under my care. At the top of the garden, the lawn gave way to beds of roses and beyond them, against the fence, grew a pair of fruit trees. The squat, stout apple did well from the first, and its bark oozed with thick gum, but I liked better the thinner, wayward pear-tree, with its glassy, pointed leaves and its sporadic white blossom that never would ripen into fruit.

It was hard for anyone from the house to see me up there, I was sure, and on spring and summer evenings the garden seemed to lengthen as the shadows gently accumulated. There might be fairies at the bottom of it, and an aunt, meaning kindly to foster the illusion, was to photograph me in Will-o'-the-Wisp costume. But the result would not have deceived the most credulous. I felt awkward, and I looked it. The costume was too tight and it prickled in embarrassing places.

Nor, in reality, was the garden any bigger than the modest standard one for the modest three-bedroomed house. It failed to expand with my expanding activities. The lawn was too small for any semblance of a tennis-court, and hopeless for playing cricket on. The closeness of the adjoining gardens made soccer socially hazardous, with furtive efforts to retrieve the ball over the fence by means of a rake. There was something tame about having to play even clock-golf in abbreviated form, but when I got a craze for archery a few years later, I exulted in shooting arrows from the garden, to soar high above the house top, and fall in the street outside. Although dubbed an archery set for children, mine had metal-tipped arrows, and their effectiveness was demonstrated when one of my less accurate shots penetrated the frosted glass of the kitchen door; I had to admire the sang-froid of my mother as she emerged to state tersely that she might have been killed.

However, the garden seemed to have no limits on those

many evenings when my father stepped into it, to join me in some hectic game of our own. It did not matter whether the ball was large or small, hard or soft, or what we played. The same principle underlay virtually all games, he said. 'Just keep your eye on the ball. The rest is easy'.

'Easy for you,' I should retort subsequently, at a time when he was seriously coaching me at tennis or trying to improve my swing on the golf course at Harrogate. And, in the garden at Leigh, watching him dribble a football, or head it effortlessly this way and that, while I longed to emulate him, I thought that the secret must lie with his own eye.

In the capricious evening light, the colour of his eyes seemed as varying and appeared as intriguing as his graceful, unshowy skills. Usually, they appeared grey or grey-blue with perhaps some tint of fawn, but on occasion, their greyness deepened to green. I had to ask my mother to tell me what colour they really were. Conscious, perhaps, of providing a less cogent answer than usual, she had finally been reduced to saying, 'They're Irish eyes.' And it was true that some of his sisters had eyes similarly-coloured, but I was left yet more puzzled. Could it be that my mother was, untypically, making a joke?

I had inherited her brown eyes, which was – I understood – a pity. It was a pity also that I had inherited her long, poorly-co-ordinated limbs, with none of the compact agility that characterised my father. She was, she insisted, hopeless at catching a ball, but whereas that mattered little for a girl, it was important for a boy to be good at games, and especially important for me, given my father.

Would you, I wanted to ask (though I didn't), when we were talking of boys and girls, have preferred to have had a daughter? I guessed that any reply to that would have stressed my father's desire for a son – as though his desire must be paramount. Actually, I sensed that what made him happy was having a child; I couldn't see him being bothered about its gender.

However, the main issue – to which my mother would soon bring us back – was the benefit for me, being a boy, in having such a man as my father. When I kicked a football, I should be aware that my father had played soccer for England and would have gone on playing longer, had his career not been cut short by incurable cramp. How cramp still affected him I knew, for I had heard him cry out in sudden agony as his leg twisted under him. A pain that drove him to betray suffering must indeed have been terrible. But then, he had the glory of having 'played for England'. I envisaged him alone on the field, or anyway captaining the side, and while unclear about what playing involved, I loved the sight my mother allowed me of his caps. There was one of ribbed white silk, for playing against Belgium, and another, of plum-coloured velvet, for playing against Spain. Strangely shallow I found them, when I attempted to put them on, but I had the thrill of contact: these were rewards won by my father in playing soccer, and through them perhaps his ability would pass to me.

Because of him, soccer was my favourite game for playing in the garden. He encouraged me, he excited me, as he dribbled the ball past me towards some rudimentary goalpost, or called for me, in possession at last, to shoot. The ball flew dangerously high, near to some freshly-planted lupins, bounced across the lawn and perhaps up into the face of my mother, who had come out to announce that supper was ready – and that I should be ready for bed.

'Just one more shot,' either of us might plead.

'Well . . . But you must both be exhausted. And you know, Otto, you've got to be up early tomorrow for the office.'

She stood there indulgently, one arm half-raised against the evening sunlight that filled the garden.

And I think – I certainly like to think – that on such evenings, the peaceful atmosphere of the scene, the beauty of nature, the sense of hopes in life fulfilled, were for a while stronger than any fears. Amid so much that was right, with much to be grateful for, even down to my father's original insistence that the back garden should face west, it may have seemed wrong to worry greatly over Thursday's lunch.

Two boys were fooling about in front of her, though to other eyes one might appear, regardless of his marvellous dexterity with a ball, merely a fattish, bald-headed man, flushed by exercise or by the setting sun. Yet he was hers, as much as was the pale child, with legs like matchsticks, despite the food she tried to cram into him, who – it had to be admitted – was healthy and energetic, in his nervy way, and by no means stupid.

Seeming hardly out of breath, my father obeyed the unspoken message that – for all their fun – our Sunday revels now must end. It was becoming darker in the garden, and cooler, and the sky had gained the serene, cloudless clarity of evening. I was to bring in the football and other games paraphernalia, while he had to prepare for Monday at the Air Ministry. But there still remained a few moments for him to approach my mother, and for them to stand, close together, surveying and savouring the domestic world they had created.

He might be moved to say, 'Perhaps I'll do some watering after supper.'

Shaking her head, she would glance up at the sky: 'It may rain in the night.'

I should suddenly feel feverishly hot. I knew I should not sleep, though I went off uncomplaining to bed. And much later, when night had come, I lay in my room, with the window wide open, but the pillows burning my cheek. Simply for coolness, I might get up and tip-toe to the window, crouching there, as I detected, rising from the garden, the blended sounds of hushed voices and the drizzle of the hose.

It made me more awake than sleepy, to think of them down below, moving with such excessive care, and myself a concealed spectator for whom even listening to the water was a cooling sensation. Tired as I was, I felt some sort of assurance in their continued existence – a pride almost parental in the two figures whom I could see well enough without having to peer out. They stood for the future: for tomorrow, when it would be cold mutton for lunch; and for other days ahead, when I should arrange to meet Trevor and we should go off together to the woods.

'I can't sleep,' I called, not too loudly, as I heard them coming upstairs with footfalls so soft that they became insistent. I left it to chance whether my mother would catch the half-ashamed mew of a cry.

Even as she quietly opened my door, I was drifting into a dozy state, though I rallied to repeat the cry.

'Is it tomorrow?' I asked, with feigned confusion.

'No. And you must go to sleep.'

But we both knew that I was seeking to receive the familiar, mysterious mantra that she must murmur, to guarantee that I did not wake until morning. Like beads, like jewels, like refreshing drops of coloured liquid, the words fell lullingly over me, and I repeated them after her, smilingly, wonderingly, as though each syllable was pristine and would soon turn tangible:

> Toodle-oo, Blue,
> Chin-chin, Pink,
> Goodnight, White.

4

Boys and Girls Come Out to Pray

It was God, giver of all things, who would be responsible for giving me encounters daily with girls in my childhood, though He would also be responsible for removing the contact soon after I had learnt to savour it. Religion would dictate where I should go to school; but just as that religion had not yet made much impact on me, so the concept of schooling seemed remote from life as I felt myself living it during the first months after we moved into our house in Braemar Crescent.

God's gifts included one that thrilled me every morning: an invisible yet unfailing alarm-clock, which went off dramatically inside me, to announce that night had gone and another day started. Before the rising sun had put any colour into the dull linen cheeks of my curtains, I was awake and alert and tingling at the prospect of the hours ahead. As palpably as the clean clothes on the bedside chair, they lay before me – holding greater promise of excitement than did the clothes.

Without leaving the bed, there was potentiality enough. Sheets and blankets and pillows easily became igloos and tropical cabins, or the canopied deck of some boat, out of which I leant luxuriously, trailing my arm along the floor as though in water. No human beings were conjured up to share my various adventures in various climes, but I had a secret crew of nameless, semi-mechanical creatures, their precise shapes undefined, who did my bidding. They lived at the bottom of the bed by night. When morning came, they swarmed wherever I commanded, and it was they not I who laboured to build those structures which had eventually, before breakfast, to be reduced again to bedclothes. While they lived (gradually, they were to fade from my imaginative world), they possessed a reality so strong that it extended to bodily functions: they urinated but did not defecate.

No two days of my existence proved to be exactly similar, and yet the days were all set in a routine familiar and fixed – as it seemed – for ever. I could compare their round to the postman's round, itself something I was beginning to be aware of. On most mornings he was visible in the Crescent, though what he was delivering could not be foreseen. In those pre-junk-mail times, and when ordinary households like ours paid few bills by post, what came through the letter-box were likely to be letters with news. News was shared, and I grew accustomed to receiving my portion of notice in greetings from people I did not recall meeting or had indeed never met. No letters came directly addressed to me but it happened one morning that the doorbell rang and a parcel was delivered: a parcel for me. It was not my birthday; nor was it Christmas. And once the event had occurred, I realised that it might happen again.

I had been ill, feverish, with a cold on my chest, for which Vick's vapour rub was the cure. I had to stay indoors though not in bed, and stay by the fire, and eat only such titbits as I wished. If that condition was what illness was, I thought I might be ill for several weeks. Even as the faint monotony of the days by the fireside was beginning to pall, while I remained untypically inert, disinclined to do anything, the parcel had arrived.

'Open it carefully,' my mother urged, uncertain about its contents and dubious about the excitement I was displaying, and also possibly about the wisdom of sending presents to small children. She, I could have guessed, never received such a parcel in her childhood.

I don't recall whether I was noisy or silent after I had torn off the wrapping paper and lifted the lid of the large box. But I was enraptured at what I discovered: a set of wild creatures in beautifully-painted metal, creatures that the majority of people, including my family, then thoughtlessly referred to as 'zoo animals'. There was a giraffe, a monkey or two and an elephant whose trunk was rubber, and they came with segments of green railing to make their enclosures.

If my mother felt any qualms as she too admired the animals, it was over the cost of the gift. With all her basic kindness of heart, she never thought of the implications of captivity for animals – still less of cruelty. And against real zoos Roman Catholicism had nothing to say, any more than it had against big-game hunting (or small-bird hunting in Italy and France). God had given man dominion over every living creature – one statement in the Book of Genesis which all Christians find convenient to invoke and which is probably repeated with relish over the *ossobuco* at the Vatican today. In creating the dolphin, God certainly gave a subject to the makers of nature films.

'That is good of him,' my mother kept saying, referring not to God but to the present-giver, someone I knew as 'Uncle Agar'. He was my father's best friend, and the friendship dated from schooldays when surnames only were permissible among boys. Guy Agar was to outlive my father and become known to my mother, who had never found him very sympathetic, by his first name. As a child, I just accepted his idiosyncratic, ironic-affectionate attitude, along with his beetle-browed appearance, as an occasional welcome novelty in my life. He was 'different' from my real uncles – different, in fact, from anyone else intimate with my parents.

A bachelor, comfortably off, whose chief amateur activity was with the Boy Scouts, he might today have been suspected if not condemned by society, without waiting for further evidence. As far as I know, his life was blameless, but it is true that he sang in male choirs, took thousands of terrifyingly competent photographs and enjoyed walking holidays (alone) in the Alps. A formidable mother and a housekeeper looked after him, and outside his work at the Board of Trade, he did exactly what he pleased. He enjoyed discriminating and commenting in a satirical way which often amused my father and perhaps mildly upset my mother. His musical preference was for *Lieder*. He adored the music of Schubert but not the travesty that was *Lilac Time*. He came to stay, which was sufficiently unusual, and went for walks with us, pointedly refusing to admire any too obvious signs of English natural beauty.

He took a few photographs of me much as he took notice of me, in a detached and humorous, curious, yet not forbidding manner, as if I were a specimen of the kind he had not previously encountered – which may be the truth. His photography and his equipment were professional compared to an aunt's efforts with a box Brownie. For him I posed relatively unselfconsciously, looking more strange than charming, with my straight hair giving a coconut look to my head, gazing out brown-eyed from among some bushes as though I were an only half-tamed, not entirely human thing.

If he bantered with me while he checked his lens and adjusted his light meter, always unhurriedly, I was not disconcerted. His precise, quizzical phraseology seemed part of him and more natural than his elaborate politeness to my mother over our simple meals (prompting me to wonder whether cold beetroot, say, was at home a favourite supper dish of his). My father enjoyed the thought of Agar indicating pedantically what he wanted in a shop with the words, 'Those are they.' And the two men lunched together regularly in their parallel Civil Service lives, swapping examples of departmental absurdity, and mocking the pomposity and ambition of their superiors.

At one such lunch, Agar had learnt of my illness, perhaps of my growing boredom. He never sent presents conventionally for Christmas or birthdays. He may scarcely have observed Christmas, for I am sure he had no religious faith.

When it pleased him, he gave me something, something carefully chosen and maybe expensive. He was little concerned about being thanked, but he was delighted when he heard that to each of the animals he had sent I had applied its share of Vick.

I expect Agar would have been pleased to answer, in sardonic fashion, some of the questions and clarifications about the wider world which I longed to have resolved. And, as I only realised much later, he could have told me much about my father as schoolboy. But there were no opportunities for me to initiate conversation with him, and I was shy of coming out with an abrupt enquiry about the 'Gold Standard', a subject which sounded alluring, and which was topical, or asking who exactly was Philip Snowden, someone also referred to frequently for a period. The name Ramsay MacDonald sounded a fine one to me, but it seemed to drop from talk at table in our house as though it had become improper, and I was to grow up ignorant about the man and his conduct.

As the decade of the 1930s began, the important man in the country was 'Mr Baldwin', always spoken of thus by my parents. But the opinion of my father about Baldwin remained opaque. Did he, emotionally a committed socialist though never a member of the Labour Party, ever bring himself to vote for Baldwin? When Churchill became Prime Minister in 1940, I was old enough to detect my father's reservations about a man whom he associated with the General Strike and possibly also with the disaster of Gallipoli. I could have predicted that he would not vote for Churchill as Prime Minister in peacetime. My mother was enthusiastic about Churchill the wartime leader, but denied having political views. The average woman of the Thirties was not supposed to trouble her head over matters of that sort, though the Equal Franchise Act (of 1928) had permitted women to vote at twenty-one. But my mother's sympathies were always with workers, not bosses, nor the rich. She became more radical as she became older, and as a widow in a Sussex village where it was presumed non-political, and anyway 'nicer', to vote Tory, she would go on resolutely voting Labour.

In Braemar Crescent in the 1930s nobody would have wished to be thought 'political' – if the word carried implications of being extreme. That was as true of my father as of our much less intelligent neighbours. He did not particularly study world events and would remain mistakenly optimistic as late as 1939 about the possibility of another war.

Yet some events refused to be ignored, and while I was at the stage of asking out of curiosity – and expecting my parents to have firm answers – many adults were asking out of anxiety. They may have asked the politicians, themselves no less anxious, and equally unable to comprehend what was happening. Mr Baldwin might be the man the country looked to – but where should he be looking, if he bothered to do so at all?

Ugly words like 'strike' and 'slump' had entered everyone's vocabulary, and my mother was instinctively sensitive to the general uneasiness and uncertainty, clinging for comfort to the fact that my father had a job. She felt herself fortunate not to be the wife of a miner or a docker. However small the salary my father earned, he had security and the promise of a pension. He was not like the many ex-service men who came to the door, in the land that was intended to be fit for heroes, selling brushes and dusters in an effort to make a living. Quite how they were reduced to this pitiful form of near-begging I could not understand, but I saw that my mother bought brushes she did not need and dusters inferior to any she would use – and with money we could ill afford. But it was, she intimated, right to do so – right in human terms, beyond the doctrine of any Church and regardless of punishment or reward in a future life.

Perhaps it was from my mother's anxieties and uncertainties about the larger world surrounding our own private one that I imbibed a sense of how different it was out there. Maybe in any decade she would have had forebodings (in her emotional climate the outlook was always unsettled), but in the 1930s they seemed entirely justified. That goodness was not a quality I should expect to find in the world was the message she inculcated, possibly more fervently than she realised. There were not many men out there like my father; Agar, although she did not say so explicitly, was more typical.

Had I known it, the ambiguities of the period were exemplified close to home – close to the office anyway, in my father's place of work, the Air Ministry. Conquest of the air was marvellous and essentially modern. To people of my grandfather's generation it must have been barely conceivable that government now included a ministry of the air, while a series of fresh achievements demonstrated almost annually that mankind had mastered that element. Lindbergh had flown the Atlantic in the year I was born, and among the names of public personalities I heard most frequently talked of in early childhood was Amy Johnson's. I had no need to ask who she was; even I knew she flew solo to countries around the globe.

My toys included a few aeroplanes, and I was particularly fond of one with a name I had to learn to get my tongue around, an 'autogiro', a version of the helicopter. But I don't think I made any connection between those toys and the aircraft being built for my father's Ministry. Although his department was that of contracts, I never asked then what that meant. He was merely a very junior official, one of many, charged with carrying out policy.

That policy itself was a matter of disagreement and controversy, for aeroplanes were part of Britain's defence against a future war. Was that a real or a remote possibility? And in either case, how many aircraft should be built? The sort of toy aircraft I played with seemed to belong with civil aviation and civilised transport of passengers. As I zoomed up and down stairs with a plane in my hand, I had no idea that in reality planes could mean fighters and bombers – and when I eventually understood as much, it was only another aspect of the fun. Bombing as an actual fact was largely hidden from me – as from many other people – before 1939.

No echoes of the bitter question of arming or disarming reached our household in my hearing. And it hardly seemed probable that British policy or the activities of the Air Ministry would disturb our quiet, content existence in Braemar Crescent, Leigh-on-Sea. Yet, while I was a very young boy at school, coping still with that alteration to my life, and apprehensive of any further alterations, I learnt that my parents were facing a dilemma, arising from my father's occupation, that could affect all our lives.

My alphabet book of countries had not bothered with Iraq, but suddenly Iraq was on the table at every meal. Like most foreign countries in English eyes at the period, it was distant and dubious, though I was delighted to discover its Eastern location and that it was the realm, often visited in stories, of the Caliph of Baghdad.

Now my father had the opportunity of going there, should he choose to. Britain took a generous, as it were paternal-colonial interest in Iraq and was helping it build aerodromes. The Air Ministry would send my father out there on promotion – which was tempting – for a period of two years, with leave, of course, but without any financial provision for coming home during that time. Whether he should and would accept the chance, and how my mother and I might manage in his prolonged absence, formed topics of constant debate, in ways more openly agonised, I expect, after I had gone to bed.

Half the implications were lost on me. The talk of months and years of not seeing my father meant nothing, and sometimes I dreamt that I should fly with him on some magic carpet and together we should land in Baghdad. But then I felt I must stand by my mother. I must truly grow up and be in lieu of a husband in the home. What I really wanted in the matter, I did not know, but I was oddly convinced about the outcome: he would go and I should have to remember to pray for him each night as I knelt to say my prayers. And praying brought with it associations of church and Christmas, and approaching the Crib in church in a heightened state of awareness, thinking this must be the nearest equivalent to entering a theatre. To try to imagine Christmas without my father was impossible. On any day of the year, he symbolised festivity, and supremely so at Christmas. But I never prayed to God that he would not go to Iraq. Go he would, I was sure. There was even excitement in the prospect. And go he did, leaving my mother and me together on our own.

We had lived on our own, effectively, before: in that period before I ever went to school and when day after day seemed extending timelessly in front of me. Even the hours which I spent with Trevor Morgan were only breaks in the daily routine my mother and I shared. And whatever the games that absorbed me as I played in the dining-room after breakfast, I remained conscious of the hum of domestic activity conveying her presence close at hand. Far as I travelled in fantasy, I had always to return for our meals together and our walks together. At a given time each morning, I expected her head to appear round the door, telling me it was time for us to go shopping together.

Those expeditions to the shops were ambivalent occasions for me, though one of the most prosaic and dull-promising, on a day too of dull weather, would prove unexpectedly momentous in my existence. For the most part, however, I accompanied my mother increasingly unwillingly to the baker's, the butcher's and the grocer's – all of whom had to be visited – and was not much appeased by the promise that we might cross the road to Mrs Jones's toyshop, where a penny could buy me something attractive, like a tin soldier or a minute celluloid doll.

Once or twice, our routine of morning outings had been interrupted, improved in my eyes, by my having a cold and being left, very briefly and amid many a warning, in the house by myself. To my mother that was, obscurely, not right, quite apart from its not being safe. To me there was a wonderful feeling of exultation on hearing the front-door shut and knowing myself the sole occupant of the house. It became mine, though nothing changed and I did not even bother to leave the hall to inspect the other rooms.

I could not explain my harmless urge but I could complain about the boredom of going each day to the same shops, with the same aims. In the baker's and the grocer's I saw lots to purchase, though anticipating they would be items we were unable to afford. At the butcher's, I merely hung around and scuffed my foot sulkily in the blood-spattered sawdust while my mother negotiated for 'best end of neck' (even the bill would be blood-stained when the meat was delivered) and I heard the plump, shirt-sleeved butcher cheerfully bringing his cleaver down to crunch on some animal's clavicle. 'Nice tripe today,' he would observe, with equal cheerfulness, oblivious of the fact that we were regular customers who never ordered anything of that kind.

'What is tripe?' I had asked my mother, and the gist of her answer was, 'Something cheap and unpleasant.'

That gave me a fresh puzzle, because – price aside – I could detect little to distinguish one hunk of dismembered carcass from another. And none looked particularly pleasant. Similarly puzzling was our habit of lunching off liver (my mother and I), while we never touched kidneys. No one, fortunately perhaps, had told me that both organs were present in my body. Anatomy and the abattoir were, like sex education, excluded from home education.

Adjoining the butcher's was the grocer's, larger and more inviting, with chairs for customers at the various counters, and where I felt altogether happier. Unaware of any connection with what I had seen next door, I watched with fascination as the bacon machine went into action, to give us the streaky rashers my father preferred. Further inside was the butter counter. On a square of cool white marble, the butter was slapped and patted and shaped by wooden spatulas, manoeuvred at speed and treated as a precious substance, which it was to us, for butter was not cheap. Margarine was cheaper, but my parents united in their belief that plain bread would be better, if we were so reduced, than eating margarine.

I thought the morning not wasted at the grocer's if my mother could be persuaded to buy at least a quarter of dried fruit. Another counter, the best of all, had me seated before it, gazing at the jars and tubs of varieties available. With scales to one side and sheets of thick blue paper at hand on the other, ready to be made into funnels, the buff-overalled assistant waited. I knew my choice would always have been candied peel, but my mother predictably chose sultanas. Raisins were objectionable because of their seeds. Glacé cherries were an extravagance, and candied peel was too sweet and sugary.

'What on earth would I do with it?' she had once asked aloud in the shop, exasperated or embarrassed by my insistence. 'Eat it,' was my muttered reply, almost salivating as I thought of getting my teeth into a piece of encrusted rind and barely mollified by being offered a sultana to munch. The rest of them, I knew, were destined to scatter what interest they could through the pale, damp texture of a succession of suet puddings.

That we could not possibly afford everything my eye coveted in the food shops, as elsewhere, I totally recognised. I had never forgotten that my father, despite his many gifts, was not made of money. When we entered Mrs Jones's crowded, dusty shop, and she came out from some cranny of it, grey and disagreeable, the embodiment of fairy-tale crone, I was quite proud of having little to spend. Let her wait while I decide – or I should walk out and put my penny towards some wine gums. Even sixpence bought no smile from her, impatient of children and looking as capable as eager to cast a malign spell over the whole race of them.

It would eventually be apparent that money was not the root of the problem represented for me by my mother. I had adjusted easily to her possession of a personality. She could drift out of focus, being just 'Mummy', in moments of emotion, usually distress, but for the most part, on most days, she was an individual as well as my mother, one with whom I talked and argued more intimately than I did with my father (though that distinction had not then occurred to me). And she talked very freely to me: about her childhood, about my father, even about what she had worn at their wedding, which, she informed me, had been 'quiet'. Her costume, as the word was, had been blue. The novelty of that seemed to linger with her, and I shared it, since I had never seen her dressed other than in brown. Already, I fretted at that restriction – not obtusely, for it typified something significant and shrinking in her character. And never would I suppose that the wedding of my parents could be other than 'quiet', in the most literal sense, even before I had heard the term commonly used. But that did not much help me to comprehend my mother. I loved her, I felt convinced, but she seemed driven by something baffling, depressing and alien to me – alien too, I should soon suspect, to other women, at least to my father's numerous sisters.

Perhaps it was in the local baker's that I first noticed cake decorations – noticed anyway small tubes of silver balls. I mentioned them to my mother, as I mentioned most of what I saw. Whether they were actually for sale may have been in my mind, since I had experienced one or two rebuffs, as I thought of them, when she had laughingly had to explain that some 'picture' of naked men and women on horseback was merely an advertisement for a tonic, and that you could not buy the pair of enormous glass bottles in the chemist's window or the gigantic, dummy box of biscuits in the grocer's.

She was anxiously engaged in seeking, as usual, good bread (white for my father, brown for her and me). It took her time to register my enquiry, and we had before had a misunderstanding in the same shop, over jam tarts. Could we not afford a few at least of them, I had asked. They blazed appealingly like miniature traffic lights with their pools of jam in yellow and green as well as red, and why my mother shuddered at sight of them I could not guess.

'It's not a matter of money,' she half-whispered, shaking her head and leading me, as though in disgrace, out of the shop.

That was another phrase to bear in mind, somewhat contradictory though it sounded: not a matter of money. On the pavement, she tried to console me over the unbought tarts. Pastry was best made at home; she would make some; my father loved jam tarts with strawberry jam. She tried hard, so I thought I must not hurt her feelings by explaining, in my turn, that hers would lack the glamour of the differently-coloured jams.

As for the silver balls, they were buyable and not expensive, but we – it appeared – had no use for them. They were just cake decoration, but not for the sort of cakes that we had. 'Why not?' I asked. And to that I received no satisfactory reply. For me to attempt to save up for them was silly and wrong; they were scarcely edible, and anyway boys did not buy cake decorations.

And so our routine visits to the routine shops began to bore me and annoy me. I could not understand why daily visits were in themselves necessary, since they seemed to give my mother more worry than pleasure. They were oddly lonely, as well. Few other people in Braemar Crescent were to be seen out shopping – few at least whom we knew. Perhaps I was company for my mother, as she hastened on, hastened back, in order to get lunch cooked (as cooked it must be) and the washing-up done, and a walk fitted in before we had tea, before the curtains were drawn and a meal got ready for my father's return from his office. Another day, she might declare, was done.

Rarely did anybody join us for tea, unless Trevor Morgan came to have tea with me. Only slowly was I beginning to realise that my mother had no friends in Leigh. A prosy, nosy, widow-neighbour, a Mrs Gapp, older than my mother and tolerated rather than welcomed by her, occasionally came and stayed until even she could not ignore the silence that had fallen over the tea-table. I was under unexpressed orders to remain present, though I sensed Mrs Gapp wished me at the top of the garden – if not further off – while I could have told her that the topic of her daughter Sylvia, just married, and Sylvia's ability to wear red ('Not every woman can wear red') could not have been worse selected for her hostess.

Yet my mother, frequently conveying exhaustion – and not just to Mrs Gapp – seemed determined that her day should contain no leisure. Leisure had connotations of idleness and frivolity, though she longed to read and re-read her books of poetry. Not until many years later did I find that she had marked, as she liked to do, some lines where a poet seemed to sum up all her own innermost feelings:

> What is this life if, full of care,
> We have no time to stand and stare?

Standing and staring enjoyably at the world of natural beauty – and also, more diffidently, at beauty in the visual arts – was a talent of hers. The pleasure of sight was keener in her than that of hearing, and her responses were at least as acute as were my father's to music, and she was much more capable of explaining her enjoyment.

However, pleasure of any kind, even the simplest, was sapped by worries and fears and doubts which seem to have run in her veins from birth – or been fatally injected into them by some horrible, tainted, blood-transfusion. Not for a single day could she shake off the conviction that all lives are 'full of care', and in particular her own life. If she felt she had no time for standing and staring, as she would have inclined to do, it was not because of external pressures but because of interior ones. She need not have limited her daily round to its busy monotony. No husband in their conventional milieu could have been less a domestic tyrant than hers. Indeed, he may often have urged her towards the impossible: to enjoy herself. Although she wanted to meet his wishes in every way, she could not obey him in that.

Ingrained or acquired was the compulsive sense that she must be sober, sedate, humble, undemanding, undemonstrative, drab in appearance, keeping people at a distance, thrifty, occupied and pre-occupied, practically concerned for tomorrow but expecting nothing from the future. Almost anything otherwise was self-indulgence, and self must be sunk in constant care for others. What had been her profession became – with good fortune, for which she would always be grateful – her personal life. Yet the instinctive pleasures of having and loving a husband and a child were inhibited and crippled – at least where the child was involved – by anxieties and uncertainty over her role in terms of duty.

Her thin, dun-hued figure, in long, flapping, tweed coat and amorphous, brown felt hat, hastening up and down Braemar Crescent, always clutching a bulky wicker-work shopping-basket, sometimes made me feel sad, as well as guilty. Too clearly did I see that I was a burden. Only rarely had I the power to lighten the load I represented and bring a smile to that sallow face, with its sharp, unrelaxed, somehow apprehensive features. I longed to whizz her around, like a top, or stick an outrageously gaudy feather in the pudding-basin hat. But she shrank from high spirits at any time and frequently quenched mine by acid observations, asking, for instance, whether I was afflicted with St Vitus's dance.

I could not articulate the complexity of my emotions or begin to understand what had damaged the flow of hers. That they did not flow freely I detected at a significantly early age. I tried to obey her injunction to grow up, leaving behind all vestiges of babyhood and enter boyhood, and in so doing I found her attitudes growing harsher. In retrospect, I am unsure whether I had even reached school age when I was struck – almost physically – and temporarily silenced by her reply to my enquiry about what she would like from me for her imminent birthday.

We were in nearby, faintly superior Westcliff, on a typical afternoon shopping expedition, so my question seemed to arise naturally enough. A negativeness spread over these excursions, for though we were meant to be seeking clothes for her, and gazed into many shop windows, nothing – as I was coming to learn – would be thought suitable and nothing would be purchased. As I put my question, she paused in the busy street, as if to consider. Then she burst out earnestly, 'That you should be good.'

'Am I so bad?' I, as earnestly, asked myself, shaken by the nullness of her response and feeling flung off at a moment meant to demonstrate my fond care for her. People around us seemed to have paused, perhaps to glare at the wicked little creature I was. The gathering crowd was more than the product of my misery. Ahead of us, it thickened and buzzed excitedly, and my mother abruptly pulled me to one side. Now what? I thought. Before I could see more, we had turned off the main shopping street.

'We'll go down here,' she said. 'There's been an accident.'

Catastrophe was what I needed, and I was sorry to be spared the spectacle.

As we retreated, I gave no thought to what her own childhood must have been like. It may have provided her with little beyond food and shelter, accompanied by a feeling that she was in the way in a narrow, remote, country household of elderly or single people. With her mother dying so young of tuberculosis, and her father a distant, drunken and possibly frightening figure, she could have fitted into some Brontë novel, and the emotional atmosphere she breathed was perhaps bleaker even than in one of those. No pattern of loving seems to have been imprinted on her, and when the experience of love came she gave it (virtually surrendered it) once and for all to my father. The common phrase about not looking at another man took on almost ludicrous reality in her life, so little could she respond in the mildest social manner to other men. As a child intrigued by nuances of adult behaviour, I used to watch some married male friend of my father's gallantly labouring to draw a spark of vivacity from her, while across the room my father managed effortlessly (on the surface) with the wife.

Yet her visual responses were not inhibited, and she commented appreciatively on men she found nice-looking, beginning – like many women in the 1930s – with Anthony Eden. I was at first disconcerted when she spoke of my schoolfellows, usually not among my friends, who were distinguished by having fine mouths or beautiful eyes. Since she seldom if ever referred to my own appearance, I soon deduced my lack of such features.

Ambivalent feelings were stirred in me when, before one of our regular walks, she occasionally allowed me into the bedroom she shared with my father, as she got ready. It was large and plain, with – above the bed – a crucifix larger than that in my room, with a plaster Christ on a cross of yellowish wood. More surprising was the large eiderdown on the double bed, a silky splash of rose-pink, and the luxurious-seeming expanse of dressing-table, glittering in its triple mirrors and glass top, on which lay big, cut-glass bowls and silver-backed brushes, and a silver hand-mirror, initialled *GML*.

I advanced towards it, fascinated to see multiple images of myself and also by the encouraging, scented atmosphere of intimacy. An exotic-looking box contained powder, and there was even a minute one which when opened revealed what my mother described as lip salve. But most of the cut-glass bowls were empty. Some of the silver items seemed useless, or unused, and it was with a sigh that she dragged the brush over her hair and perfunctorily lifted the weighty hand-mirror. The cosmetics were gifts, I understood, kindly meant but not really to be applied, at least not by her.

It was more in monologue than as conversation that she complained of her thin hair that was unable to retain hairpins and picked up the tasselled scent-spray, which I was tempted to handle, remarking that she loathed anything 'heavy' in perfumes. She offered me a sniff at the toilet-water, which was lavender or something equally light and flowery, and I had to hide my disappointment at her rejection of all the appurtenances and possibilities of glamour. Quick to perceive my mood, she would remark that we were merely going for a walk. There was no reason to dress up. But I was not deceived, and nor perhaps was she. There never would come a day for her to dress up – not even on Christmas Day at 'Homeleigh', where the 'Girls' threw off their normal cares and disagreements, and each descended the stairs smiling and freshly smelling, each celebrating in her own style the occasion with something new, if only a pair of slippers or a blouse.

My mother was right to stress that we should be going for an ordinary walk, but it was the ordinariness which oppressed me. The woods were too far, and so was the sea-front, itself dingy and devoid of appeal. Like self-appointed sentries, we therefore made the round of roads on our estate, passing the monotonous lines of newly-built, semi-detached houses where any deviation, any glimpse of humanity, was wonderful and welcome. Here and there, an old house survived – old by comparison with its surroundings – and seemed in disgrace with its untidy garden and cottage air. One had a border of tiger-lilies, as I learnt they were called, and I at once loved the house and the orange flowers.

Walking further one afternoon, we accidentally discovered a whole road with its own character, and since we had to go somewhere, I begged that we should go there again and again. When my mother asked why, I pointed out that most of the houses were masked by dark evergreens and high shrubs, giving the street a secluded, secret feel. Long before the onset of twilight, the effect was of dusk, of privacy and of snugness. Nobody ever seemed to come out of the houses, and we never encountered passers-by.

When, behind the shrubberies, a window was lit, the sense of seclusion only deepened.

It was a moment of triumph when I realised that I had made my mother see something of what I saw. She agreed the road had unusual character, though to live in it would be gloomy. I had anticipated that objection and could have guessed that she believed shrubs growing close to a house made it damp.

Another triumph was to follow, unexpectedly, on a dull, overcast morning on the dull routine of going shopping for food. My reluctance about these visits had quietened into a generalised sulkiness, and it was out of boredom that I looked up at the flat surface of wall flanking the familiar row of shops, on which was painted a firm's advertisement in large letters.

Without thinking, I spoke aloud the words: 'A and B Kind', probably not managing the next word, 'Builders'. But I had said enough to make my mother halt and glance sharply at me.

'Oh,' she exclaimed. 'You can read.'

I had known for some time that I was tired of my alphabet blocks, though not forgetting that 'I' was for Ibex. And I had become ashamed of the rag books which had been my first books. The books in the bookcase in the dining-room were what I preferred to play with, but I did not consciously read them. And while I was glad of my morning's success, I was not confident of being able to repeat it. Luck had played its part, not least in the builders' initials. Yet my father's delight, when he heard the news that evening, gave me confidence. He would buy me a book to celebrate my achievement – several books – and soon I should be struggling to read them, and then not struggling, just reading. It was a new, sustained excitement which bore me along, into worlds that sometimes disturbed me as well as puzzled me, so I did not always feel enjoyment. And I hated the occasions when I brought out in talk some word I had read, only to learn that I had mispronounced it.

My mother approved of reading, in moderation. It should not keep me indoors on a fine day, and when reading it was important to have good light (she believed her own eyesight had suffered from poor lamplight in her childhood). I was not to be too eager to read everything. Some books were more suitable for adults than for children. Fortunately, nowadays there were nice, illustrated books for children of a kind not available when she was a girl, and there were always fairy tales, which children loved.

My parents gave me one or two books by Beatrix Potter, and they seemed to like what they saw in the illustrations of rabbits in checked aprons pouring tea from tea-pots, but neither the illustrations nor the stories charmed me. They made me uneasy, though I dared not confess as much. It was more satisfying to believe in fairies than in dressed-up animals who got chased by humans. I detected something frightening behind, if not in, the stories – in perhaps the imagination of the author. And my opinion has not changed.

Fairy tales I expected to be just that: tales of fairy beings and no more alarming than was 'The Piper of Dreams'. My own imagination was quickly stimulated and stirred by what I read – sometimes even haunted by it. A sumptuous book arrived – my second surprise present – from a rich spinster in Northumberland once nursed by my mother, with whom she had kept in contact. It was an edition of folk stories, based on those of the Brothers Grimm, with full-page colour illustrations by Rackham or Dulac. My mother was flattered, almost flustered, by the generosity. She told me that this was a book to treat very carefully (and it may have had pretentious tissue-paper insertions covering the plates), a book any child should treasure.

However, when I began to read some of the stories, helped perhaps by her, I was terrified. Much of the cruelty was incomprehensible to me. I had no idea what a step-mother was, or a dwarf, or why so many people in the stories acted out of sheer malevolence. It was enough to sense that the book was crammed with unhappiness and horror. Once I had read one such story, I could not rid my mind of images of the girl whose pet horse was decapitated and nailed up over a town gateway, from which the head spoke to her as she passed under. I said nothing of what I thought, though I wanted no more books of stories judged suitable for children. The tortuous elaboration of the illustrations displeased me, as it had from the first. And my over-active imagination, heated by what I had been reading, went back to some of the nursery rhymes I had learnt automatically. 'Miss Muffet' had not lost its charm, and I was more fond than afraid of spiders. But what of those three mice who were blind and had their tails cut off by the farmer's wife? What had they done to be punished like that?

If I ever hinted to my mother my feelings of bewilderment and apprehension, she was prompt to dismiss anything of that kind as merely my imagination. Arguably, I was reading too much, and certainly I was reading too literally. This or that was just a story. Yet I noticed she could provide no further explanation, and I resented the dismissal of something which possessed real power over me as the product 'merely' of my imagination.

The world in which I had cocooned myself was being intruded on by more than reading. There were signs that I must face up to encountering life in new, strange and alarming ways, and the pace of my existence was accelerating.

I was old enough now, it seemed, to go to church on Sundays. And so the three of us set out early in the morning (before breakfast, if my parents wished to go to Holy Communion), caught a bus into Leigh, hurried up a hill from the inconvenient bus stop and arrived at eight o'clock Mass. I had had no concept of what a church would be like, and I was unprepared to see and take a place among so many people, tightly packed into narrow pews. What was going on at the altar was remote and obscure, and altogether there was less to look at than I had supposed. I was intensely aware of a lack of air, of feelings of dizziness – and more than once, with a crash, I fainted. After that, it was thought better that I should attend a later Mass, after breakfast, the Mass that included a sermon. By the time we had journeyed back from that, most of Sunday morning had evaporated.

The sermon was the only portion of the service in English, but it spoke to me no more eloquently than the Latin of the Mass. It interrupted that ritual with its woolly, would-be colloquial appeal, to which I sensed the listeners attached much less importance than they did to what took place on the altar. Old or young – and usually he was old – the priest clambered with difficulty into the pulpit, impeded by his vestments. He seemed to face us as though facing an ordeal. Momentarily, a silent struggle seemed to be going on over whether he would launch himself into speech at all. And then, giving us his text, he was away, wandering among time-filling exhortations to remember always, and bear in mind, and never forget, or lose sight of, the infinite something of God (his patience perhaps). I felt free to wander too, letting my glance rove around the building.

Set in a churchyard of prunus trees, the church looked from the outside grey and venerable, but inside it was disconcertingly light, new and shiny, with windows of clear glass and plain stone walls. On either side of the high altar were two chapels, one of which I would soon find was dedicated to Our Lady, and I might be allowed to visit it after Mass was over. Meanwhile, we the worshippers sat and stood and knelt in our pews, and the murmur of the Mass continued. A bell tinkled on the altar, and I had to be especially quiet, but sometimes a baby wailed or a prayer-book was accidentally dislodged. Little though I could perceive of what was occurring in front of me, I knew I must not yield to the temptation of turning round. And at last signs of stirring came surreptitiously from the congregation, and a greater stir came as the doors at the back of the church were opened, bringing currents of delightfully cool air into the building. One or two devout people might stay kneeling in prayer, but the majority rose, released, relieved, and drifted slowly towards the doors.

It was as a kind of reward that my mother (and it always was my mother) took me to light a candle before the slim, blue and white statue of Our Lady, standing like a vision in a sort of grotto. I was meant to say a prayer to her, as the Mother of God, but most of my concern went into the business of putting a penny in the box attached to the iron-wrought candelabrum, and selecting a new candle, lighting it from one already burning and then sticking it firmly on a spike. Proximity to the flaring, guttering candles and the smell of hot, dripping wax induced in me feelings of goodness and purity. I felt I even moved in a spiritual way, as I crossed myself and genuflected, and modestly tip-toed from the chapel, not unconscious that in the now emptied church I presented to any remaining observer the spectacle of boyish piety.

If this was what going to church every Sunday involved, I thought it not unpleasant, despite some tedium. But there were other objects in the building, more central to my sight. Only when the congregation was seated had I been able to register fully the series of compositions, looking as though they were modelled in plasticine, which studded the walls at intervals. I looked yet without wanting to look more closely, because I saw that each scene showed Jesus suffering as he carried his cross. The connection was re-stated, reinforced, by the group of three big, brilliantly-painted statues, standing high on a beam above the main altar and dominating the nave. A male saint and Our Lady, hooded now and no longer slim and serene, seemed writhing in grief beside the cross on which the naked, bleeding body of Jesus was stretched out in agony.

By comparison, the tiny metal crucifix in my room at home was tame in its impact; anyway, it had dwindled to being just part of the furnishings. But this brightly-coloured, strongly-sculpted group was so lifelike in its pain and suffering that it seemed unavoidable, unforgettable: with me in fact or in my imagination. As we left the church, I knew I must be prepared to see it on the following Sunday, and so onwards, and that it would never entirely lose its power to frighten me. Perhaps that was why it had been set up there with such prominence.

As yet, I had not been instructed that it incarnated God's infinite goodness to sinful mankind. Nobody had told me that all human beings are miserable sinners, condemned to eternal damnation without the grace of God. That Our Lady was relegated to a side chapel did not then seem of any significance. I simply preferred her blandly agreeable statue, unaware that she too was invoked in the same belief, interceding with her Son on behalf of evil humanity.

Mass was for me at first a ritual being mumbled distantly and undramatically on the altar below and beyond the three-dimensional group of the crucified Jesus. I could not possibly make any connection between what the priest was doing and what was carved overhead. I had not yet learnt that the Mass was a form of sacrifice – ominous, atavistic word – and that its emphasis was on the tearing of flesh and the shedding of blood, and that it constituted – of all things – a meal. Images of agony and cruelty entered my mind long before anyone attempted to give them a doctrinal meaning. Perhaps for that reason, I could never quite quell my revulsion when confronted by them, and even after I had accepted that they were at the core of Christian faith, and I of course was a Christian, I never believed that Jesus had had to undergo his Passion and Crucifixion because of my sins. I felt no guilt and saw no need for atonement.

Doctrinal matters were never discussed in our household – were never even alluded to. All such affairs were in the hands of priests, who instructed the young, after which rites took over: the Mass and the sacraments were guaranteed to see one through all the events of life, inclusive of matrimony, and, in the form of extreme unction, be at one's deathbed, conferring the final boon of a good death. The essential facts of Catholicism were not facts but mysteries, and hence were incapable of explanation. The necessary state was one of faith, and whatever St Paul might have said, the greatest of the virtues was Faith.

Faith was what I had been provided with by my parents at birth, just as they had provided me with clothes. It was their duty to ensure that I did not go through the world without wearing both, and unquestioningly.

Devout as I perceived my mother to be, and anxious that I also should be devout, I knew that the prime mover in all our religious observances was my father. There was no apparent change in his temperament or his demeanour on a Sunday morning before church: no gloom or repression. Yet, though I scarcely thought about it, I detected determination and concentration as he led us through the sleeping streets, to the bus stop, and up the hill, to Mass. He carried no gun or sword, just a discreetly-hidden prayer-book, but he was engaged in a fight: against sin and sloth and worldly values. Only when the act of worship was over, almost in going down the hill, did he resume his characteristic everyday, easy-going charm of manner. I might have thought that I was fancying all this, were it not that one period of the year gave me an indication of the stern nature of his faith, when sternness was directed unremittingly towards himself.

I had reached the age of reason somehow aware that there was a cheerful day in very early spring called 'Pancake Day'. A first surprise was learning that the following day was kept, at least in our household, as 'Ash Wednesday', and it was the opposite of cheerful. It signalled the beginning of a long period, of six weeks, called Lent. And we marked it by eating a small amount of fish for lunch on that Wednesday.

Nothing much seemed to mark the existence of Lent in church, until the Sunday when we went to Mass and I was surprised to find the big central group of the Crucifixion muffled in purple cloth. As I looked around, I I saw that all the other statues were similarly muffled. It was Passion

Sunday. Not until Easter, I understood, would they be unveiled.

The six-week period would have meant little to me, had it not been that at home my father observed Lent by fasting and abstinence – words which took on grim reality as I saw he deprived himself of taking pleasure in eating. He never smoked and he could not swallow alcohol. He and my mother rarely went to the theatre, rarely indulged in anything recognisable as a 'treat'. About the only thing he could give up for Lent was eating sweet things and sweets, in particular chocolate. Like his sisters, the 'Girls', he loved chocolates and selecting good chocolates, and recalling the exotic-sounding sweets (like 'Persian Biscuits') available in his late-Victorian childhood. It was no light penance or mortification which he inflicted on himself. Over the weeks it made even him irritable. He struggled under it, and – had I known it – some of my aunts at 'Homeleigh' were struggling similarly, desperate for Easter Sunday to arrive. But at Easter there would be something special to eat, and sweets again, and Easter Eggs. Everyone celebrated Easter. Trevor Morgan and his family would be having Easter Eggs, though Trevor had never heard of families doing anything about Lent.

By Good Friday I felt celebrations could start. It was not a day I had previously been aware of, but now I saw it as virtually ending Lent. And my father was at home for the first day of his Easter break. I skipped downstairs expectantly, sniffing the spicy scent of hot cross buns as I entered the dining-room. 'What shall we do today?' I was about to ask, before I realised that my father was in no mood for cheerful questions. A look from my mother nervously warned me to be silent, and though the curtains were drawn only metaphorically the atmosphere was dark and subdued.

At last I understood that this was the day on which Jesus had expired in agony on the cross. It was a day reserved with us for mourning, and I was unclear whether we were permitted to enjoy eating our hot cross buns or whether they were part of the mourning process. As for what we should do, I was amazed to learn that we were going to church in the middle of the afternoon. For the first time in my life I should be attending the ceremony of the Stations of the Cross.

All day I dreaded it. But I had not foreseen how crowded the church would be and how hard it was, as a child, to tell what was happening as the priest slowly proceeded around it, pausing for meditation at each of the fourteen Stations. With one movement, the congregation turned as he turned, sang or muttered responses and otherwise remained in brooding, oppressive silence. I had no difficulty in hearing what was happening, for the priest's voice rang out plangently, enunciating the successive stages of the way to Calvary: Jesus falls for the second time under the weight of the Cross; Jesus meets His afflicted Mother; Jesus is stripped of His garments . . .

It might have been better seeing something, apart from the forest of adult legs, rather than hearing the high-flown but horribly graphic phrases which the priest recited at each pause, compelling us to plunge deeper and deeper into the Passion. How could I not listen as his voice rose and fell, savouring every morsel of detail?

'Regardless of His desperate weakness, and the blood that flowed from His numerous wounds, His barbaric tormentors did not hesitate to inflict yet further indignities upon the bruised body of Our Saviour . . .'

I did not faint. I could hear in the intervals of silence the clang of the trams outside on the Leigh high road. In the churchyard, the prunus trees were just coming into pink blossom, and I thought of Trevor Morgan and how he might be spending the afternoon, playing with his brother or having tea with his grandmother. I wondered if I should ever return to the normality of Braemar Crescent and the blessed dullness of routine visits to the shops. Even the butcher's was preferable to this unending catalogue of cruelty lingered over so lovingly: 'Some of his garments had adhered to His flesh, and in their wickedness those evil men tore . . .'

Jesus was crucified, dead and buried. And then he rose again, on Easter Sunday, when we were encouraged to relax, be joyful and celebrate. But never could the atmosphere in church equal the intensity of the grieving mood of Good Friday. Glorious as the Resurrection was proclaimed to be, it was far outside human experience, a mystery, needing the natural accessible associations of spring and fluffy lambs and birds – and eggs – to become a complete celebration.

My father had imaginative presents for me. There was not only a large chocolate Easter Egg, opening to reveal smaller chocolate eggs inside, but a box of delicately-speckled sugar eggs, birds' eggs, with each species carefully identified. Perhaps that was the year when my presents also included the lifelike clockwork chick. And always essential to our celebration of Easter, of renewal and of young creatures, was a real chicken: the one killed for us which we sat down to eat at lunch.

Among the congregation in the church at Leigh were nuns, stately Sisters of the Order of Saint Vincent de Paul. It was one of them, Sister Theresa, pale and tall, and among the stateliest, whom my father consulted about my schooling. She recommended my going to the nuns' local convent school, St Edith's. My father greatly respected Sister Theresa, and possibly he detected or elicited a glint of humour under her stately manner. Anyway, he took her advice. I should go to St Edith's.

In those days there was no sensible procedure for preliminary visits by children to chosen schools. After a few weeks of awareness of what was impending, and having made one wild, half-unconscious effort to escape school altogether, I set off for my first day at St Edith's, accompanied by my mother. On the way to the necessary bus stop, we passed the Morgans' house, but I did not look for Trevor. He had gone or was going to a different school, one much nearer, the 'Elementary' one.

I was apprehensive yet resigned and mute. At the school-gate, I paused to say a subdued and final-seeming farewell to my mother. A teacher was there to greet me, and my first pleasant shock was to see that she was not a nun. With her straight brown hair in a bun, and wearing spectacles, she looked reassuring, like a younger sister of my mother's. But I gazed beyond her smiling face, gazing at the convent grounds.

My idea of a convent school had been of something church-like, grey and grim. Perhaps the buildings were, but what I saw was a grassy slope and trees, with children of all ages freely and noisily running around. Some were boys. But the majority were girls. There were more girls than I had ever seen, girls in bright dresses darting by, shouting and laughing, or standing in groups talking confidently.

None of them glanced towards me but that allowed me to go on looking, less shyly. So this, being surrounded by girls, was school. I began to feel I should enjoy it. Perhaps my mother had been right after all when she tried to cheer me up beforehand by saying – for the first time – that your schooldays are the happiest days of your life.

5

'Enter Oberon, King of Fairies'

Within five minutes of my arriving at St Edith's, it was working upon me as a school. Gently but remorselessly, it pushed me towards total acceptance of its version of reality, so that I began to doubt whether I had lived a previous existence or had a home to go to when the day was done. That was presumably why I had been sent to school. It was essentially a preparation for 'real' life, which in my case would mean life as a practising Roman Catholic.

If there had been any discussion between Sister Theresa and my parents about the nature of the new pupil coming to St Edith's, I expect it touched on my nervy, dreamy temperament, and stressed that I was an 'only' child – as though the adjective was descriptive of me, rather than of my circumstances, and belonged in the same category as my being skinny or having brown hair. Even as a small boy, ignorant of sexual matters, I found it curious that my mother could remark of me that I was an 'only' child, with such detachment. 'Only' was a word that carried overtones of apology: only a scratch meal, only one of some item left . . . And when I knew that I was being looked at in the light of my only-ness, often by a person hesitating about how to reply, I wondered whether an apology was due from me. Perhaps I was only a foundling or a changeling, a prince mislaid at birth and swapped by the fairies, or only a pauper child kindly taken into their home by the people I thought of as my mother and father.

I never heard my father refer to me in that 'only' sense – despite his experience of a childhood almost too rich in siblings. I suppose my mother had anxiously read what purported to be popular child-guidance books of the period (an advance, perhaps, on the earlier absence of such books), in which the 'only' child came trailing clouds of dilemma, especially in the matter of not being spoilt. I can believe she will have earnestly assured Sister Theresa that she and my father were doing all they could not to spoil me; and if Sister Theresa possessed any shrewdness about parents, she probably saw that my mother was a naturally apprehensive one and my father one naturally confident.

In any event, both parents could have every confidence in St Edith's. Although it took boys only while they were very young, it mixed boys and girls in its classes, it provided plenty of outdoor exercise, it taught a basic, secular curriculum but it also guided children in their faith, preparing them for Confession and First Communion.

It appeared to be the ideal school for a boy who – though no longer saying as much aloud – still continued to believe in fairies. And St Edith's pressed on me its own immediate agenda in the actual world throughout the first morning, banishing any dreams of fairyland or indeed dreams of any kind. I felt the pressure physically, as the sharp edge of the bench of the desk shared with another boy bit into the back of my bare knees. Even without the admonishment to pay attention, I paid attention, since a constant, bewildering series of demands had to be met. I must pay attention to our teacher, Miss Springfield, who seemed friendly yet commanding; to the blackboard by which she stood and to the books she handed out; and to the looming problems of where was the boys', as opposed to the girls', lavatory, and where we were meant to go for school dinner.

However, even as I shifted my bottom on the wooden bench, keeping my legs as far away as possible from the other boy's, I felt I might become fond of St Edith's, once the preliminary problems were solved. I anticipated getting to know some of the girls who shared the classroom but who, I had quickly noticed, did not share our desks. They were herded together, in the further part of the room. Now that I was positively there, I was eager to join in the experience of school, for all its unknown quantity. It was bigger and also more exciting than the life I had known at home. If it loomed around me, as a testing, slightly perilous world, it was at least one where I confronted the tests and perils on my own.

I certainly had much to learn at St Edith's, and most of it I learnt joyfully – though I could not and would not learn to enjoy what was served up as school dinner. But beyond that disgusting experience, and the curriculum, and the routine, and my tentative encounters with a variety of girls, St Edith's was to offer me something less tangible and so wonderful that it would affect me for the rest of my life.

The experience did not come from religious teaching, and not from the novel, agreeable attendance at chapel for Bene-diction, a service which seemed almost too sensuous and stifling, with the singing and the incense and the prostrating of ourselves before the Host. It was devotional and harmless – and brief. I liked the afternoons when lessons were cut short because we were to crowd into the chapel, with the nuns, for Benediction.

It was out in the open air, under a tree near the school-gate, that I first became aware that some of the older girls were rehearsing a play. I was quick to detect that it was a fairy play, and the person who dominated it was Oberon, King of Fairies. Oberon was played by a big, dark girl, Elsie Dines by name, who lived quite close to us, in Stirling Avenue. She wore a red cloak and had about her a pert, bold, gipsy air which I found more alarming than appealing. She was not at all my idea of a fairy king, though perhaps her very boldness and resolute unsoppiness were just what was wanted for the part.

I must have witnessed her first, scornful clash with who-ever played Titania and her despatch of Puck to fetch the 'little western flower'. But it was the preceding dialogue between Puck and Titania's fairy attendant which, once heard, went on haunting me. As I listened to it, I instinctively transferred the wood near Athens to the woods I knew around Belfairs golf course, where I had often picked up acorn cups and easily envisaged them being crept into by elves. I had never seen cowslips growing, but I expected flowers of all kinds to be visited by fairies; and there was nothing surprising in a fairy's duty to 'hang a pearl in every cowslip's ear'. Like the rubies she referred to as spots on the cowslip, the pearls were not fanciful to me (I missed the fact that they were dewdrops) but actual, palpable jewels. But nothing to me was more intensely real than the glade where Oberon and Titania had been wont to meet, a glade that I was sure I had stumbled on myself in the local woods but which glowed in my mind's eye with eerie green fire, its grass and trees transfigured by 'spangled starlight sheen'.

Those three words lit their own fire in me. It burnt with a fierceness that shrivelled the pretty water-colour compositions of Margaret Tarrant and other fairy illustrators of whom I had been fond. And it made a mockery of my continual attempts to create a setting for the play out of pots of poster-paint and tinsel and torch bulbs masked by green paper. It would whirl me on to the last scene, unconscious that I was obeying the play's rhythm, bringing one back to the location of the first scene, in the palace of Duke Theseus.

I should long go on striving to mount the play somehow, more and more frustrated at my failure to find any visual equivalent for the atmosphere conjured up by the marvellous final effect – one of the most marvellous in all literature – when the fairy world benevolently invades the human one, and into the silent, darkened house Oberon enters, to command every elf and every sprite to trip through it, blessing the sleeping mortals. It had, I can truthfully say, its holiness for me. It is a vision which professional stages can seldom realise – and I had only a shoe-box. But I

saw it all in the theatre of my imagination. The shadowy
figures shed a magic phosphorescence as they moved, and
a muted radiance seemed to bathe the whole play in what
Oberon characterises as 'glimmering light'. Whether I had
enquired or been told, I had learnt that the play was called
A Midsummer Night's Dream – 'Shakespeare's Midsummer
Night's Dream', I expect they said. That gave me a clue,
for my father owned a fat volume dauntingly entitled *The
Complete Plays of Shakespeare.*

It was agreed that I could borrow the volume and read
the play – if that really was my wish. Unlikely though my
mother thought it, I was even free to read other plays in
it, with the exception of one too horrible for a child, *Titus
Andronicus.* I went first, of course, to that, but its horrors
barely registered, or they seemed tedious, and its plot was
incomprehensible. Nor was *A Midsummer Night's Dream*
as accessible as I had assumed it would be. I had been
unprepared for the mechanicals' portion of the play (which
never would seem to me very funny) and for the difficulty
of the language throughout when confronted on the page.
Even after I came to learn by heart some of the speeches,
I remained none too clear about what the words meant,
supposing that Oberon's 'Tarry, rash wanton!', addressed to
Titania, was some form of expletive, to be delivered without
pause. I went around the house chanting exuberantly what
I had learnt, and it would be years before I appreciated the
irony of detaining my mother – on her way out shopping –
as I spoke that line, before I launched into Titania's lyrical
response.

What I did understand was that ordinary existence had
been enhanced by my acquaintance with the play. It was as
if something had been added – almost physically added – to
the single cell that constituted my life. It was an extension of
life rather than a retreat, because it enormously enhanced my
sense of enjoying existence. And I went on with my reading
of Shakespeare's plays with the same sense of enjoyment and
expansion. All of them, even eventually *Titus Andronicus,*

simply excited me. I wanted to see them all, partly to gauge the difference between my ideas and the realisation on a stage, and partly – as I perhaps hardly grasped – to have confirmation that I was right to feel the excitement which I did when reading them. When acted out in public, they must cease to be figments 'merely' of my imagination, and I should not feel alone in my excitement.

My English history would begin with the plays, and so would my Roman history. I instinctively thought it right that history dealt with great personages, preferably with their downfall. Tragedy appealed to me far more than comedy, and the plays that then left me quite indifferent were such masterpieces as *Twelfth Night* and *Much Ado about Nothing*. From very early on, I was always attracted to anything Egyptian, and – in parenthesis – my debt of gratitude to the Army must include its kindness in transporting me to Egypt (where I only just missed seeing the film of *Caesar and Cleopatra* in Alexandria). *Antony and Cleopatra* thrilled me from the first. I felt Cleopatra was the very symbol of hot, exotic, alluring Egypt, and the whole play seemed metaphorically wrapped, like her, in gold tissue. It ended not sadly but splendidly; and as I reached the close, I saw Cleopatra seated hieratic and instantaneously mummified, with eternity in her gilded eyes.

However, none of the plays enveloped me more completely than did *A Midsummer Night's Dream*. It was the play I had been looking for, the play that fused the normal world and the supernatural fairy one in a way that I found entirely true, and therefore entirely serious. If I was too young to perceive the strong resilience of its structure, or realise that its shimmering surface hid shafts of steel and that its crystalline quality was like quartz embedded in earth, I could yet recognise its artistic validity – without using such big words. Nobody had to urge me to enter its realm. It sprang up before me like a rapidly-erected circus tent – not so much before me as around me. I had entered it without thinking and inhaled its heady atmosphere of enchantment without effort.

And the play has continued to exist as part of my own existence. All that has changed down the years is that its dimensions have expanded as I have been able to see further into it. Now I can recognise it as one sustained celebration of love as the binding, generative force in human affairs (and in fairy ones). The ducal pair united in marriage at the end of the play are promised the eternity of having offspring who 'Ever shall be fortunate', just as the three newly-wedded couples themselves shall 'Ever true in loving be'. Natural forces and human beings are linked in a cosmic harmony – much as they are at the end of Mozart's opera *The Magic Flute* – and although Oberon and Titania do not (cannot?) have their own offspring, they share a surrogate child in that Indian boy whom Oberon receives paternally from his foster-mother, Titania, as a symbol of amity and unity again in Fairyland (that is, in nature) at the close of the play. Far from all this being a flimsy, whimsy, trivial theme, it is as serious a cosmic vision as Dante's or, indeed, as that of the Roman poet Lucretius in his *De Rerum Natura*, with its great opening invocation to Venus, goddess of love, who 'alone guides the nature of things'.

How lucky I was in coming on the play not on the page, not as a duty, but as acted out under a tree and catching my attention virtually by chance. And I was lucky in my first Oberon. Elsie Dines may not have been the most accomplished performer of the role, but in plunging me vigorously into the action, with no fancy, simpering airs, she was perfect.

I was at a vulnerable moment in my life, an intermediate moment between the protection of home and the first exposure to school. As a schoolboy, I was learning – among other things – that beyond my personal predilections was public opinion. And already I sensed conflict. Very easily could I have been swayed to accept what was probably the majority view among the pupils at St Edith's that *A*

Midsummer Night's Dream was a lot of rubbish, suitable in the boys' eyes only for girls, and hardly more tolerated by the girls, except for the opportunity to dress up.

However, I could not help my total absorption in it, though I might manage to keep much of that absorption to myself. At home I should continue planning and preparing my own production. When I began to have pocket-money, I spent some of it at Woolworth's on artificial flowers which would serve to create a fairy bower out of a deck-chair. At my next school after St Edith's, I tried to persuade reluctant boys to make up a cast, and I copied out their parts, with cues in red ink, some of which unfortunately splashed on the pages of my father's volume. At boarding-school I was delighted when it was announced that a group of us would perform scenes from the play at the end of term. I had not guessed that these would centre on the mechanicals' own play. Nobody was required to play Oberon, and I was given the role of the bellows-mender, Francis Flute, who acts Thisbe.

A Midsummer Night's Dream was the first play of Shakespeare's to which I was taken, while we lived at Leigh-on-Sea. It was a thoroughly Victorian production, still vivid to me, with the fairies at the end moving as points of artificial light in the cardboard architecture of Theseus' palace. Long after the curtain had come down, I sat on, unwilling to leave the theatre.

It seemed the culmination of my own dream when posters in Leigh announced a film of the play, Max Reinhardt's famous one. But my parents declined to take me, despite all my pleas. They were convinced that the film must be vulgar simply because it was a film (and they then never went to the cinema) and was associated with Hollywood, itself a term of denigration. Daily on my way home from school I passed, with difficulty, the exclamatory posters: 'See James Cagney as never before . . . Laugh with Mickey Rooney's Puck . . . Marvel over Magic Scenic Effects'.

I was old when I finally saw the film, and I winced at its

vulgarities on behalf of my parents. Rooney is excruciating, though Cagney is confident and impressive. Hollywood at its crassest and clumsiest often tramples on Reinhardt's imaginative ideas. But I still found something to enjoy, and I know how profound would have been my enjoyment could I have seen the film when I was a child.

The natural world was the first world I discovered, and long before I became aware of the wood near Athens I had come to love the Belfairs woods in which I walked sedately with my parents or explored more excitingly in the company of Trevor. There was a magic about them which awoke something wild and woodland in me, something which exulted in crashing through the high ferns and half falling against the rough trunks of the massive trees. It would be not frightening but thrilling to be lost among them, whereas I was intensely conscious that I must not get lost when my mother took me down into the town of Leigh. To lose her, even temporarily in a shop, was a terrifying possibility – one she accidentally fostered by her own often-expressed anxiety that we might get separated. But although it was playful, and a diversion on a weekend walk, I liked the sense that I was 'lost' to my parents as I crouched in the undergrowth or concealed myself behind some bush, while earth and stalks of stiff grass and spiky branches pressed themselves on me and into me, and I – who was so susceptible to any threat of pain – hardly minded being scratched.

I felt sure that Trevor would be no more understanding than my parents about my exultation, which could, however, be easily disguised when with him by general horse-play. Besides, Trevor and I were finding that our natures were very different, as we grew more familiar with each other. He was robust and practical; I was withdrawn and dreamy. Although we would later go occasionally on local trips together, we were getting ready to separate. And a strange fusion of small incidents, fused at least in recollection, showed me that I was happier alone.

One morning, before I ever went to school, and privately
believing I should never have to go, I had asked Trevor to
come with me to the woods. I was not pleased at his refusal
and by his declaring that he and his grandmother were going
there that afternoon, to pick bluebells, and that I should not
be welcome to join them.

I revealed nothing of this near-quarrel to my mother. But
during the afternoon I took care to play near the gate,
waiting until I heard voices that were recognisably those
of Trevor and his grandmother approaching. I had already
planned that I would hide and then follow them down the
Crescent to the woods.

It was a sort of game with myself, and I thought I
was not taking it seriously, even as I crouched down on
glimpsing Trevor's fair head and his grandmother's black
hat, surprisingly close to me, before they passed along the
pavement. But then the lure of shadowing them was too
strong. And since I knew the way they would go, I could
afford to dawdle far behind. In the glade of bluebells I should
come upon them.

There was something wanton, as I knew very well, in
picking the flowers. My mother had pointed out to me
how easy it was to uproot the slim bulbs as you pulled at
their long, white stalks and how rarely anyway the bluebells
survived in water. I agreed that they were beautiful just left
growing under the trees, and yet I wanted to be of the party
of pickers represented by Trevor and his grandmother.

By the time I reached the woods, I had lost track of
them. The bluebell glade where I expected to find them
was deserted, and the woods themselves were quiet and
unpeopled on a sunny weekday. Perhaps a pair of golfers
approached a nearby green, chatting between strokes, con-
centrating on their putts, and then they strolled away to the
next tee, leaving me yet more conscious of being alone.

Almost in defiance, I picked a few bluebells. I felt aimless
and yet content to wander in the alternate patches of sunlight
and shade among the trees. I paused over the giant ants'

nests, where so many insects toiled, gave them a stir with a fallen branch and stroked the soft, glowing moss that covered the twisted roots of the trees. I admitted nothing to myself, but I knew that I was not going home – at least, that I was not going to school. If necessary, I should remain in the woods. And so I wandered on, until I could sense that the light was slowly lessening, and the woods seemed quieter and more shadowy. I crossed the smooth green of a fairway, seeing no one and nothing in the distance except the flag of some far-off hole. On the fringe of the trees, where the rough grass began, I found a log. It seemed sensible to sit down on it. I was more tired than I had realised. I let the bluebells fall from my hands, and soon I was asleep. There, some hours later, a conventionally plump and beaming policeman, looking the picture of a story-book bobby, discovered me.

He administered no anaesthetic, but it was in a tranquillised state that I went back with him to Braemar Crescent. I seemed to accept return as inevitable, with no sense of pleasure or fear or apprehension of what my parents would say. And, perhaps out of sheer relief, they said remarkably little. I don't remember being scolded or required to explain why I had slipped away. Vaguely, I murmured something about following Trevor and his grandmother to the woods and then getting lost. After that, it seemed tacitly agreed that the incident was over. I can't remember even being made to promise that I would never do anything similar again.

Perhaps there was a reason for treating the whole affair in a deliberately low-key, undramatic fashion. Although it cannot, I think, have been on the very next morning, it was definitely soon afterwards that I set out for my first day at St Edith's Convent.

By my second or third day at St Edith's, I felt highly confident. And I was sure enough of enjoying school to decide to take with me, slung round my shoulder on a piece of string, a miniature wallet I had made myself, containing a selection of coloured, jewelled as I thought them, toothbrush handles. Even while I was putting it on, my mother asked me whether I was wise to take it. I reassured her rather coldly and went off proud of my collection and pleased to think that I should have something so personal with me in the classroom.

It was as we were closing our exercise books and getting up for break that the string suddenly snapped and the toothbrush handles tumbled over the floor. Miss Springfield looked surprised but smiled. Feeling more annoyed than embarrassed at first, I bent down to gather them. Only as I did so did I become conscious of the laughter of the whole class. I spent a miserable, lonely break, thinking desperately of ways in which I could dispose of the ridiculous objects. And when I was home again, although I could not bear to throw them out, I felt that some of my joy in looking at them had gone for ever.

Ours seemed to me a big class, and Miss Springfield was responsible for almost all our instruction, including handicrafts and singing. I was particularly eager to please her. She mattered to me more than any of my male classmates, with none of whom did I make friends, though it was with them that I shared books and class activities.

Miss Springfield was always kindly, but I felt myself a disappointment to her much of the time. A first awkward experience had come when she tested a group of us, in front of the rest of the class, for singing. I sang away happily with the group until she stopped us. One boy was badly out of tune, and that was I. The rest could go on singing, without me. As it happens, something similar occurred during the schooldays of Tito Gobbi, according to his autobiography, but with a rather different sequel in adult life. Not all Miss Springfield's natural kindness could soften my humiliation, and I learnt that in future any singing by me should be soundless, whether in class or chapel – or, leaping somewhat ahead, in the back of a three-ton army lorry.

Even at handicraft I was less deft than I had expected. This late-afternoon activity signalled relaxation, though I was disappointed to find that segregation still continued – indeed, it was emphasised by giving the girls raffia, with which to sew table mats, while the boys were given cork circles on which to paint for the same purpose. Lime and black were the colours I chose for my design, a typically early-Thirties pattern of interlocking curves, drawn with the aid of a penny. But despite all my care, and repeated efforts, a smudge always seemed to appear on one of the segments before I had finished.

'Try again, dear,' Miss Springfield said, issuing me with yet another blank piece of cork. Nobody else seemed to have had to try quite so hard publicly, or else nobody minded as much as I did.

When we had what were called 'sums', I could sense my attention slipping into speculation about who exactly were John and Mary, one of whom had six loaves but gave two to the other before being given three by Henry. Mary seemed dominant. She had seven pence, whereas Henry had only three. If John was Mary's brother, I supposed Henry was their friend. But I was unprepared suddenly to answer aloud the riddle of how many loaves or pence Mary, or possibly John, now had. Willingly would I have written, had it been required, a story about the three children. When we did write something called an essay, the topic was seldom so vital.

What I could do, better perhaps than most of the others, was learn a poem by heart. Memorising anything in a book caused me no difficulty, and if there was an opportunity of reciting it afterwards – and even if there was not – I was ready to oblige. When Miss Springfield told us to learn the first two verses of some poem by the end of the week, I came back the next morning with the whole poem learnt, partly by practising on my mother before and after supper. She too became proficient in reciting lines of pseudo-nature poetry, embodying the pathetic fallacy at its most coy, with echoes of my heavy emphasis on the metre: 'And through their green curtains the violets peep'. My arm was up almost before Miss Springfield had called for someone to begin the recitation, and I was quite hurt when she moved on to the next person while I was still on my feet and in full spate.

My happiest times at St Edith's were when the bell rang and break began. There must have been days on which it rained but – as is normal – my memories are of sunny mornings and of our rushing out into the convent grounds. Admittedly, after that immediate impulse, I often hesitated over what to do next. The girls were an attraction but also a challenge, for I found that they were not necessarily eager to mingle and talk with the boys, however eager some of us might be. They tended to form their own coteries, going and sitting in a detached, consciously superior way on a grassy bank and tittering at any approach by a boy. That only helped to coarsen our behaviour. Another boy and I (a boy with whom I was not otherwise friendly and whose name I have forgotten) used to amuse ourselves by trying to detect the colour of the girls' knickers as they sat in that exposed position, tittering ourselves at our own daring as we exchanged cheeky comments.

There was one girl, Una Woodward, whom I shyly liked very much. With her thin fair hair and pretty, pointed face, she was or she ought to have been one of the fairies in Titania's train – the Fairy perhaps who encounters Puck. I promised myself that hers was a skirt up which I would not look, though in Puck-like manner I did. Her father must have been a colleague of my father's, for I was to meet Una Woodward again, as a teenager, in wartime Harrogate. I made no reference to our days at St Edith's when we went out one morning on an emotionally awkward, tongue-tied walk, each of us constrained (I especially). My life in Harrogate was horribly lonely, and I needed a girl-friend. But our walk created no rapport and was never repeated.

At St Edith's I was more openly friendly with a cheerful, ginger-haired girl called Sylvia, but that was easier as I felt no physical attraction towards her. Yet I enjoyed being with her. She was one of the few girls who was, for some reason, a boarder at the Convent, and I can remember being in a firelit room with her one evening after school, waiting to be collected by my mother and modelling a dragon for Sylvia out of plasticine. She had shown me a necklace of hers, of glass beads, which had become unthreaded and spilled over the carpet. As she watched approvingly, I took a handful of the tiny beads and used them to create a glittering carapace for the creature I had made her.

However, the girl I cared for most at St Edith's, Alma, seemed indifferent to gifts of my own devising – and I had nothing else worth giving her. Out of silver paper I made her more than one goblet, which she accepted with the same indifference she displayed towards my eagerness to be with her whenever I could. She was tiny and pale, looking the paler in her customary scrap of black velvet dress, with ringlets of hair so pale that they might have been peroxided. And altogether there was something about her, including her passivity, which gave her the air of being a miniature version of the fashionable peroxide blonde of the period.

Her blondeness, her fragility, her dumbness, were all part of her appeal for me. Whenever we as a class went out on walks in Leigh, in crocodile, I always chose to walk beside Alma. She accepted the proximity, without any show of emotion. I told her all sorts of things about myself, and I nudged her to look in such interesting shop windows as that of the pet shop, in which finches and parakeets could be seen fluttering animatedly around. Not even they stirred her out of that anaemic passivity which I found so fascinating. Alma was my favourite person at school, I informed my mother. Even as I pronounced her name, I detected my mother's silent demur. She was careful to say nothing, but in the carefulness I read, rightly or wrongly, a hint of disapproval. Perhaps she did not care for my being so fond of any girl so early in my life. Perhaps she did not care for the girl I pointed out to her one day at the school-gate. When she next referred to Alma, her tone conveyed an impression to my nervous ears that in the name itself she thought there was something cheap. It was a personal, emotional situation, involving sex (though of course ours was not a milieu in which the thought could be permitted where children were concerned, and still less could the word be uttered). And my mother shrank from such a situation. Her fear became a sort of generalised disapproval, which would have its inhibiting and thus damaging effect upon me.

A practical situation, however, she could face. Not quite seeing where it would lead, I presented her with one when I – as she would say – 'harped' on the awfulness of the school dinners at St Edith's. I blamed the cook, who was also the person who served the food and who managed to suggest that it was an insult not to eat what she provided.

Alice in Wonderland had by then come my way, and the combination of Carroll's text and Tenniel's illustrations made it an enduringly absorbing book to me. Between the Duchess's irate cook and ours at St Edith's I could see little difference. Ours also was perpetually hot and red-faced and on the verge of losing her temper. Her name was Mary Dignam, and she was Irish.

One afternoon as she collected me at school, my mother said that she had decided, after all my complaints, that she would have a quiet word with Mary Dignam. She would explain that I was a finicky eater even at home, but perhaps the school could provide something simple and light for me – at least not suet dumplings in gravy (which I was physically unable to swallow).

I waited in the playground while the interview took place, pleased by my mother's intervention but curious about what was going to occur. I wondered rather guiltily if I had adequately briefed her over Mary Dignam's temper. Or had I perhaps, as was my tendency, exaggerated it? After all, I was just a child, a thoroughly tiresome one, who had done an Oliver Twist in reverse to an adult in authority.

It cannot have been that my mother emerged from the kitchen region actually pursued by oaths or objects hurled at her by Mary Dignam, but she emerged looking physically bruised. I saw at once that there had been a battle, which she – we – had lost. She took me by the hand but it was I who guided her out of the school grounds and to the safety of the bus stop. 'Never have I been spoken to like that before,' she said at last, trying to appear less flustered. 'How the nuns can put up with it . . .'

'Thanks anyway,' I muttered. At least I could not be accused of exaggerating about Mary Dignam's temper.

Only when the bus came did we seem out of her glare and able to relax. My mother recovered to the point of managing a brief smile.

'Irish people do tend to have terrible tempers,' she remarked, as she relived the incident, beginning with her polite approach and the immediate fury of Mary Dignam at the insult to her cooking.

'But,' I objected, 'Daddy is Irish.'

'Half Irish,' she retorted.

We both sat there, each clearly thinking that his view of the affair was what we wanted. And he was at once sympathetic and amused. After all, there was plenty of food which he could not eat.

'Suet in greasy gravy *and* tapioca,' I emphasised, to indicate the disgusting nature of Mary Dignam's meals. I knew my father had never even tasted a milk pudding.

'She sounds like a character out of an O'Casey play,' he said to my mother. '"The world's in a terrible state of chassis."'

That made her laugh but it baffled me.

I was still rather baffled after my father had taken the trouble to explain the allusion to me. *Juno and the Paycock* remained a puzzle, and I had not previously encountered the word 'chaos'. Yet I responded to associations with Dublin, because that was where our family came from, and wasn't I named Michael after my great-grandfather, Richard Michael, who had been conductor at the Theatre Royal, Dublin? O'Casey and Synge, and the Abbey Theatre, and some of its leading players, would become merged in my mind with him as part of my heritage. Excluded from it, because excluded from the interest of my father and my aunts, were Yeats and Shaw, for the most part, and definitely Joyce. But Dublin was a city which we were going to visit one day, my father, my mother and I, and that was still a prospect being talked about when the Second World War broke out.

It was significant that my father bothered to explain to me about O'Casey and about 'chassis'. I had reached a new stage in life, to be marked in numerous ways: I had reached the age of reason.

I doubt whether I should have known as much had it not been spoken about, especially in (of all things) a religious context. Along with my classmates at St Edith's, I was now qualified and to be prepared for making my first Confession and First Communion. After that, though I was slow to grasp the fact, the convent finished its educating of a boy. He must go on to some other school.

I thought of the age I had reached, seven or so, as one not so much of reason as of reading. If questioned on the point, I should have said that the two were opposites. Reason had implications of duty, while reading was pleasure. And with reading I classed listening to stories told on the wireless, preferably when they were acted out and when they concerned not contemporary children, not contemporary life at all, but people from the distant, classical past. Among my father's books, I had discovered one which he had had at school, a severely-bound, sparsely-illustrated text-book, which retold in factual terms the myths and legends of ancient Greece and Rome. It was not a book he claimed to have read enthusiastically but I made up for that, learning almost by heart its very turns of (late Victorian) phrase.

I was in no danger of believing in the gods and goddesses whose lives it chronicled. Mere chance introduced me to them while I was learning the Roman Catholic catechism and hearing about God, and about the future life in Heaven, or Hell. I was at an age of reading when I could equally and enthusiastically embrace stories from all these sources. I liked to read about Venus (who I knew was Aphrodite in Greek), but I should proclaim my devotion to Our Lady, soon after my First Communion, by buying a statue of her and creating an altar on the chest of drawers in my bedroom. Neither extreme of enthusiasm would really be approved by my mother, although I could sense that a delicate problem, never to be resolved, arose more from my manifestation of fervent piety than from my fondness for classical mythology.

Yet the latter had its power to disturb as well as to delight me. The BBC's *Children's Hour* broadcast a series of playlets, dramatising ancient classical myths, to which I listened with intense fascination. Ingenious sound effects accompanied the story of how Danae and her infant son, Perseus, were imprisoned in a chest which was then cast on the waves – and before the moment arrived of their happy rescue from the sea, I had experienced a claustrophobic panic, induced by the relentless boom of the waves and tossing of the chest. I had to rush into the kitchen, where my mother was ironing, and pretend that I was just looking in to see what was for supper. But she at once noticed how pale I was, and how frightened.

It seemed sometimes that the age of reason, in the grown-up sense of calm behaviour, was eluding me, despite my advancing years. So much went on happening in my imagination. But it was precisely my imagination which it appeared I should by now have outgrown. And what increased my feeling of shame was the unexpectedness of those imaginative fits.

My father had long before kept his promise that one day I should have a rocking-horse. I found it in my bedroom one Christmas morning. But as I began excitedly unwrapping it, I gradually saw how shiny and hard and wooden it was, how far removed from the black horse as seen from my pram in the shop window in Wimbledon and lovingly enhanced by memory. I tried as I went downstairs to feel thrilled and grateful, and I think I succeeded at least in displaying gratitude. But the object itself never charmed me, and a convenient fiction took root that I was too old by then for such an object.

There was that other promise made by my father, a promise of burning importance to me, that we should one day go to the theatre. And one evening he told me that this had been arranged. We were going on the following Saturday afternoon to a play called *Treasure Island*, which was being performed at Westcliff. The title alone served to enchant me, and I was not greatly troubled by my mother asking aloud how on earth she was to cope with the boy until Saturday arrived.

It was a real theatre to which we went, which was excitement enough. We sat in the dress circle (and my father told me that he always preferred that to the stalls). From the programme I saw that the actual island, the focus of my interest, was not reached until after a preliminary scene or two. I was sitting as comfortably as my emotions allowed when suddenly the lights went out and the curtain rose, on the interior of an inn. Men came and went, talking roughly, and the surroundings of the solid theatre faded under the impact of what was happening on stage. Somebody was expected at the inn. He was called Blind Pew, and everyone fell silent, listening tensely for his coming. I leant forward no less tensely, and then I heard, with mounting terror, the tapping of a stick which seemed to quicken as did the beating of my heart.

'Are you all right?' my mother whispered, and as she did so the tension broke and Blind Pew finally appeared on the scene. It had been a close thing with me to keep from screaming, and the rest of the play passed almost as an anti-climax. I enjoyed it, but it never again took possession of me as it had done for those few terrifying seconds.

'I'm not sure you should often go to the theatre,' my mother declared afterwards. 'It frightened you too much.'

'Only at first,' I said, carelessly. 'I really loved it. I loved the island, and I loved the parrot. Daddy, can we go to another play again very soon?'

At St Edith's it seemed to me that each term brought fresh events. There was the Empire Day pageant, when groups of pupils mimed all the flags of the Colonies, and I represented, briefly, a portion of Australia. There were those rehearsals for *A Midsummer Night's Dream*, which fascinated me more perhaps than an actual performance. And, as the weekend approached of first Confession and First Communion for a number of us in my class, we were not only being told about the Sacraments and tackling the Catechism but going to church to practise on the spot entering the confessional and receiving Communion.

Under Mary Dignam's regime, school dinners continued to revolt me, but now I simply exercised my own form of abstinence. She herself had ceased to be a terrifying figure. She had become as absurd and as personally harmless to me as the Cook or the Duchess in *Alice in Wonderland*. Since my father's amused attitude, and perhaps as a result of reaching the age of reason, I had become aware of a new way of seeing people and life. It was not at all my mother's way, though she could be persuaded to share it because it was so much my father's.

His sense of humour constantly punctured situations which might appear otherwise serious and reduced unpleasant, pompous and overbearing people to their due, ridiculous unimportance. I was only just beginning to realise that what he read was as revealing of him as my mother's reading was of her. Except for Shakespeare, he never read poetry (and his Shakespeare was entirely the dramatist). Prose – stylish, ironic, humorous prose in short stories and novels – was what he savoured and repeatedly alluded to. Saki and P. G. Wodehouse provided endless pleasure (Wodehouse fortunately never failing annually, as it seemed, to publish a new book), and he delighted in daily life approximating to their art. If his devout, inner ideal was of a Sister Theresa, his view of ordinary secular existence included the Mary Dignams, who unwittingly added greatly to its gaiety. St Edith's happened to contain both samples. Had I possessed the acumen to comment on that, I expect he would have told me that I should find the convent a good microcosm of the world.

This world, however, was of less immediate concern, if I followed correctly the doctrines we were being taught, than the future one. Without trying to, I had learnt by heart passages of the Catechism. I think we had anyway been chanting them in class. And I accepted everything the Catechism said. I knew, therefore, that God had made me. He had made me to love, honour and serve Him in this world and be with Him in the next.

That seemed clear enough. I was interested in the scope of the promised next world and disappointed that the Catechism, which was precise about the torments of Hell, opted out over evoking Heaven ('The eye hath not seen, nor the ear heard, nor hath it entered into the heart of man to conceive what joys God has prepared for those that love Him'). But the promise of punishment and of reward seemed fairly similar to daily life, though I remained obstinately, if privately, unable to be frightened by the idea of my natural sinfulness and the possibility of eternal damnation.

To ensure that we, children still at the most rudimentary stage of conventional education, understood the alternative before us (imbibed it, rather than understood it), we had to attend classes at church on Sunday afternoons, in the final run-up to taking the two Sacraments. It was the first time that I had felt rebellious at surrendering my agreeable leisure to receive a dose of religion. The priest instructing us seemed dourly insistent on every child's need for penitence. We could proceed to the sanctity of Holy Communion only after undergoing Confession, of all our sins – without which there was no state of grace. No state of grace meant, in my immediate perspective, not wearing a white shirt and white armband on Sunday and not joining the other boys at the altar rail to open my mouth and receive this time no unconsecrated wafer but the body and blood of Our Blessed Lord. Such failure would not merely disappoint but profoundly disturb my parents. And I had not sufficiently attained an age of reason to question the whole system which was about to grip me.

I looked forward to my First Communion, not least to the sense of occasion. Boy and girl communicants would sit together in pews at the front of the church, and the girls would be dressed entirely in white, with muslin veils, like brides. Alma was perhaps too young to be among them but Una Woodward would be there. We might have gone up to the altar rails as a pair, I thought, before learning that segregation applied, and that the boys went up only after the charming, white cloud of girls had demurely risen, received Communion and returned to their places, to an almost audible murmur of admiration from the congregation.

First Confession proved to be an ordeal. I entered the confessional half-ashamed at the pitiful lack of sins I had to offer. The priest too, behind the grille, seemed irritated by my meagre list and hesitant attitude. I thought wildly of mentioning that I had read *Titus Andronicus*, and I might have added that spilling red ink on the Shakespeare volume had caused some trouble at home. At last I decided to sum up boldly, declaring 'I have been naughty several times.'

'Say "disobedient",' the priest's stern voice came back in the confined space. I was so disconcerted that I scarcely took in whether my penance was two Our Fathers and one Hail Mary, or the other way around. Even after I had dutifully said two of each, to be on the safe side, I felt more ruffled and querulous than in a state of grace.

Of course I believed that I was now ready for the next Sacrament, on Sunday. I could not postulate any alternative to believing – any more than I could to life with my parents in Braemar Crescent. I believed what they told me. I believed in Father Christmas, especially as I had once caught a glimpse of him at the front door at 'Homeleigh', as he arrived with a sack of presents for my cousins and myself. And as I returned to the pew, with the other boys, after my First Communion, I felt blissfully enrolled in the Church and permitted access to another largely unseen realm: of God and His saints, of Our Lord and Our Lady, all of whom I felt eager to believe in and obey.

When I gained some additional pocket-money, I purchased another statue for the top of the chest of drawers. It was one not easily found, even in the religious repository shop facing the church in Leigh, and was of my patron saint, the Archangel Michael, in armour, with raised sword. And then the fervency of my faith required a red glass lamp, with oil and floating wick, to burn in front of the statues while each night and morning I knelt to say my prayers.

I seemed already in my life to have done a lot of kneeling in prayer. Praying, I had been taught, was something God required daily of me. It was part of the worship which he must receive unceasingly from human beings – and which, one might suspect, was necessary to his holding and retaining a dominant place in human affairs. To pray for specific human ends was not merely permissible. It was encouraged. It gave purpose to prayers that might otherwise seem, even to the most credulous, monotonous and meaningless in their diet of praise. It was hard to conceive of God – any god in any religious creed – not tiring of solely being praised for eternity. But I was early warned that God did not always answer our prayers – not, at least, always in the manner we expected. That helped, of course, to ensure that we went on praying, with greater fervour and with fresh praise of a God who knew better than ourselves. And thus, in total acceptance of this primitive, addictive form of reassurance (in which God is guaranteed always to be right) to assist me through life, I went down on my knees in my bedroom, as I should do similarly in churches and chapels throughout my childhood and into my adult years. It was like playing with my toy telephone; I enjoyed picking up the receiver and talking, though there was nobody at the other end.

An aura of approval seemed to emanate from my family generally since I had made my First Communion. One aunt staying with us on the Sunday snapped me on my bicycle, proudly displaying my sleeve with its white armband, though the angle of her hasty shot sliced off the top of my head. Another, the most shy, silent and retiring of the 'Girls', but the one with the most sonorous series of names, Valentina Rose Blanche (Vally, to the family), sent me a special 'holy picture', a small composition of Christ administering the Sacrament to a smartly-suited boy. She had bothered to write on the back of the 'happy day' it commemorated, and to put a touching postscript, which I gladly obeyed, when I remembered, and which seemed recognition of my new status in the world that God had created: 'Sometimes say a little prayer for me.'

But permanently lodged in my imagination was Oberon; I gained so much from his existence, and yet he required nothing from me.

6

Family Matters and Family Myths

One summer day in 1894 my father's father, Haydn Handel Levey, assembled his children for a group photograph in the garden of 'Homeleigh'. He and his wife had often been photographed, occasionally with some of the children and occasionally on their own. And more than once he had been photographed playing the cello. One particularly evocative photograph shows him in the drawing-room at 'Homeleigh', playing with friends in the quartet he regularly organised.

The photograph of 1894 was a final and complete record of his surviving progeny – all fifteen of them, ranging from the eldest, Florence, then a girl of eighteen, to the youngest, Otto, my father, who appears as a boy of barely a year old, seated on his mother's lap. One of his sailor-suited brothers sits on their father's knee. Most of the children look, with varying degrees of cheerfulness, towards the camera. Only my father's head is slightly blurred. He obviously moved during the protracted taking of the photograph. Florence has a detached air, which is explicable, since in fact she was out of England at the time and a separate photograph of her had to be skilfully integrated into the composition.

The result is a typical document of late-Victorian family life. As I study it nowadays, I ask myself whether its instigator ever studied it and pondered on what would be the fate of all those sons and daughters of whom, I assume, he was so proud. On Sunday mornings, the progress of the family through the hushed streets of Brixton to the nearby church of Corpus Christi, an unfinished work by Bentley, must have been a notable sight. Two pews bore the Levey name, and often enough did I as a child kneel where my grandfather and his children had knelt.

My grandmother would not have been among them, for she was not a Roman Catholic. But she is to me the heroic figure in the group photograph. She looks clear-eyed and serene, with handsome, somewhat masculine features, apparently unbowed by constant child-bearing and child-rearing and all her other domestic responsibilities. We have her likeness but hers is, typically for a middle-class Victorian wife, a character forever hidden. What is known is that she was not my grandfather's first love. When she married him after the premature death of his first wife, she accepted instant maternity, taking care of the five children who survived from that romantic match. And a year later she gave birth to Madge, the first of her own yet more numerous brood of children.

She was a London girl, born Fanny Elizabeth Suter, from an ordinary, probably 'humble' background. How she came to meet my grandfather is not known, but in 1877, at the age of approximately twenty-five, she married him in the Roman Catholic church at Lambeth. It may or may not have been a factor in her willingness to marry him that her father, Emanuel Suter, had died early in her childhood and that her mother, a witness at her wedding, had subsequently remarried and been again widowed.

Whatever her dreams or hopes as a young girl, she is unlikely to have foreseen marriage to a Roman Catholic Irish widower in his mid-thirties, with five children under the age of twelve. However, he was good-looking, cultivated, confident and vigorous, rising in prosperity and clearly eager to re-marry and establish a new family.

I presume that theirs was a contented partnership, in which her role remained subordinate – though important in maternal terms. Ten of her children lived into adulthood.

To help her, first perhaps as nursemaid, a young country girl called Julia joined the 'Homeleigh' household. She would leave it only at death decades later, during the Second World War, by which time several of the children she had known as babies were themselves parents, whose children in turn had come to think of her as an essential element of life at 'Homeleigh'.

My father may have received a bigger share of his mother's attention and affection than had most of his siblings. She was over forty at his birth, and there must have been every reason to accept that he was to be her last child. If his temperament is any evidence, she was a profoundly affectionate mother, in addition to being a profoundly experienced one. Although he said tantalisingly little about her, he had obviously reciprocated her affection – and he admired her too. He did tell me how she always took him as a young boy with her on charitable expeditions to poor families in Brixton, explaining to him later that his presence, and inevitable chat about children between her and other mothers, helped to banish any hint of patronage from those visits. And that concept of unobtrusive, considerate generosity would also characterise him.

Everything suggests that my grandmother was calmly capable, emotionally assured and faintly amused by life. She had married a man with his own vein of humour, perhaps inherited, along with musical gifts, from a father who was something of a Dublin wag, if not a wit. Her eldest daughter recollected that on visits to London 'the old gentleman' enjoyed making jokes in public and was not above seeking mildly to embarrass his English daughter-in-law. According to another daughter, my slightly sentimental yet sweet-natured aunt, Senta, she had laughed a lot when young Senta confessed that she quite liked the idea of marriage though not of sharing her bed with a man. But that is a rare anecdote, and although photographs convey her dignified appearance, her clothes and her jewellery, little or nothing speaks of her real personality. It was perhaps inevitable that in my aunts' collective memory the male figure of Papa was more dynamic and dominant. His books, his opinions, his taste in wine and cravats, and his own considerable personal jewellery, were all treasured at 'Homeleigh', and his charisma lingered there as long as the household survived.

Where there seems a marked emotional hiatus is in the image presented, to the girls of both his marriages, of marriage as a desirable state, at least for them. Perhaps my grandfather was so vivid and charming, though possibly also demanding, that they could not contemplate linking themselves to another man.

Or perhaps other reasons existed why the majority of his daughters, all of whom had their own distinct characters, remained unmarried. It is a notable statistic that out of nine girls, only two – the two youngest and the two prettiest – sought or found husbands. Even the prosaic financial implications of spinsterhood for the other seven were considerable. My grandfather bequeathed equal sums of money (I think) to them all, but he probably realised that they would have difficulty living separate lives, whatever their wishes, and that continuing a joint household, at 'Homeleigh', was the best economic solution. And he may have guessed that even then some of them would need to earn money to keep it going.

In contrast to their sisters, the six boys all married, and all had children – though not as prolifically as had their Victorian father.

Haydn Handel Levey started life in 1841 with unusual, significant baptismal names (in fact, they appear in reverse order in the baptismal entry). Family tradition spoke of them as the names of his father's favourite composers, and the boy directly inherited his musical talent, though he would never make professional use of it. His own favourite composer seems to have been Beethoven. Beethoven's quartets were probably those played most often on musical evenings at 'Homeleigh'. But his fondness for early Wagner was proclaimed by the names he chose to give three of his daughters, and the 'Girls' recollected that he had visited Bayreuth; somewhere in the house, they vaguely believed, was a journal he had kept of his visits. Of other opera composers, I know only that Mozart was represented for him, as for most of his generation, by *Don Giovanni*, a predilection passed on to my father.

By the time I realised the interest of Haydn Handel writing about visits to Bayreuth, his journal could not be found. I had begun to feel that altogether the mythic charm of 'Homeleigh' was diminishing, and I suspected that the journal was one of those things that had never existed. Writing was not an activity I associated with my grandfather, whose life seemed anyway full enough. He had continued to go daily to his office in the City up to the day of his death in 1920. He had his music and his love of Rhine wines, and his numerous family. And late photographs of him show a mellow, distinguished, white-haired paterfamilias, exuding a quiet consciousness that life has treated him well.

I knew the story of how, when very young in Dublin, he had fallen in love with an actress, Annie Coates, eventually tracing her to London – and marrying her. She was to die in 1874. Five of their six children grew up and formed the 'first' family, and my grandmother had had to be a mother to them all.

What I did not know for many years was that one manuscript written by my grandfather did exist. In the early 1870s, he had bothered to set down at length the tale of how he first saw Annie, and fell in love with her, and how he despaired of ever seeing her again, and how he managed to get to London and find her, finding also that his love was reciprocated. He ends his memoir with the words: 'thus I was exquisitely – completely – & without exception perfectly happy'.

As this sentence suggests, the writer lacks ease of style and is obviously unused to expressing his feelings on paper.

Nor is it clear whether he was writing with any definite audience in mind, although at one point he mentions his duty to 'my readers'. But he knows he has a good and touching story to tell, and he must have experienced an urge to leave some record, however stilted, of the central emotional event in his life. Most touching of all, given Annie's premature death, is his expressed thought that one day she may come to read this story of his love.

He also happens to allow us a few glimpses – too few – of his family circumstances in mid-Victorian Dublin. It was his father, Richard Michael, who unwittingly provided him with his first sight of Annie Coates. Had Richard Michael not been rehearsing his new pantomime to open on St Stephen's Day (Boxing Day) in 1856, and had he not accidentally left his baton at home that morning, there would probably have been no meeting between his fifteen-year-old son and the actress, and thus no later marriage.

The memoir opens with the boy on holiday in Dublin, strolling on that frosty morning to a friend's house. He heard someone whistle behind him but paid no heed until he realised that the person was whistling to attract his attention and was his own father, 'the only individual who had a right', as he facetiously puts it, 'to call me in that canine way'.

Aware of having forgotten his baton and spotting his son in the street, Richard Michael asked him to dash home, collect it and bring it to the theatre. When the boy arrived there, he stayed on for a while, amused by all the bustle of rehearsal. The pantomime's heroine was seated downstage, and suddenly he saw approaching her a young girl. It was Fate, it was Destiny, the man assures us, recalling his immediate reaction. At mere sight of the girl, the schoolboy had fallen in love.

After this dramatic start to a true-life romance, it is disconcerting to discover that the only existing likeness of Annie shows a sad-faced woman, with a mouth slightly askew, devoid of beauty and not conventionally pretty. And something of those features lived on in her daughters.

However, from the memoir there is a good deal to be learnt or deduced about her husband, the writer. He openly states that his thoughts as a boy were to become a musician. But his father, he says, warned him off that profession, remarking that enough members of the family were already struggling in it. His next thought – a surprising one for the future father of fifteen children – was to become a priest. There was somebody in Dublin, according to him, who would have facilitated his studies and even arranged for him to go to Rome. But finally he took an unpaid job in a business firm, offered to him by one of his cousins. There he stayed for more than two unsatisfactory years, at the end of which he learnt that his cousin rated his proficiency as non-existent and declined to give him a salary. And he quotes the opinion, expressed presumably by his cousin, that he was somebody who 'would never set the Liffey on fire'.

Settled in London, and happily married, he could afford by the 1870s to look back and smile at that assessment. In a way, he could be grateful for it, since it had helped to deepen his resolve to leave Dublin for London, to seek out his Annie and obtain a post in some good commercial firm there. It must have taken greater courage than he quite conveys to break out of the family constraints, especially those placed on him by his father who seems to have gone on treating him as, in his own words, 'the errand boy – the Valet', expected to be on call first thing in the morning and last thing at night, '& fifty times during the day'.

In writing with such emphasis, he hardly conceals traces of resentment. And when he describes his eventual, approved departure for London, in July 1860, at the age of nineteen, it is notable that he mentions saying farewell to his father, without any affectionate qualification, while referring to his 'poor' mother, his three 'darling' sisters and his 'good' cousin, Lizzie, who had been his chief helper and confidante.

It is clear that he was glad to be leaving Dublin behind him, although he records understandable pangs of lone-liness en route to the totally unknown city of London. But a remarkable inner confidence about his future, pro-fessionally as well as personally, seems to have sustained him. And it was to be triumphantly justified. He found his Annie, learnt of her reciprocal love for him and entered a business house, Ellis Everington & Co., of St Paul's Churchyard. Like the young hero at the end of a Dickens novel, and without the benefit of any plot manipulation, he had gained happiness and prosperity.

At some date he established his own firm of H. H. Levey, dealing in the import of silks and ribbons, and building up connections which became those of friendship no less than business with family firms in Switzerland. One such Swiss friend was Otto Senn, after whom my father was named, and the Senn family would retain its links down the years with later generations of the Levey family. My grandfather took his two eldest sons into the firm, and they continued to keep it surviving for more than a decade after his death. Indeed, it gave them a standard of living considerably above that of the sons of his second marriage.

I am uncertain whether Haydn Handel ever went back to see his family in Dublin. Psychologically, it makes sense that he should not. His life as an adult was centred in London, from which he had extracted the emotional and practical essentials for an independent existence. And, above all, he had demonstrated to anyone who cared to look that he was an individual far from doomed to inferiority – or poverty. Materially, he was probably the most successful member of his family. By daring to escape from provincial Dublin, he escaped from narrow conditions and petty pressures.

As a result, he would ultimately enjoy the best of several worlds. He was the successful, cosmopolitan, self-made business man, with devoted wife and crowd of children, who at home could still satisfy something of his early, instinctive urge to be a musician. His chosen instrument, the cello, was one that required more than casual, amateur strumming, while not offering such popular opportunities for virtuoso effects as did the violin, played professionally by his elder brother and, more significantly perhaps in the context, by his father.

Richard Michael Levey, the man who whistled 'in that canine way' to attract his son's attention in the street, was clearly a personality who expected to have his wishes promptly obeyed and who imposed himself on his family as much as on his orchestra and on Dublin society. Haydn Handel had strong, positive reasons for leaving Dublin, but no less strong among negative ones may have been the need to be out of his father's proximity. No doubt Richard Michael Levey was a charming, genial and attractive person to know, with patently 'Irish' qualities of conviviality and gaiety, as well as being a gifted musician with some creative energy as a composer, in addition to his skill as a performer on the violin, and his work as a teacher whose pupils would include the composer Charles Villiers Stanford. The social aspects of music-making seem central to all his many activities. He lived long and had a good, fertile memory of theatrical and musical events in Dublin from the late 1820s, and he himself became prominent on the musical, theatrical, social scene there. He was famous enough to have his portrait painted and to be gently caricatured as 'Ireland's Eye' in a series by 'Spex' which owes much to the similar semi-cartoons in England by 'Spy'. But, just because he was so considerable a personality, he may – for all his gifts and his geniality – have been a rather heavy father, especially to a son.

In his own right, he sounds fascinating enough. He wrote some account of the stars he had known or watched (*Annals of the Theatre Royal*), but probably his anecdotes in conversation were even more lively, and they could have been very wide-ranging, for he, who had seen Edmund Kean and Paganini (visiting Ireland in 1831), was later to be involved in a partnership with G. J. Vandeleur Lee, the mysterious and mesmeric singing-teacher of Bessie Shaw, mother of George Bernard Shaw. He and Lee produced Bellini's opera *La Sonnambula* in Dublin in 1873, when the taxing role of Amina, the sleep-walking heroine, was taken by Shaw's sister, Lucy.

Mysteries exist in the life, or at least in the origins, of Richard Michael Levey. He is stated (in, for example, Grove's *Dictionary of Music and Musicians*) to have been born in 1811, in Dublin. And it is always said that his real name was O'Shaughnessy. Family tradition that this was our true name was firm in my childhood and was frequently invoked by my aunts. They had various reasons for explaining why my great-grandfather had made the change, which nobody called an improvement, to Levey. Sometimes, I was told that it was because O'Shaughnessy was too difficult to pronounce when he conducted or performed in England. At other times, a franker explanation seemed to be that the Irish were unpopular in England. The choice of 'Levey' was explained as being a tribute to his first music-teacher, of that name.

When I was a boy, I accepted the general story of the change of name, though I told my aunts often that as soon as I grew up I should change my name back to its proper form and become Michael O'Shaughnessy. This was an intention each of the sisters still living at 'Homeleigh' approved of, but none was more enthusiastic about it than my aunt Madge, the most Celtically-inclined of the whole family, who was fond of using Gaelic script and green ink, who took her holidays in Connemara and always had fresh shamrocks sent over from Ireland for St Patrick's Day. Although not my godmother, she was to assume a godmotherly role in aesthetic matters as I grew out of boyhood. She introduced me to such sophisticated pleasures, quite beyond my parents' range of interest, as visiting art exhibitions after gourmet lunches at first-rate restaurants. She alone seemed to make a cult of the family and its Irish links, and she distributed to the younger generation, including myself, items of jewellery and so on which had belonged to our grandfather. Although far too generously affectionate ever to hint at any disappointment, she must have noticed that I reached the age of twenty-one enthused by her enthusiasms and yet without taking action to alter my name.

Somehow, I should never get around to it, though I have frequently pondered whether I would have been perceived differently had I, for instance, appeared in public under the name Michael O'Shaughnessy. Any books by me set in the slums of Belfast or Dublin would have been raved about by English reviewers, with their love of the ethnic, usually mistaken by them for the authentic, which is their chief criterion nowadays for judging fiction. The BBC, always offering oxygen to self-publicists, would have allowed me constant opportunities to rediscover my roots in Ireland, and I would have been wise to acquire a hint of Irish accent to accompany my lyrical celebrations of the Emerald Isle, of Guinness and 'soft' days in Galway or wherever.

I can see that I might greatly have enjoyed that persona, in addition to or even as replacement of the one I was to possess as Michael Levey. Many of the traits in my character could have been attributed to my Irish origin, whereas my name alone presupposes that I am of Jewish descent, and hence the same traits may plausibly be explained as typically Jewish. Granted the still current though no longer openly expressed stereotypes, I have probably gained on occasion, rather than lost, by being thought to have an intelligence 'Jewish', not 'Irish', in its calibre. And there is something quite funny about the actual likely truth, presented to me only very late in life, a truth suitable for one born under Gemini: that I partake of the two races.

Irish records are patchy, since many were destroyed in the uprising of 1916 in Dublin. That may be the reason why it is difficult to trace the place and date of birth of Richard Michael (O'Shaughnessy) Levey and to establish who precisely were his parents. He probably was born, whether or not in Dublin, in 1811. He did not die until 1899, when his obituary notices were oddly silent about his background. Diligent recent research (not by me) has failed to produce an O'Shaughnessy who can be satisfactorily identified as his father. What has emerged is the likelihood that his father was a certain Richard Levey, a solicitor in Dublin. And that in itself must raise a presumption of Jewish blood.

On looking back, I think I detect in my aunts at 'Homeleigh' an unexpressed, even unconscious determination not to consider any such possibility. One might surmise that in their fervent Roman Catholicism, itself held genuinely enough, they were rebutting any hint of Jewishness. Again and again, it was also a matter of importance in the family, extending to my father, to stress that 'Levey' was spelled with two 'e's. The spelling and the pronunciation 'Levy' had to be avoided – though it seldom was. And it might have been better to opt for spelling the name 'Leavey', which had some Irish resonance, or even create an amusing. Joycean variation, with impeccable associations of Dublin, 'Liffey'.

Instead, a shadowy, endemic hint of Jewishness, needing to be rebutted before it could find open expression, hung over the 'adopted' name, and it even affected my mother, I should notice, when having to give it in shops or on the telephone. It was almost as though she, like the rest of the family, longed to launch into the story of how our real name was O'Shaughnessy and how my great-grandfather had been persuaded to change it. Yet in conventional English eyes, the Irish were by no means necessarily more respectable than the Jews, and obtaining a correct spelling of the Irish name might have had its own problems.

O'Shaughnessy was certainly a name my great-grandfather must have thought himself entitled somehow to use, though he did not do so on such documents as his marriage certificates. But at his death in 1899 he was registered as 'Richard M. O'Shaughnessy (Levey)', which explains nothing and which yet may represent some truth, perhaps that the thoroughly Irish name had been that of his mother. If so, it is rather bizarre that one published account of him (in 1910) should refer to something semitic in his appearance being attributed by a friend to Jewish blood on his mother's side.

Whatever the exact facts, now unlikely to be fully established, he seems to have been uninhibited by his background and a man of energy and considerable will-power under a jovial, jokey exterior. 'I beat time' was an often-repeated witticism of his to explain his longevity. As well as becoming prominent and popular as a conductor, he showed facility, if nothing else, in composing overtures to annual pantomimes which total fifty (according to Grove). More seriously, he was involved in founding the Royal Irish Academy of Music and in numerous other, more ephemeral musical ventures in which he performed as leading violinist. His private life was, in its way, equally busy. He married three times and had numerous children.

One of the most famous stories connected with him has him rehearsing the Theatre Royal orchestra when a servant-girl arrives to announce that his wife has given birth to a son. The rehearsal breaks off while he receives congratulations. A few minutes later the servant returns, to say another boy has been born, and more congratulations follow before the rehearsal resumes. Then the girl rushes back again, to say, 'It's triplets.' My great-grandfather lays down his baton. 'Gentlemen,' he tells the orchestra, 'I must go home and put a stop to this.'

The story doubtless gained from frequent repetition, but it is a fact that by one of his wives (not my great-grandmother) he did have triplets. And clearly he was a source and fund of such stories in Dublin circles.

Something of his delight in the amusing, as well as in the musical and the theatrical, was inherited by his immediate descendants. In those people I knew well, like my father and several of his sisters, I think one can detect a fascination too with stage performance, regardless of the category of entertainment. They were all remarkably, admirably, unsnobbish about what they enjoyed, especially where music was concerned. That was perhaps partly a nineteenth-century attitude, which made fewer distinctions between the opera, the pantomime and the drawing-room ballad.

A more subtle inheritance came, I believe, from Richard Michael, distributed variously among his grandchildren, and that was an effortless capacity to enjoy life itself. I suspect it passed directly through Haydn Handel, arguably a man of greater refinement than his father, to sparkle openly in my own father. He lacked the urge to perform publicly in any area and would probably have thought his Irish grandfather a dreadful show-off, not least socially; even compared with that of his father, Haydn Handel, his personality appears reticent and shy and ungregarious. But within any family context he was quietly yet confidently at ease, and although he was the youngest of all the children, in time he took on the emotional responsibility of being a father, one resolutely unheavy but good, wise and loving, to his sisters at 'Homeleigh'. And circumstances would increase his paternal role more widely in the family.

As quite a small boy, I was always delighted when my father agreed to recite chronologically the litany of names of his father's children, and I too learnt to chant it: Florrie, Molly, Byl (sic), Vally, Bob, Madge, Elsa, Senta, Bertie, Ernie, Winnie, Jeanne, Fritz, Eva, Otto.

Most of the names were of people familiar to me – but not all. Fritz, of course, was dead, though he had left a widow and two sons with whom my father kept in touch but whom I never met. Bertie had early gone out to Australia, leaving behind associations – rightly or wrongly – of being a 'black sheep'. Certainly, his name was seldom mentioned in my hearing, yet my father sometimes referred to one further brother, Wilfred, who had died in childhood and, as I gathered, had been an epileptic.

Geographically distant but very much alive and often talked of admiringly was my aunt Florrie, who lived in Poland and only rarely came on visits to England. She was to be caught in Poland at the outbreak of the Second World War, being then in her early seventies. News of her plight filtered through only sporadically, and there were times when it seemed unlikely that she would be seen again by her family. Yet she marvellously survived adventures of every kind, and I met her first in London after the War, to be enthralled by her calm, mental clarity, her humour, her crisp, slightly foreign-sounding speech, and an agelessness enhanced rather than diminished by her wiry white hair. It was easy to believe the stories of how she had marched miles to escape the Bolsheviks, as she called them, and how at some point she had bribed a German general with a bottle of whisky. For long she had been a legendary personage to me, and then someone for whose safety my aunts anxiously prayed. At 'Homeleigh', her arrival once, in happier, pre-war days, with a present of black bread from Poland, would frequently be recalled, along with her astonishment at finding after a while that nobody would touch what she described as 'my lovely pumpernickel'. For some reason, this story and that exotic word 'pumpernickel' made my cousin Bernard and myself shriek with joy as children, and the vigorous old lady who settled in England for the final years of her life had perhaps by then become more at home abroad than here.

Growing up in the realisation that I possessed a large number of aunts and uncles, as well as cousins too, I made no distinction between the children of Annie Coates and those of Fanny Suter. Indeed, I was probably none too clear that my grandfather had married twice; and that fact seemed not to influence the varying degrees of affection existing among the two lots of siblings.

Only gradually did I learn to see the physical differences

that separated them. Paradoxically, it was the children of Annie Coates, who had died so young, who tended to have strong constitutions and to enjoy longevity, outliving their younger half-brothers and sisters sometimes by many years. Fanny Suter's children were plumper, and they may often have looked healthier. But most of them suffered, knowingly or not, from heart conditions. They might, like my father, die very suddenly, with no previous illness; and none of them lived beyond the age of seventy-two.

I think other, more nuanced differences were detectable between the two sets of children, although it is easy to invent distinctions of that kind and, after all, every one of them had had the same father. Yet even in their shared characteristic of keen humour, I discern two different styles of expression, almost according with physical appearance. Humour was dryer and less exuberant in the older group, in some at least of whom there seemed altogether more emotional reticence, though greater intellectual energy. But even in writing that, I am conscious of exceptions and contradictions. My musically talented uncle Bob, a good amateur singer, the last child of Annie Coates, born only shortly before her death, was as openly and affectionately genial as any of his half-sisters – and as plump. And my own father's intellectual powers were unmatched elsewhere in the family.

Whatever the mix of personality, and however sad some of the fates of the fifteen children, those I came to know as aunts and uncles were endlessly entertaining in my eyes – possibly more, on occasion, than they intended.

Of his two half-brothers, Byl and Bob, my father seemed to prefer Bob. Perhaps proximity played its part when my parents were first married, since Bob and his stately wife, Maud, with their three attractive children, occupied a house nearby in Wimbledon. While I have no clear-cut recollections of visits there, I have a generalised feeling of familiarity, more with the large-seeming house and Uncle Bob than with his children, considerably older than me, or with his wife. Rather short, bald, rubicund and virtually a humming-top of good temper and hospitality, he seemed ideally avuncular, even to his jaunty bow-tie, and a perfect incarnation of the cheery, proverbial assurance, 'Bob's your uncle'. And as such he truly remained right up to the period of my own marriage.

By that date I had come to know and savour the whimsical, fastidious, cooler and perhaps more complex personality of his brother, Byl. He was a slim, slight man, neatly-dressed and with neatly-parted hair, whose delicate wit seemed perpetually in play, as if quizzing life itself. At times he would exercise it airily on his highly animated, socially-inclined wife, Winnie, and on their daughter, Diana, who was very much the forthright, sophisticated product of two such apparently disparate individuals.

Byl kept himself aloof from the rest of the family as represented by 'Homeleigh'. I never witnessed any of the few, flying descents made there by Diana and her mother, though with what my aunt Senta dubbed my 'blotting-paper ears', I caught something of the stir and the mildly satiric comments generated by those visits. I was intrigued by talk of this cousin who as a child had once created a notorious scene by declining to give a farewell kiss to her aunt Vally and who as a young girl in the Thirties moved in London circles that at 'Homeleigh' were spoken of, disapprovingly, as 'fashionable'. Yet it was better that we should not meet until I was grown-up and my character had developed sufficiently to appreciate – without being too overwhelmed by – all Diana's bright energy. Then I could also appreciate the prescience of her parents in giving her that name at birth.

The outward circumstances of the lives of Vally and her elder sister Molly could not have been more different, and that difference was reflected in their temperaments. Vally remained all her life at 'Homeleigh'. She was unfitted for existence outside a sheltered environment and often seemed vague to the point of what the idiom of that day not unkindly characterised as 'dippy'. The fiction was that she shared with her half-sister Senta domestic responsibility, though in reality her role was nominal. She was the most silent member of the household. When she spoke her voice was unexpectedly gruff, and with her somewhat crumpled features and mauveish, powdered face she could appear at first disconcerting. Yet nearly everyone, her siblings and most of her nephews and nieces, rightly found her lovable. She had, too, a knack of coping sensibly when the occasion required. Accosted in the street by some would-be mugger or drunk, she had repulsed him firmly, and effectively, with the words, 'Go away, you silly man.' The drawing-room drama of Diana's refusal to kiss her had been heightened by Diana's mother declaring that they would not leave until her daughter obeyed. After Diana eventually capitulated and the pair had departed, Vally was asked about the kiss. Sportingly, she only then, and gruffly, revealed the truth: 'She gave me a lick.'

Molly must early have left 'Homeleigh', partly to earn her living as a governess, like her sister Florrie. But no sense lingered of her being missed, and she herself never visited there, as far as I know, or showed any interest in the household's existence. At once fiercely independent and yet needing human contacts and indeed offers of hospitality, she seemed sadly fated to be more tolerated by friends and family than positively welcomed. Physically, she was small and painfully fragile, but mentally she was tough. She lived alone, bravely struggling on very little income, determined never to touch the small, sacred sum of capital bequeathed by her father and destined by her for favourite nephews and nieces. In that well-meant but slightly perverse attitude, much about her was revealed. She was articulate and sharply intelligent, and by nature affectionate. That was as undoubted as was her tendency, increased by living alone, to express her views with an outspokenness which rarely took into account the feelings of other people.

Bizarre incidents somehow attached themselves to her and her reputation within the family. Thus, when taking a coach for Cambridge, where she was then living, she had managed to get on one that carried her, as she realised too late, to Oxford. While that might happen to anybody, she alone, perhaps, would imply that the fault lay with the driver. And the story was often told at 'Homeleigh' of her going into the hat department of Liberty's in London, asking to see every item in stock and then, dissatisfied, flinging down the final hat with the remark, 'I see you have nothing.'

I accompanied her back to our local dairy when some cream she had bought proved to have gone bad. She began a spirited volley of reproach, cut short when the indignant woman behind the counter pointed out that we had come to the wrong dairy. An even more humiliating occasion was our retreat from a crowded restaurant in Kensington, where she had planned to offer lunch to my mother and me, when she abruptly concluded that the menu looked inadequate. With less than her usual frankness, she told the waitress loudly as we rose, 'The little boy can find nothing he likes.'

She was a familiar presence throughout my childhood, since she had fixed on my parents as endlessly willing to put her up – and, though she may not have formulated it in that way, to put up with her. She was grateful, though gratitude did not check her freedom in commenting upon my mother's housekeeping or my table-manners, sometimes in comparison with the households and children of friends, or former employers, whom she as regularly visited.

Perhaps it was the pedagogue in her that prompted the flow of well-intentioned criticisms. She must have been a good governess, in her fashion, for she was knowledgeable and talked directly to children, without condescension. She knew how to stimulate interest and rather enjoyed the child who spoke up – like my perceptive, quick-witted cousin, Bernard – even if in contradiction to her. I was not his equal in repartee but she noted, for example, my fondness for history and promptly took me on my first visit to the National Portrait Gallery. Afterwards, as we had a little time to spare, she took me to the adjoining institution in Trafalgar Square, the National Gallery, where her own interest in the paintings was slighter but where mine was significantly kindled.

Both my parents found in Molly a person more odd and piquant than irritating. They understood, above all, that she refused to be pitied or patronised. That she must consider literally every penny she expended was comprehensible, though my father delighted to recall how she had once cautiously informed him, apropos some major horse-race, that if he knew of a certainty at long odds, she would risk a shilling. Great had been her astonishment at his swift response that in such a case he would put everything he owned on the animal.

The four 'Girls' at 'Homeleigh', Madge, Elsa, Senta and Winnie, who were my father's full sisters, were to occupy, along with Julia, a central place in my heart and imagination. They were entwined in the process of my growing up, and I reserve for the next chapter any sketch of the group they formed.

There remained my father's three married siblings, Ernie, Jeanne and Eva. He was very attached to Eva, and Ernie and Jeanne were my godparents. No doubt they would have generously taken me into their families had my parents died, for they were outgoing, affectionate, 'family' people. Yet I never attracted much attention from either of them. And as a boy I tended to resent that lack, especially when I watched my cousins being lavishly fêted on their birthdays and at Christmas by their godmothers, who were my unmarried aunts.

I seldom saw Ernie, who had been severely crippled by polio in childhood. He had to drag himself around on crutches which in those days were of heavy wood and cumbersome – almost as much a hindrance as a help.

He scraped some sort of living from a small sweetshop in Forest Hill, assisted – I feel fairly sure – by discreet sums from his sisters at 'Homeleigh' and perhaps occasionally also by my father. I barely knew his three children, who were cousins older and younger than me, and I have only the faintest recollection of his wife.

I can, however, recall my father taking me across London to the shop, where Ernie's daughter, Josephine, the precociously responsible, eldest child, would often help out. It seemed exciting in prospect. I knew that my aunts were anxiously fond of their brother, and they frequently expressed their admiration for Josephine. The sound of 'Forest Hill' had not prepared me for the grey, grimly unrustic nature of the district. Nor had I supposed that behind the shop the family would be living in such dark, cramped conditions. The whole physical environment depressed me, embarrassed me and made me unresponsive to the point of sulkiness.

Even then, however, I could not miss the impact of Ernie's remarkable personality. Circumstances and his condition seemed not to have diminished his traits of cheerfulness, friendliness and keen humour. Indeed, they shone out the more brightly, and I understood why his siblings admired as well as loved him. I could see, too, strong similarities between him and my more fortunate father, and selection of him as my godfather began slowly to make sense to me.

In addition to kinship, there were affinities and sympathies which bound together my father and his two married sisters. He would choose the elder, Jeanne, to be my godmother and had himself previously been chosen as godfather to the one child of the younger, Eva. He enjoyed the company of both their husbands, especially Eva's. And after I was born links between their families and ours naturally became closer. Jeanne was married to a journalist known generally as 'Tim' (his surname was Timmins), a clever, literate man, frequently concealed behind thick pipe-smoke and secluded from his boisterous, convivial family of four children, at work in his book-lined study. When he emerged, it was with a certain dry, wry detachment. Theirs was a household I had entered first before I have any memories, but I should always find its atmosphere warmly welcoming, invigorating – and slightly hectic.

My godmother embodied it. As she flung open the front door and stood there, with her striking, often untidy, mass of red-gold hair and bright blue eyes, she seemed smilingly prepared for anything, except people who were slow and undecided, or 'finicky' over their meals, or excessively house-proud, or who expected much of her time and attention. Her manner spoke for her as she served up a hearty tea for twelve or gladly contrived a spare bed for yet another stray guest: 'Take it or leave it.'

In wartime London she was an even more welcoming presence. With the break-up of the family at 'Homeleigh', she had taken in two of her sisters, and she would find temporary space for me on my journeys to and from Harrogate. The large windows of the pleasant house in Streatham were criss-crossed with brown paper strips. I must have naïvely asked why. 'Against blast, of course.' If only inwardly, I winced, though after the night's air-raid I was with my cousins excitedly collecting fallen shrapnel.

This group of cousins I grew up knowing and instinctively loving. The arrival of the whole Timmins family at 'Homeleigh' on Christmas Day was a memorable moment of the morning in my early childhood. It was equalled only by the ensuing excitement when there came a thunderous knock on the door, and adults as well as children rushed into the hall: it was Father Christmas. One year I actually glimpsed the red-cloaked, bearded figure, as I kept afterwards telling my cousin Bernard.

'But hadn't you noticed who had disappeared?' he asked impatiently. 'It was Uncle Tim.'

'Our tribe', was the way in which his wife liked to refer to their four children. Jeanette and John, the two elder, were always kind to me, though in my eyes they seemed almost grown-up, and I was rather awed by Jeanette's vivid, inherited, much-praised prettiness. With the two younger children, Margaret and Gerard, only slightly older than me, I felt more relaxed. Gerard was nice enough but pasty-faced and permanently subdued, with an air often mistaken by our aunts for profound piety. They detected in him a vocation for the priesthood, and I was quite jealous when his godmother, Madge, promised him the jewels from one of her rings for his chalice; I was tempted to be similarly 'called'. In fact, Gerard was destined for a happy marriage and children of his own.

So was Margaret, but nobody ever supposed she would become a nun. Pretty, if arguably less pretty than her sister, she had the same blue eyes and a more obviously animated, teasing, dancing, attractive manner. I increasingly responded to its appeal while I was increasingly tongue-tied under her rapid, topical, teenage banter. Nobody had told me about the latest catchy tunes (not yet termed pop songs), and I could never be sure what 'Swing' was – even less whether, in the words of an often-played record of a Crosby-Mercer exchange, 'it was here to stay'.

Coming under Margaret's attention, if only teasingly, was novel, delightful and, as it were, educational. It gave me an inkling of what it was like to have a sister, and from another cousin I had already gained, more profoundly, the sense of what it was like to have a brother.

Only two years older than my father was his sister Eva, a fair-haired and blue-eyed girl, less robust and, I presume, of a less lively character than Jeanne. Photographs of her in adulthood may do little justice to her colouring but they suggest that she was not so much pretty as beautiful. She too married a journalist, Jack Hoole. His family was friendly with the Levey family, and his sister Mary became my Uncle Ernie's wife. In 1926 Eva gave birth to a son, Bernard, as blond and blue-eyed as herself, with an attractive, amusing temperament, and an acute intelligence to match. In the following year my mother gave birth to me, at least in physical appearance a total contrast. And it was a contrast often manifest as the two families met and went on holiday together, and the two little boys were photographed together.

My mother would find Eva the most immediately sympathetic of her sisters-in-law when she encountered the massed family in what must have been, on the first occasion, a considerable ordeal. In marrying my father, she was to be endowed with not solely his few worldly goods but his many relations and their extensive range of friends and the whole social ethos that radiated around 'Homeleigh'.

She and Eva were women who became mothers only in their thirties, and they may well have shared confidences and apprehensions over the raising of their sons – and plans for their future. It came as the gravest shock to her and to my father when Eva died in 1931, at the age of thirty-nine. She had been ill, possibly with pneumonia, but her death – communicated to us by letter – was devastating in its implications: for Jack and his very young boy, for the boy's godmother, my unmarried aunt Senta, and for the family generally.

Eva was the youngest of Haydn Handel's daughters – a tiny girl in a pinafore, seated close to her half-sister Molly in the group photograph of 1894. And she was the first to die.

Witnessing my parents' distress, I was bewildered but unable – despite all they repeatedly said – to recall my aunt and our seaside holidays, or even bring Bernard clearly to mind. Death itself meant nothing to me. I had never heard of it before and I could not properly understand why we were to grieve.

Without realising it, however, I had received a first, sad lesson, helping me perhaps towards seeing that our family, for all its sense of vitality, and all its lively, intriguing individuals, was not exempt from a sudden, fatal blow. And, tragic as the circumstances had been, I would sometimes think later that they played a part in bringing Bernard more prominently into my childhood life, enormously enhancing my pleasure in it.

7

Growing Pleasures

'Bernard is coming to stay for a few days' were words I would hear my mother say often enough, but in tones so neutral that she might have been echoing those of an announcer on the wireless, giving out a weather report for the attention of all shipping.

I knew she was fond of him, and deeply sympathetic too, though no overt reference must ever be made to his mother's death. But she showed none of my voluble excitement at the prospect of his stay. Indeed, apart from expressing greater concern over what we should eat, she seemed to feel no emotion, unless mild, largely-concealed anxiety. Perhaps she would have recognised the analogy with the weather report and been inclined to issue one privately on the lines of, 'Squalls may arise without warning.'

Nor should I have disagreed. That there would be something to stir the even tenor of our ways at Braemar Crescent was what I anticipated and welcomed about the news of his stay. It was unlikely that we should quarrel – or anyway not for long – despite the basic differences in our interests and our natures. Rather, we should be able to conspire together, if only in conversation, against the settled adult world which under his influence I would see as frequently absurd.

As the younger boy, and the one whom life had left unscathed, I should in any case perhaps have been inferior in knowledge and initiative. But it was not so much age as personality which made Bernard dominant – and dominant in a lively, amusing way which adults had to take notice of and had on occasion cause to fear. For him to reduce me to hysterical giggles of homage was not difficult. But I perceived how his pithy observations about people and things struck everyone around us. His pale blue eyes, reminding me of a jay's, and his straight, blond hair, seemed to convey how clear-headed he was, and how hard-headed too.

He had his feelings under much better control than I had mine. Feelings as such he rarely revealed, at least to me, and though I might look forward to confiding in him, I was aware that he would be quite uninterested in my confidences.

His indifference did not hurt me, and though I admired his wit and pluck, and his ability to hold his own among adults, my admiration was surprisingly untinged with envy. Partly, that was because I was sure – sure beyond any need to give the matter thought – of unspoken mutual affection. 'Bonding' was not then a word in the current vocabulary, but I had been bonded with him from our earliest years, and a casual, sunny snap, taken when we were around the age of two or three, shows us seated side by side, with his hand firmly, steadyingly, grasping my shoulder.

His coming to stay always increased my consciousness of my own individuality. No longer was I a small child being educated at a convent. I was a schoolboy, with blazer and cap and satchel, who went daily to an all-male private school down in Leigh, Mr Palmerstone's, a small, amateurish academy, where educational standards were to be drastically improved when it was taken over by the Christian Brothers. Even under Mr Palmerstone we did homework, and we were taught Latin and French, though the Latin master sometimes had to supervise the cooking. I learnt to mingle with other boys, to scuffle with them, to mock or be mocked by them, and to make friends.

I was growing up. I was seven and then, imperceptibly, eight, going on nine, soon to be ten, and among my many pleasures was that of growing physically. I could almost sense the regular increase in my stature. I was growing taller, if not much fatter. I was ready to exchange the uncomfortable short flannel trousers of the period, with their complement of thick, knee-length woollen socks, for the ease and grown-up suavity associated with long ones ('longs'). I had new, sudden, growing enthusiasms. I sent off for birds' eggs from catalogues and collected (that is, killed) butterflies. I formed the nucleus of a traditional museum, including stones that I was convinced must be fossils. I had, too, a drawer of dressing-up clothes and a make-up box with false hair for beards and spirit gum for sticking them on. Then I went through a phase of needing a chemistry set, chiefly because of the appeal of the phial of copper sulphate crystals but also to burn sulphur to make my own variation on a popular joke product, the 'stink bomb'. Bernard and I were united in eagerness to visit the big joke shop in Holborn where the attraction lay in buying those items already in bad taste which, like stink bombs, carried whiffs of social anarchy.

I wanted to own unusual pets. I acquired a slippery, unresponsive grass-snake, which hissed when disturbed and which had created a *frisson* when I opened its box in a crowded railway carriage. I don't think it was very happy with me. It constantly escaped into neighbouring gardens, and there would come complaints on the telephone with the request that I go at once and remove it.

More conventionally, I even collected stamps for a period and was eager to own not just an ordinary album but the one described as 'de Luxe'. Colour and size were the guiding principles behind my collection, and Azerbaijan, I think, provided the best combination, though I was fond of the triangular stamps issued by the Cape of Good Hope. And Belgium produced an unexpectedly romantic set, in sugary tints but black-edged, to commemorate the death, in a car accident, of beautiful Queen Astrid in 1935.

In those years, which tended to blur as they passed, there seemed so many pleasures to experience, absorb or eventually grow out of. Even the most significant event of all, the period of my father's absence in Iraq, which opened with the agony of the day of his departure, became tolerable because unusual and interesting – or was thoughtfully made so for me by his attitude and my mother's.

The actual day, however, had been the worst ordeal of my life so far: sitting with her in the primitive environment of a typical 1930s café in Victoria, after we had seen him leave on the boat train. The wet rings on the tiled table came not from my tears but from slopped cups, and I took miserable pleasure in expanding them with one finger, while she could not rally herself sufficiently to check me.

In our soreness of spirits, we rubbed unbearably against each other, boding the worst for our relationship in the two years that lay ahead. But her stoicism soon asserted itself, and gradually it had its bracing effect on me. I never doubted that hers was the greater hardship, staying behind, than had been his in going. And each acted in accord with their temperament. The situation brought out the strength of her character. In some ways, it suited her, psychologically, better than a round of feasts. She might feel nervous and lonely and bereft. But those feelings only increased her determination not to repine. She had something to struggle against, and a duty to do so for the sake of her child. To me she made it appear, for the most part, as if my father had gone off to enjoy fascinating and exotic adventures, while privately she worried about not receiving his weekly letter or about how to pay the next gas bill.

During that prolonged period of his absence, I began very slowly to recognise a new, unselfish pleasure: that of being able to share her worries and even occasionally to ease them. When no letter had come for several weeks, I impulsively slipped a note under her bedroom door, saying that I was sure it was because of the post and not of some disaster to Daddy. I was filled with a novel sense of pride when, the next morning, she thanked me and said that it had helped her a lot. A day or so later, two letters, one accidentally delayed, arrived together.

It was another mark of growing up that my father wrote letters directly to me, often describing picturesque local sights or telling some story connected with his devoted personal attendant, his 'Bearer', Gabriel, who was obviously surprised to be treated not as inferior but as a fellow human being.

To my mother he often wrote letters with rather different emphases, conveying what it was like to live in a would-be British Raj-style mess in the middle of the desert, with a group of men, and some of their wives, who were enjoying the unaccustomed experience of being waited on and the opportunity to humiliate the native servants. Whatever material advantages these people were meant to be bringing to Iraq, they were by their behaviour helping to foster later antagonism – the old story of Colonial Britain. Anyway, social occasions cannot have been very agreeable to him, not drinking or smoking. For all his love of music, he did not dance. He probably seemed to his compatriots to have gone 'native', given his interest in the local scene and his taking trouble to learn a certain amount of simple Arabic.

Perhaps it is only imagination which makes me see him preferring to pass many an evening in his tent, writing letters home, while the mess grew rowdy. But certainly his comments had satiric bite – and, I should now say, touches of puritanism and even of misogyny. He was seldom entirely at ease with women socially and was quicker than he perhaps realised to stigmatise vivacity and sophistication in them as indications of silliness. It was an undercurrent of unconscious hostility which chimed with the presentation of women in two of his favourite authors, Wodehouse and Saki.

My mother hardly needed reassurance that his existence was chaste and sober. Only when an occasional letter arrived expatiating on some delightful expedition – such as going duck-shooting with a party of men – did she, as it seemed to me, feel tempted to contrast the comparative pleasures of his life abroad with the routine of hers in Braemar Crescent. But if she was momentarily so tempted, she quickly repressed it.

For me it was not only his letters that eased his absence. At intervals came exotic presents, usually linked to something he had already mentioned: a crate of oranges, a silver napkin ring on which my name had been inscribed in Arabic and, most splendid of all, a complete set of authentic Arab robes made to my size. My mother had the nice idea that I should be professionally photographed in my robes and the results sent out to my father. As the boy Lawrence of Leigh-on-Sea, I posed not before the privacy of the bathroom mirror but in the tiny, prosaically-lit studio of the busy local photographer. A humiliating, toothy self-consciousness pervaded the prints, much as I had feared. My mother could not hide her chagrin. She was disappointed to be reminded of my physical resemblance to her, and I felt obscurely at fault.

Suddenly, the tempo of life quickened with the news that my father was on his way home. We went down to Tilbury to meet him. Along with other excited people, we stood on the quayside and scanned the packed rails of the liner. And there among the crowd of faces was his face, unmistakable and tanned and smiling. The distance was too great for speech, so we waved and he waved. And we went on waving back and forth for what seemed like hours before disembarkation began. A slight weariness crept into the animation on both sides, though it vanished when we were eventually united and seated together in the boat train to London.

I had a thousand things to tell my father, whether or not he already knew them. I had actually seen the King and Queen in the Silver Jubilee procession, and the Indian Princes who rode in it. And there was a terribly funny current form of joke, which began 'Knock, knock', and you asked 'Who's there?' . . . But I was laughing too much to explain the nub of it, and abruptly I realised my chatter had reached boring point and that I must shut up. By then we were travelling in the unusual luxury of a taxi from Leigh station, and my mother had scarcely managed to say a word. The happiness and relief of my father's return needed no words. And the emotions lasted for days. All could be read in my mother's demeanour and in his own frankly expressed delight in the simplest aspects of being in his own home again. He was eager himself to talk and especially eager to show us the various Middle Eastern items he had brought back for the house.

It was a major event, occupying a whole morning. My mother and I sat as audience while he unrolled and unwrapped in our buff and cream dining-room embroidered bedspreads, blue, red and gold cushion-covers, a beaten copper jug and circular tray, and two magnificent Persian carpets, for which there was not sufficient space on the floor.

So bewitched was I by the sumptuousness of the array that I failed for a time to notice my mother's gathering gloom. Her lack of enthusiasm became puzzling, then awkward, and finally – to my amazement – it turned into outright near-anger.

'What on earth would we want with such stuff in this house?' she exclaimed. 'I'd never use garish things like these, and I don't know how you ever thought I would.'

Although she reluctantly agreed that the carpets were in themselves beautiful, and no doubt of fine quality, she refused to consider most of the rest of the items. 'Michael can have them for dressing-up clothes,' she said.

But even that proposition did not console me. For the first and virtually the last time, I witnessed a violent clash between my parents. I felt overwhelmed with shame at being present, particularly when I saw how hurt my father was. Just for something to do, I bent and stroked the gilt thread woven into one of the red and blue cushion-covers.

Only a few moments before, I had been listening as he described bargaining for it in some bazaar. Now it looked rejected, outlandish and indeed garish in the setting. I thought I could understand both my parents' viewpoints, but all the confused, pent-up emotions after so long an absence escaped me. What I did not miss was a new, creeping sense of how, even amid rejoicing, there could emerge a chill tinge of disappointment and disillusion.

Inevitably, I experienced in those years knocks and bruises and cuts that were sometimes actual as well as metaphorical. Still, had I been asked, I should have said – truthfully enough – that I was more conscious of growing pleasures than of growing pains.

Although my cousin Bernard was a permanent element in my life, he occurred as a presence only at holiday periods. Holidays and special occasions were what I associated him with, and the very fact that it was on this irregular basis that we met – sometimes quite briefly – sustained my sense of excited anticipation.

He came to stay with or without his godmother, my aunt Senta, a woman obsessively devoted to him yet with plenty of affection to spare for me. She was simple and certainly not clever, 'not brainy', as she frequently observed. Chronic deafness afflicted her. She bore it patiently and even cheerfully, forever experimenting with new deaf aids, which rarely did much to help. Yet she went on smiling through a tangle of wires, the bore of headphones and the handicap of a box which would suddenly emit embarrassing squawks in the silence of church. By nature she was warm-hearted, more maternal, I can now recognise, than any of her unmarried sisters, and far more demonstratively affectionate than my own mother.

I was astounded, almost disconcerted, when one day at Leigh she suddenly praised the lights in my hair. 'Nice silky hair,' she murmured, 'lovely auburn tints.' The word 'auburn' was new to me – as new as the idea that some physical attribute of mine might be appealing.

Senta was fond of my mother, and during my father's absence in Iraq the four of us went on a summer holiday to Rottingdean, in Sussex. We stayed in a ghastly boarding-house, with inedible food and peculiar permanent inmates, about whose appearance Bernard's comments soon had Senta and my mother laughing helplessly while they tried to shush him.

Day after day, it poured with rain, but to compensate there were thrillingly high seas, with waves curling white and tall over the front, and we two boys enjoyed getting drenched. As a holiday it was near-fiasco, however, and it closed acrimoniously with the landlady accusing me of having drawn in coloured pencil on the staircase wall. I had brought my crayons with me, and marks there certainly were. But I was not conscious of having made them. The incident remained inexplicable. What struck me during the painful sessions of recrimination was that Senta showed herself much more robust than my mother in defending my plea of innocence.

Knowing I would see Bermard at 'Homeleigh' added to the pleasure of any visit there. But the real joy was to stay the night and share a bedroom at the top of the house, whispering in the darkness, perhaps on Christmas Eve, until some adult at the door insisted, not for the first time, 'You boys must go to sleep.'

That seemed a waste, especially as the clock of St Saviour's, the church nearby, would ring out hourly at the approach to Christmas Day, and Bernard had not finished recounting to me the latest horrific science fiction story he had read, and I was thinking up some mild anecdote from my life to tell him in exchange.

Hilarious, in retrospect, was the night when our talk drifted to the subject of sex. He asked me if I had not noticed a pleasant sensation when I stroked myself, 'down there'. This was a totally new idea to me and I thought I would immediately put it to the test. 'Yes,' I whispered back delightedly, as I let my hand wander very slowly across my stomach.

Of Bernard's life when we were apart I knew little at that

stage, though I was aware of his going to a 'good' Catholic boarding-school. And at some point I became aware that his father was re-marrying. My blotting-paper ears had picked up that fact, along with a sense that the 'Girls' at 'Homeleigh' did not really approve. The second wife worked in the same newspaper office as his father and she was not a Catholic.

Without Bernard's company, I yet never felt my life lonely or dull. The change from St Edith's Convent to Mr Palmerstone's private school had gone unexpectedly smoothly. It seemed a part of growing up that I must learn to do without girls, and in some unexplained way it was essential to avoid anything that might be termed 'girlish'.

I suppose that Mr Palmerstone's was basically a Roman Catholic establishment. Other boys from the convent had moved on with me, though those with whom I became most friendly cannot, I think, have been Catholic and were not to be seen in church on Sundays. Perhaps the school's 'private' nature explained why some parents had chosen it and were willing to pay for their sons' education there. Its tone was more genteel than overtly religious. It seemed free from harshness or bullying. In my class was a shy, gentle Indian boy, the only boy of his race in the school, and I cannot recall that he was ever picked on for his colour or condescended to or treated as different from the rest of us. That ought not to need saying, of course, but it was perhaps remarkable in the place and for the period. Most of us, I at least, wore with pride our uniform of black cap and black blazer, with its badge in silver, but we seldom felt exclusive, though we may in some ways have been excluded from the rougher elements of life.

Every afternoon, as I went home on the bus, I passed the elementary school, where the pupils were coming out from the two buildings prominently marked as separate: Boys and Girls. I guessed, rather than knew or bothered, about the differences in ethos and education from my school. Obviously, ours was smaller, and it occupied a couple of what had been private houses. Instead of a large tarmac playground, we had a pleasantly tangled garden to enjoy in breaks. And for organised games, where I already felt doomed to remain a shivering outsider, we borrowed fields further away in Leigh.

Whatever the subject, all teaching was by rote – in which, regardless of curriculum, it was probably similar to the system at any elementary school. The learning of tables of arithmetic, tenses of French verbs, passages of English verse and Latin mnemonics presented no problem to me. The problem was that I frequently failed to comprehend or apply what I had learnt – and was extremely reluctant to draw attention to my failure.

It would take the arrival of the Christian Brothers and a tough, stocky, naturally talented Irish teacher, Brother Finbar, to detect the trouble with me. Licking a whole class into shape, with the licking carried out physically, when necessary, with a strap on the open palm, was what he relished. He was quick-tempered but no sadist, humorous, confident, committed and perceptive. We partly feared him but we also respected him. I have often wished I could have stayed longer under his rigorous, inspired discipline, but we moved from Leigh before he had finished making something of me. When we were leaving, however, he intimated to my father that I had – if properly directed – potential intellectual ability.

Before Brother Finbar started, pugnaciously, almost pugilistically, to take us on, we got by well or badly depending mainly on our own initiative and our liking for a subject. I was eager to learn French but it became as dead a language as Latin – or even more dead – under the existing system, because we never advanced beyond the grammar book and were writing sentences involving the imperfect subjunctive before we knew how to ask for a train ticket or a loaf of bread in a shop.

I was first up the next morning after we had been told to learn overnight the present tense of *être*.

'Je sweeze,' I began confidently, surprised to hear around me suppressed tittering. I flushed at the response and staggered on. But when I sat down I could remember only that my mother had 'heard' me over supper and pronounced me word-perfect.

I never made such a public fool of myself over Latin, which we all found hard. In fact, I was anxious to progress and to make use of some of the less common prepositions that clustered together in unhelpful mnemonics at the back of (I think) *Kennedy's Latin Primer*. Even today I can locate in some obscure mental compartment the equivalent of a drawer of dead flies, containing a jumble that starts: '*A, ab, absque, coram, de, palam, clam, cum, ex* and *e*. Rather like the ingredients of a recipe, 'Add *super, subter, sub* and *in* / When state not motion 'tis they mean'.

During Maths classes, I suffered a form of dyslexia – or I would understand only as long as the problem remained on the blackboard. When the master went to rub it out, before proceeding (having dutifully asked if we all understood), a comparable process wiped it out in my brain.

For some strange reason, Geography and History seemed ranked together, scholastically speaking, though not in my estimation. In Geography, we began with the earth's surface originally cooling and shrinking, and we never got much further. The process was compared to a baked apple; that I grasped quickly enough, because I was fond of the baked apples cooked by my mother. History I felt positively excited about. I supplemented the knowledge I had gained from reading Shakespeare with the information printed on the back of my cigarette card collection of the Kings and Queens of England, much of which I knew by heart.

Without quite realising it, I was developing something of a fixation on royalty and regalia. Before the Silver Jubilee celebrations began to fire me, my enthusiasm had caused my mother to feel ashamed in front of Trevor Morgan and his mother. On an uneasy outing by the four of us to Westcliff Pier – the last of such friendly occasions – we visited the waxwork museum. Even I could not be frightened by the tatty presentation of old-time tortures, where the dummies drooped around braziers filled with red paper and the instruments they brandished looked very like the poker and tongs on the hearth at home. But, dashing ahead, I discovered the final tableau of all: George V and Queen Mary, dressed in their coronation robes and brilliantly illuminated against dark velvet drapery. Back I ran to the other three, to announce breathlessly, 'Their Majesties, the King and Queen.'

Trevor Morgan seemed sturdily unimpressed, and Mrs Morgan may have laughed good-naturedly. But my mother glared at me in an agony of reproach and embarrassment. And afterwards, when we were alone, she complained about my outburst. I felt sorry, without being repentant. My mind was occupied by thoughts of bending some perforated strips of metal in my Meccano set into crowns resembling those worn by the early Kings of England.

History at school started early enough, but with a different approach, in some medieval period where we concentrated on villeins and the tenure of land. And there we remained. When I went on to other schools, it was always to find that we should be studying the villeins again. It was a shock in my teens when suddenly the topic jumped to Whigs and Tories in the eighteenth century.

If there had been rarely a hint that French was a language being spoken, even as we sat at our desks, by thousands of people living across the Channel, so – to a greater degree – Europe was excluded from our history lessons. As for the larger world, that got the odd, glancing mention in text-book lists of battles fought by the British. But from an encyclopaedia which I was lucky to have been given, I learnt of other times and other countries: of ancient Egypt and Renaissance Italy, of peasant costume in Latvia, as illustrated, of the climate in the Andes, and of the Etruscans. A haunting photograph of the statue of an armed Etruscan warrior was captioned as representative of 'a mysterious people of whom we know little'. That virtually summed up British attitudes in the 1930s to the rest of the world – and it extended far beyond the classroom. English was at least our own native language. And there was our literature. From it we were assigned reading, in the days of Mr Palmerstone, Scott's *The Lady of the Lake*, a poem in interminable cantos, with presumably some sort of dénouement, or end, though one never reached by us. But its jogtrot lines of verse were horribly easy to memorise – indeed, difficult to forget – and for anyone wanting to acquire knowledge of Highland place-names it was a useful study.

Mr Palmerstone himself deigned to take some of the classes in English. He would sweep in with great style. Gingery whiskers, large signet-ring and a gown billowing out over slightly flamboyant, sporty clothes all helped to proclaim him the headmaster. We could bet that it would not be long before he displayed his tendency to bursts of irritation, flinging out his hands as he did so. Off would fly his signet-ring, and then, with its recovery, he usually recovered his composure.

It would not have been possible or desirable to convey at home how diverted we were at school by such minor occurrences. Besides, apart from stories in the comics we all read, we had no standard of comparison for what constituted a normal school. Japes and pranks and 'swots', and permanently angry though also absurd 'beaks', filled the pages of what almost passed as newspapers to us (a copy of my current favourite weekly would be delivered with my parents' paper).

It hardly mattered that the school concerned might be a boarding-school, with much that was unfamiliar to us, from dormitories to tuck-boxes, and perhaps a Chemistry master known as 'Old Stinks'. We responded to the implicit assumption that the best of school life went on outside the classroom, while in it the general routine, or tedium, was constantly relieved by funny incidents not communicable to anyone else. To those involved, whether in fiction or in actuality, the upsetting of an ink pot (and quantities of liquid ink were prevalent in classrooms) could become an event of endless amusement.

In Mr Palmerstone we recognised the qualification to be the 'Head' in some school yarn. He had the necessary idiosyncracies, extending to possession of a Chinese man-servant who impassively served the far from Orientally-inspired school-dinners. 'Crikey!': the implications of what that sinister Eastern figure might be secretly plotting could even have engaged the attention of Bulldog Drummond. Only the prosaic arrival of the Christian Brothers put an end to such possibilities.

Before that, a new, previously unguessed-at and soon rapidly growing pleasure, that of the cinema, had come to me through a schoolfriend. My best friend was Eric Moxon, Eric Vladimir Moxon in full, though 'Moxon' was *de rigueur* during school hours. It was his Russian mother, thinking perhaps to occupy time before providing tea at their house, who took us one afternoon to see a film.

Eric may well have been in a cinema before. Anyway, it would have been in character for him to give such an impression. But on me the effect was overpowering, from the moment we moved from the glass ticket-booth in the foyer into the magically shadowy interior, where a film was already in progress.

The occasional flickering silent cartoon-film, tentatively projected in somebody's poorly-darkened drawing-room as a birthday party treat, had been no preparation for what I now experienced. Immediately I was engulfed and absorbed by the scale of the images that unrolled before me so smoothly and flawlessly and, as it seemed, unendingly. Any sense of being a spectator dropped away. I forgot Eric and Mrs Moxon and life outside the cinema, pondering only, as I settled ecstatically back, that this experience was available every afternoon, without preparatory fuss or great expense. How could my parents have kept the fact from me?

I could hardly put the question to Mrs Moxon. She seemed as amused as pleased by my reaction when we came out – out into the plain daylight of Leigh which looked both plain and alien. I was still there, not in the cinema but in the jungle; I had just seen *Tarzan of the Apes*.

I had also seen the trailer for next week's main feature (was it *Elephant Boy?*), and I determined that my mother should take me. And, none too willingly, she did, though believing that cinemas were literally pits for fleas. This time, the trailer was for Errol Flynn in *The Charge of the Light Brigade*, and I begged that we should not miss it. As an ultimate concession, she agreed. After that, I depended upon Eric and his mother, who perhaps dozed through a medley of films which included at least one gritty drama of American prison-escape so thrilling that Eric and I had to re-enact it after tea. As he was firing a tommy-gun from an upstairs window of their house on the front, I hurled myself down on the gravel of the garden-path, dying with such conviction that I badly grazed my knee.

The movies really moved in that era. One reason why films then moved so fast was because they were not shackled by tradition – that regular clog on action and on active thought in any sphere. They had sprung up as a new form of entertainment, brash and slick but mercifully without pretension and theorising and pastiche and wearisome attempts by directors to win awards for camera 'artistry'. The very convention of black and white photography was a restriction which helped. It required style and confidence to manage, since in it there could be no easy 'realistic' effects. And those films, whether comedies or tragedies, or just adventures of some sort, not merely entertained thousands of us as we grew up – and adult audiences too – but at their best retain the power still to entertain.

Without the Moxons I might have gone on for years ignorant of or despising what Hollywood – and primarily it *was* Hollywood – had to offer. But I feel grateful to them for taking me out of myself and my immediate environment in other ways.

Their household was so different from ours – more sophisticated, I should now say, and more glamorous. I did not want to swap my parents for Captain and Mrs Moxon, but they had their fascination for me. I was slightly afraid of him as moustached and aggressively masculine, and slightly in awe of her as dark and beautiful and foreign, thoroughly 'Russian' in recollection, where she figures as permanently clad in furs. I seem often to have been at their handsome house, with its garden facing the sea: an attender at a lavish birthday party for Eric, too shy to enjoy the occasion; more relaxed when Eric and I could fool around together; and always hoping for a sight of Nadia, who might smile but hardly recognised my existence. I never forgot how I first saw her.

Eric and I had been walking away from school one afternoon when we were joined by a girl, taller, obviously older, who dismounted from her bicycle and walked casually beside us. Gradually I realised – not least from his equally casual attitude – that this dark, attractive, poised girl, who seemed lightly amused by our conversation, must be his sister, Nadia.

Even my parents had to agree that Nadia was beautiful. They had already pronounced Eric to be 'bumptious', a sweeping term meant severely, which I privately rejected on his behalf, while aware that he was indeed sure enough of himself to be quite indifferent to their opinion. If Nadia could be said to 'take after' her mother, the implication was that Eric 'took after' his father.

Encounters between the two sets of parents were rare, but one occurred after a weekend Eric had spent with us. Captain and Mrs Moxon had been in Paris – maybe they had flown over – and they motored up to Braemar Crescent to collect him. There were greetings and semi-facetious enquiries ('Has he behaved himself?') and profuse thanks for putting up with him. Some hint of Paris clung to the very manner of the Moxons, culminating in Mrs Moxon producing a gift for my mother of the largest bottle of scent I had ever seen. Somehow, it crystallised the non-meeting of temperaments under the polite exchanges. As the Moxons' car drove away, I could predict the fate of that elegant, extravagant, greenish-yellow glass bottle: to remain on my mother's dressing-table, unused.

Perhaps what I enjoyed about Eric's company was the quality that to my parents seemed bumptiousness. He was lively and he looked cheeky. It might be harder to define what interest I had for him as a companion, but we played happily together. He gave his own slant to my theatrical obsessions, concerned less with history and dressing-up than with acting out some modern thriller. But he was much better than I was at games like cricket. And he discouraged the sentimental notion I had of our continuing our schooling together. After I once risked blurting out my hopes of that, he coolly remarked, 'Oh, no. I'm going on to Haileybury, where my father went.' I think he was quite pleased that I needed to have the reference explicated.

Eric and my cousin Bernard never met. Impulsive as I tended to be, I knew better than to precipitate such a meeting. But for a time in my life each perhaps was some reflection of the other. It seems sad that Eric, a boy of under ten, and harmless enough, could frighten my parents into clumsy, near-moral reactions – for fright they showed. What if he did put brilliantine on his hair? Not even the Roman Catholic Church pronounced that to require contrition, absolution and penance. It was as if a tennis ball had bounced into the neatly-kept parental flower-bed. Neither then, nor later, did they want a child of theirs to start bouncing comparably – or perhaps at all. And as yet I was far off adolescence, never mind adulthood.

Bernard, fortunately, was liked by both my parents. He and my father shared a taste in humour that savoured the turns of phrase in Wodehouse, as well as the ludicrous mishaps of characters like Bingo Little. Meals became more fun while these were recapitulated, leading often to the familiar yet still diverting anecdotes, almost worthy of Wodehouse, involving our aunt Molly. And he had devised a form for our escaping early from the table, especially the tea-table, by chanting in unison: 'Please may we descend?'

He devised much else. Utilising that esoteric word 'Pumpernickel', he had created a race of robot-style aliens who inhabited the planet Pluto. When I was allowed to share in that world, I drew the Pumpernickels – doubtless to his specification. I began to imagine a court, with the King of the Pumpernickels in ermine-trimmed robes. But he thought that irrelevant, if not silly. What mattered was the internal wiring system of those beings and how they travelled from their planet to Earth.

Nor were we to waste time dressing-up as Indian princes – indeed, dressing-up had no appeal whatsoever for him. We could be rival gangsters, however, and we purchased cap pistols for the purpose and rode our bicycles up and down Braemar Crescent, firing viciously.

His single most surreal device was thought up on a day Molly was due to come to Leigh for lunch. Very frequently did her normal conversation invoke her friend Amabel, who had said this and decided on that, and who – in truth – became a dreaded name to the rest of us, adults in addition to children. It was a fair guess that we should be hearing of her activities.

All morning Bernard worked, with me as assistant half-disqualified by fits of giggles, in piling junk on the roof of our garden shed. The whole structure was carefully contrived to rest on a framework to which was attached a length of string.

Molly arrived. Her tiny figure was almost smothered in the excited welcome of kisses and cries. Bernard's presence particularly delighted her, but she was bewildered by talk of Amabel. 'Amabel here?' she kept asking, as she was led into the garden. 'How can she be?'

By now Bernard and I were laughing so wildly that he

nearly forgot to pull the string that brought the apparatus on the roof crashing to the ground.

'It's Amabel,' we shrieked. 'It's Amabel!'

Although bemused, she was not cross. She shook her head and murmured something about boys being boys.

My mother, who had been looking on apprehensively, hastened to declare that lunch was ready. And the meal seemed to gain animation from the incident; hardly any mention occurred of Amabel. Even I was inspired to repartee, after being sharply questioned by Molly on some peculiarity in my eating habits, answering, 'I like tomatoes and I like marmalade. But I don't like them together.'

I felt pleased – tame though it was by Bernard's standards. To my lasting admiration, he had even stemmed, for a while, my mother's daily stream of anxious instructions and admonishments to us by saying airily, 'In future I shall call you Miss Snip.' The aptness was beyond question, and she was forced to acknowledge it with a smile.

Although a visit to 'Homeleigh' would be enhanced for me if Bernard happened to be there, and his presence always brightened the household, I enjoyed my visits at any time, particularly in the period before the Second World War.

The aunts led lives that may not have been as agreeable as they sometimes appeared but were busy, partly diverse and partly united in social activity. There was always news to exchange about members of the family and about friends. There was always something happening, whether it was sherry for the new Irish curate or the prospect of the gifted, youthful, not yet famous George Malcolm coming in the evening to play the piano. And for nephews and nieces visiting the house it was the kitchen, rather than the drawing-room, which provided a special attraction, for there was to be found Julia.

'Yes,' an aunt would say. 'You may go and see her. She hoped you would.'

It was not so much a formality, in the sense of being taken

for granted, as formal permission to walk down the dark passage to the kitchen, a step short in reality but seeming to keep far apart two totally different spheres. In her sphere, Julia received a visitor without effusive greetings or even much animation on her gaunt, lined face. Her grey hair was scraped into a bun, and under an apron she wore a floor-length black dress. She was usually at work, sometimes attended in pre-war days by a maid, a girl who invariably seemed skittish in comparison, whatever her true character, and liable to give notice.

The very conditions in which she and the maid worked were part of the charm, for children. The kitchen was not much lighter than the passage, and its chief window was barred. But it contained a ceiling-high dresser, a cooking range, a small iron machine for mincing and for making breadcrumbs, and – most appealing of all – a large, drum-shaped contraption, with a handle, for sharpening knives. To permit some knives to be sharpened, though they were already of surgical sharpness, was one of the privileges Julia usually granted.

In character and outlook she might appear severe and rigidly circumscribed, as was the pattern of her existence. She rarely seemed to leave the house, and then always by the side, servants' entrance. But once a year she went away to spend two weeks with her sister, Minnie, in Bedfordshire. We children knew these things, and we knew too, without being told, that Julia liked granting our requests to 'help', perhaps by grinding some breadcrumbs or licking the spoon after she had prepared a cake-mixture. Although the dishing-up of Sunday lunch was a hot, elaborate process, she allowed you to rush in and scoop some gravy from the sizzling joint with a morsel of bread.

'That's what your father used to enjoy doing,' she told me.

I always felt she was kind towards me because I was my father's child, but I expect the other nephews and nieces felt similarly. And she never showed favouritism.

I remember one occasion, however, when I was informed at the end of a stay that Julia wished to see me, to say goodbye. She met me in the passage, where it was so dark that seeing each other was quite difficult. Saying little, she just took my hand and pressed something into it, before retreating to the kitchen. And when I was in the hall again, I discovered, with a thrill, that she had given me a shilling.

Perhaps I spoilt it by proclaiming the fact too loudly.

More than once, my over-excitement in the environment of 'Homeleigh', especially during some festivity, had boiled over and dampened the event, embarrassing everyone. It was a pity that I should, one Christmas, have upset the most imaginative and aesthetic of the aunts, Madge, with whom I sensed such rapport. Her custom was to organise ingenious tableaux of the children available in the house, to surprise and possibly to stimulate the adults on Christmas afternoon. What we would represent must naturally be kept secret from them, but she confided to me that one tableau would consist solely of me as St Francis of Assisi with the birds. She may even have given me advance sight of the brown crêpe-paper habit she had cut out and the plaster robins to balance on my arm.

Unable to keep the news to myself for a few hours, I ruined the surprise element; and by the time I posed with the robins by the window in the dining-room, I felt no saint – just miserable and in disgrace, and relieved when the ordeal was over.

Of course I was forgiven. The aunts readily forgave, and the normal mood of the house was one of resolute cheerfulness, whatever the underlying strains. As the eldest daughter there, apart from Vally, Madge might have become its household head, but that would have bored her and anyway she was too individualistic for the role. Much more suited to it was the next sister, Elsa, almost my father's twin in her humorous enjoyment of life, her calm sense of responsibility and her excellent financial brain. While she lived to guide it, 'Homeleigh' seemed safe as well as happy.

Elsa held a responsible position as cashier-accountant for a large commercial firm, with offices that overlooked Oxford Street (hence she had been able to get me a direct view of the Silver Jubilee procession). Madge also went out to work, as receptionist to a successful American osteopath. As interpreted by her, the job took on a social, extremely stylish aspect, and her clothes (often utilising Irish tweed) were consistently stylish. She delighted in the people she met and brought home amusing anecdotes about them. If Elsa seemed ideally placed in the practical, bustling world represented by Oxford Street, Madge was equally well placed, not far away in fact, in the quieter, more refined location of Cavendish Square. But both of them made long journeys across London each weekday, begining by taking a tram at Brixton. Perhaps they travelled together, though that would be misleading, since their temperaments and tastes were very different.

At 'Homeleigh', Senta remained with Vally, in charge of household arrangements, highly competent at her task and also a resource to her sisters as their dressmaker. Any tendency to irritation, when her deafness led her to ask for yet another repetition of a joke or a passing remark, would vanish with the production of a length of material. Then she would be cunningly invited to admire its quality and colour before the inevitable request. But she loved being of use and was naturally inventive: she had immediately responded to my wish she would contrive wigs for me to wear as my two favourite monarchs, Charles II and Queen Elizabeth I, and saw nothing peculiar in the request.

Rather different was the contribution to the atmosphere provided by the youngest sister, Winnie. Like her brother, Ernie, she had been struck by polio in childhood, and she always wore a high, surgical boot. In colouring she resembled my godmother, Jeanne, with blue eyes and hair of a brilliant red-gold tint, and when she unobtrusively limped into the drawing-room, wearing a simple dress of pure blue, the effect was startling. But to me as a child she often appeared white, tired, bitter and forbiddingly pietistic. Of all my maiden aunts, she was the only one for whom I had no real fondness – nor, I think, had she any for me. And although she liked and respected my father, she seemed at best guarded in her attitude to my mother, whose own relationship with her was markedly reserved, if not uneasy, in contrast to the affectionate one established with the remainder of her sisters-in-law.

Winnie also had to go out to work, in some humdrum book-keeping capacity, and no doubt for her it was particularly wearisome. She was intelligent – too intelligent probably for the job. And she was an industrious correspondent, unlike most of her sisters, keeping in touch with scattered members of the family. The family mattered to her, and she seemed the chief contact with the widow and sons of the dead brother, Fritz. She may also have read more assiduously than was normal at 'Homeleigh'. I remember during the Spanish Civil War she read – sometimes aloud – the Catholic Sunday papers, all favouring General Franco, with horror at every outrage reported on nuns and priests but no sympathy for humanity on the other side. She fervently supported missionaries in Africa. Regularly each year she made the pilgrimage to Lourdes, helping to look after the sick but hoping in her heart, I suppose, to be herself miraculously cured. In her final days, after the break-up of 'Homeleigh', she chose to retire to a convent in the country.

The hedonism frankly embodied in Elsa found expression more naïvely in Senta and more idiosyncratically in Madge but seemed absent in Winnie. When Madge brought down a book of Boucher engravings to show me one Sunday evening, Winnie was doubly horrified. Yet all of them were pious women, and Senta had her pet saint, the adolescent martyr St Philomena, to whom she must often have prayed for a miracle over her deafness. Happily, she was dead before Rome expunged St Philomena's name from the calendar of saints as that of somebody who never existed.

'Homeleigh' was a joint home to which each sister there contributed, even if at times the contribution was a criticism. Madge might be judged fey and over-self-centred. Elsa perhaps ate more than was good for her and was becoming dangerously stout. Senta missed so much of what was happening. Winnie's devotion to the curate threatened to be an embarrassment. But it probably seemed to them all that they would somehow go on living until death in the home where they had been born.

Their investments drastically dwindled. Julia was ageing, and maids were hard to obtain. The garden had been abandoned to marauding cats. And Brixton was not the area it had been in Papa's time. But it was to 'Homeleigh' that other members of the family came, to sit in the drawing-room with its unchanging blue and grey silk upholstery and on the mantelpiece the elegant glass-sided clock with blue enamel pillars. For visiting children there would be a treat when Madge, who had mysteriously taken possession of several of their father's personal relics, brought down the Swiss music-box from which sprang out a tiny, feathered bird, opening its minute beak as it trilled, before disappearing with a sudden snap.

For Bernard and me, staying in the house, there were certain abiding pleasures. After we had been allowed to descend from table, we might go to the tall bookcase where the books included a set of natural history volumes, with beautiful, factual plates, and the fourteen volumes of the Henry Irving Shakespeare. In armchairs on either side of the fireplace, we had each our preference, while the grown-ups went on talking and I was never too absorbed in a play to neglect eavesdropping on their murmured conversation.

I had grown – in height and experience – by the time I accompanied my father on a visit to 'Homeleigh' in the late summer of 1938. Much had happened in our immediate lives, and yet more was happening in the larger world. Everyone now knew the name of Hitler. People spoke openly of a possible war with Germany, though our prime minister, Mr Chamberlain, believed it could yet be averted. And my father was convinced there would be no war.

We had moved from Leigh to Coulsdon, an outlying suburb of London, and lived in an estate agent's dream of a modest house, distinctly separate from its neighbours, with truly 'individual features' and a long garden sloping steeply down from a terrace and two lawns to a jumbled screen of trees. Daily I exchanged it for the bewilderingly big, soulless-seeming John Fisher School in nearby Purley.

Experience had given me a keener sense of how pleasures and pain were often intermingled. I delighted in everything to do with our new house but in the icy, swimming-bath environment of the school I felt my individuality was drowning.

'Homeleigh' looked the same as ever, as the door opened, but inside the atmosphere was hushed and sombre. My aunt Elsa was seriously ill – too ill certainly to see me, if that had been mooted. With an effort at cheerfulness, my father went up to her bedroom. He came down in a way that revealed at once that he had said his final farewell to her. And on 7 September, 'Fortified by the Rites of Holy Church', she died.

I remembered her as so full of life, always beaming and bountiful. She had once arrived at Leigh station, coming for Guy Fawkes Night, with an enormous box of fireworks that seemed to symbolise all her generous, exuberant qualities. And I could have wished that my blotting-paper ears had not picked up one poignant irony of her last illness: that in delirium, she was convinced that downstairs they were holding a party.

Her death foretold the end of 'Homeleigh'. Then came the war. When the household broke up, and the contents were to be sold, the surviving 'Girls' asked my father whether he would like some memento. He chose the drawing-room clock, and as a favour he asked also that I might have the

Henry Irving set of Shakespeare's plays. He never got the clock, mislaid or stolen, in wartime conditions, but the fourteen books reached me; and they are beside me as I write.

8

Prep, Soaks and Palestrina

I looked forward enormously to the coming of the new year, 1939.

Although January was not the usual month in which to begin, I was beginning a new school, a boarding-school in Berkshire – the same one as my cousin Bernard went to. Getting ready to go there had meant, among other things, that I had to have a complete set of new clothes, including a specially-tailored Sunday suit in a special blue material, and every item had to bear my name and school number.

Among my acquisitions was a new diary. Indeed, I may not have owned a proper one before. I was now eleven, and I could look back with amusement to the small boy who had once started a notebook on which he had written 'Dairy'. I felt sure that there would be plenty of exciting events to chronicle in 1939; and I was not entirely wrong.

From Bernard I had learnt what seemed a great deal about my new school, though he wisely cautioned me that I had much more learning to do, and that that could be done only on the spot. But already I had a few words of the lingo. Henceforward, what had been homework would be 'prep'. I knew that young louts coming up from the nearby town of Reading, to invade the school grounds, were described as 'Brummers', and that an official lie-in on the morning of Sunday or a weekday holiday was a 'soak'.

Above all, Bernard had cautioned me in important negative ways: primarily, I must always remember to address him and refer to him in public as 'Hoole' – and most of school life would be in public. Nor must I rush up to him with letters from home, about our aunts, for example, or what my parents might be doing, even if they were coming down to see us. He ranked as a distinctly older boy, was perhaps due to be a perfect, and generally moved within his own circle of friends. I must make my own. Everything he told me, I eagerly accepted as part of the new lore. It all added to my excitement.

In a mild daze, and still unsure whether I was to become a pupil there, I had for one memorable afternoon been on the spot. The grey bulk of the main building stood prominently and impressively on a hill overlooking Reading, and from the train window that silhouette would become a familiar sight. But on the suavely-conducted preliminary tour given to my parents and me by the headmaster, I had noticed little about the school except for its grounds.

I had never visited a country house and so I was unprepared for the effect as we were led out through a glass door on to a gravel path, to gaze across the wide Thames Valley panorama. Formal gardens lay immediately below us, but I also took in what could be seen of a lake and a long, hedge-lined vista closed at the end by a small temple. And, near at hand, was a massive, ancient-looking cedar with heavy boughs sweeping low.

The headmaster indicated it half-dismissively as we strolled.

'It's often supposed,' he remarked, 'to be the tree under which Charles I said farewell to his children, but that's probably just legend. It can't really be as old as that, and those stories are so common, aren't they?'

That was the moment, I think, when I knew that here was the school for me.

But I was not yet a pupil at it. I still went to the John Fisher School in Purley, a day-school around which I felt I would never – in any sense – find my way. Whatever the process of growing entailed, and the process went on, I could not grow accustomed to existence there.

I doubt, however, if I told my parents as much. I had become more chary of revealing my feelings to them. Increasingly, I wanted privacy and apartness, though I did not see that as any diminution of my love for them. And by now I was more keenly aware of emotional fluctuations and fissures, often quite minor ones, that occurred between the trio of us. At one moment I might seem, simply by expressing an opinion, to be siding with my father, and at the next I was on my mother's side. Or it might be that they united in a way that left me feeling isolated. And all this might arise over the question merely of whether to go for a walk or stay in the garden.

There would be nothing so definite as a quarrel. But I felt tensions which made me long for us to be a larger, less tightly-knit group, one where I alone was not the inevitable shuttlecock. Oh, for a sibling, I thought, who would take some of the concentration and responsibility off myself.

In wanting to leave Leigh-on-Sea, however, we had been totally united. There was no single cause perhaps for our gradual dissatisfaction, although the estate around Braemar Crescent kept expanding as inexorably and as unappealingly as a cemetery. Notionally, at least, the woods and fields we had known seemed to have been reduced to a distant, diminishing fringe. We had exhausted the health-giving properties associated with the mud of Leigh, and my parents had never cared for the town. Nor had they made any friends there.

Since his years in Iraq, my father was earning a slightly better salary. He had returned with hopes for a more agreeable environment, a more individual house, and a garden not overlooked by neighbouring ones. And, he would have added, the virtual absence of neighbours altogether. My mother shared these hopes, in a less active way; and she wished for closer access to London, chiefly for my father's sake. As for me, I just longed for change and all that change would bring.

It is significant that I can recall nothing about our

departure from Leigh in 1938. Such farewells as we made must have been muted and devoid of even conventional talk of keeping in touch. Apart from Eric Moxon, there was nobody I was going to miss at school, and Eric was Haileybury-bound. I was not, but I felt equally confident in contemplating my future. With the larger house and the larger garden, I should be gaining a larger bedroom. That I was about to go to a much larger school appeared in prospect one more facet of an enlarged existence.

A similar mood of pleasant anticipation bound my parents and me in moving and as we entered our new home. It was an irony unnoticed that we saw ourselves enjoying a brighter, more comfortable domestic life at the very period when world events were darkening, almost hour by hour, the lives of everyone. It may be that my father's optimism about the unlikelihood of war had been accidentally strengthened by his personal circumstances. All the greater, for the three of us, would be the eventual shock and upheaval.

Yet nothing could banish some sense of unease. I think my mother was never entirely convinced that war would not come. Her innate pessimism served her well. And it was hard to believe that all was normal when gas masks were being issued to every household. The mundane cardboard boxes in which they came did not disguise but rather increased the impact of the ugly tin and rubber snout contained inside. Long before any poison gas seeped up from the town of Coulsdon, I should have suffocated, I was certain, being unable to breathe – or indeed see – when I put on my mask.

Coulsdon was a small, agreeably nondescript town, combining aspects of the urban and the countrified. It provided the necessary Catholic church for us in a brash new building on a bare stretch of land. The necessary Catholic school was provided at nearby Purley, a bus-ride away. Coulsdon was also the site of a lunatic asylum – a fact I could never get out of my mind. The asylum itself was hidden amid thick trees, but its winding drive, with luxuriant shrubbery, lay open and easily visible. I dreaded the sight of it. But I never spoke of my fears, and I never fully articulated them to myself. There were times at night when I thought I heard the sound of the hooter that signalled the escape of a lunatic – or did I imagine that?

In any case, it symbolised the secret worries which I felt lying below the surface of our assured-seeming new life. Most mornings I awoke to realisation that the John Fisher School had to be attended – and that I could not reasonably complain of anything about it, except that it appeared to me a remorselessly efficient, impersonal workshop for the sole manufacture of academically accomplished pupils. For the two or three terms that I was there, it stretched me hard enough to delight Brother Finbar. I never doubted that I was learning a lot as I laboured in its competitive atmosphere. The pity was that I failed to capitalise on what I learnt, and when I went on to a boarding-school with a less demanding regime I squandered what I had acquired. But I was far happier.

The John Fisher School took its name from the Bishop of Rochester who had been executed under Henry VIII. He happened to be a familiar figure to me from the days at Leigh. After he and Sir Thomas More were canonised by the Pope in 1935, a stained-glass window depicting the two martyrs had been inserted in the nave of the church, considerably improving it in my view.

The school was notably free from any oppressively religious air. If anything, it seemed secular. Most of the masters were lay, and even the weekly service of Benediction was performed coolly, rather than with any excessive, incense-laden piety. And the school in my experience was notably free from bullying or ragging of any kind. It was almost as though there was no time for high jinks or low japes; but then there was hardly time, I found, to get to know any of my classmates.

Time was the god we worshipped – or at least obeyed. We arrived and anxiously scanned the sheaf of timetables and instructions which fluttered on the big notice-boards, before the working day began and the staircases were jammed with boys commuting from classroom to classroom. We paused at lunch (which I think we brought for ourselves). In the afternoon, we had organised games and we resumed lessons and we took down our homework, before jostling and shoving and streaming out of the school, down the road to our different destinations.

It did not help that I lived in Coulsdon, when the majority of boys came from Purley. But I thought I might become friendly with a boy in my class called Gorman. He seemed calm, slow and monosyllabic, ruminative, almost rustic, and he looked like a flaxen-haired peasant in some Victorian painting. I did not know him very well, but I asked him to tea at home, meaning to be kind and to introduce him to our nicely-furnished house and spacious garden.

He accepted and came one afternoon. My mother was relieved that I had a friend at last and she gave us a splendid spread. But Gorman, though far from shy, spoke even less than usual. He appeared uninterested in most of what I had to show him, and after tea the occasion languished. We leant against the doors of the empty garage, both of us silently wondering how soon he could say that he must catch the bus to the obscure place where his family lived.

I did not expect a return invitation, but he gave me one, with directions for getting off at the right bus stop. He was waiting for me as I stepped down in what seemed deep, uninhabited country. He led me through scrub and copses, and we crossed a rivulet, and all the time we were on the way to his home. It was wonderful land for playing in, as he agreed with more liveliness than usual. We could play there that afternoon. And very slowly I absorbed the fact that where we were walking belonged to his father.

I had understood that the family was large – and Irish. He had elder brothers, sisters too perhaps, but nobody would be at home, he intimated, when we reached the plain, white-washed house. I could, I realised, forget my party manners. His mother, or someone, had left us bread and jam on plates in the kitchen, to eat when we liked. That was how the family tended to behave.

How strange it was, I reflected on the bus back to Coulsdon, after reluctantly leaving, that this meeting had proved so very enjoyable. And how strange, almost sly, of Gorman not to have hinted before about his family's land. My cheeks burnt at the recollection of showing him the really large tree at the bottom of our garden, and the steps to the two patches of lawn from the terrace that was part-rockery.

'Oh, yes,' I replied impatiently, when my mother asked if I had had a nice time. What I felt I had somehow had was a lesson.

At last, January 1939 arrived. My trunk was packed, and just as in the typical school story, I also possessed a tuck-box. I was ready to leave home. Aware of my own natural timidity, I surprised myself by having no regrets and no qualms. My mother was more apprehensive – if not for me then about me (was I good enough for such a 'good' school?), and about the social implications which joining it seemed to bring.

'We like to have the parents gather beforehand, for a glass of sherry at the Great Western Hotel,' the headmaster had explained, when setting out the arrangements for assembling at Paddington Station on the first day of term.

He may not positively have added, 'It seems more civilised', but his manner said it for him. I was soon to discover that being civilised was his main aim for pupils as well as for himself, though its interpretation frequently seemed capricious, indeed perplexing, and was always subject to his fluctuating moods.

That he was charming, my mother had decided on first meeting him. He spoke so pleasantly and urbanely, with a trace of drawl. He looked distinguished too, with crinkled grey hair, and grey-blue eyes in an attractive face whose complexion was of a faint, incipient, raspberry tint. He wore elegantly-cut double-breasted suits of blue or grey, with a hint of silk handkerchief displayed if not in the top pocket then in his sleeve. Despite the grey hair, he was not old, though nor was he young. He looked youthfully mature, ideally fitted in age and appearance to be headmaster of a small but select preparatory school where boys would be guided on their way to becoming good Catholic gentlemen.

He certainly set a stylish standard as host in a room at the Great Western Hotel, greeting every parent with graceful attention – subtly more marked when the parent was a young mother. Schools and even trains – he seemed to convey – could wait, while he proposed more sherry and nonchalantly waved his long ivory cigarette-holder in the direction of the drinks tray.

My mother had been appalled on receiving the clothes list sent by the school when it accepted me. There was the cost; but there was also the business of journeys to London, to the designated outfitters in Bond Street, for the blazer and jersey, the shirts with detachable collars, and the necessary measuring of me for the Sunday suit. It was no help to her that the suit represented a modification of the previous regulation one, an 'Eton' suit, as worn earlier by my cousin.

That my father had all his suits tailored was in the natural order of things. But she felt differently about me, a mere boy, whose clothes she had always chosen on strictly practical and slightly retarded lines. My eagerness for a proper suit was if not suspect at least something not to be encouraged. And the whole matter of my clothes had, by chance, already become an issue between us in circumstances mildly ironic.

My father went to a talented and extremely successful London tailor, Roy Clarke, with whom he had first become friendly in the Army. Roy Clarke admired my father and was anyway a generous man, and he must have cut his prices, along with the cloth, to permit someone on a modest Civil Service salary to be among his clients.

It was their friendly relationship that led to a joint holiday in North Wales for the two families in the summer after my father returned from Iraq. The Clarkes had only the one child, a boy a year or two older than me, and with that symmetry and the affinity between the two men, based partly on a shared sense of humour, the plan seemed attractive – at least to them. I too looked forward to it, especially when I heard we should be driven around in Roy Clarke's large American car and be staying at a 'good' hotel, where I should be expected to join the rest of the party at dinner each night. Expected? It was all I could have hoped for.

From the first, my mother was dubious. For her taste, Roy Clarke was perhaps rather too determinedly a comedian, despite all his kindness. And undeniably, she and Mrs Clarke had, as she must have declared often enough in the run-up to the holiday, 'nothing in common'. Even I could see that, and it only added to the fascination I felt just looking at Eve Clarke. She was always beautifully dressed, manicured and coiffeured, with waved, prematurely silver hair, slim and small ('petite' in period terminology), and almost a caricature of the type of Thirties woman, the obsessionally, narcissistically feminine. Yet, as I used privately to remind myself, she was also a mother.

Russell Clarke and I had, as it turned out, equally nothing in common, though he was pleasant in a dull sort of way. He seemed to have inherited much of his mother's self-absorption, with only a dash of his father's humour. In material terms, both parents could be said to spoil him, for he appeared to possess everything he desired, as I had noticed on a first visit to the Clarke home in Watford. But he had been polite, if detached in manner, and generous, making me a present of some toy of his when I left.

As my mother got out some clothes for me to wear

at dinner in the hotel in Wales, I could envisage Russell coming down in a series of suits, inevitably well-tailored, which would emphasise his maturity and the age gap between us. A pair of navy shorts and a short-sleeved Aertex shirt in egg-yellow were not, in any case, my idea of hotel dinner-wear, though I lacked the authority and knowledge to state what for me would be. And eventually, under protest, I wore the clothes. My mother thought I had made a fuss about nothing. But not even the combined social tact of the Clarkes could prevent me from feeling ludicrously juvenile as I sat down to dinner with bare knees. Quite apart from that, the holidaying together – in stunningly picturesque mountainous scenery – proved a taut, bumpy affair emotionally, and an experience the adults must have tacitly decided never to repeat.

Clothes were only one symptom of the flawed relationship that had developed between my mother and myself by the time I was eleven. I think we both recognised it and had both decided to keep the fact from my father. It therefore played no part in his proposal that I should join Bernard at boarding-school, but it explained to me why I welcomed the prospect of leaving home.

My mother and I had conflicting slides to put into the projector to illustrate my adult future. Mine were misty and enchantingly coloured, and true to my nature. Hers were intended to be solid and sober, but they told more about her than about me. And where I had hopes, she seemed increasingly to have only fears.

'Artist, actor, author', was the formula I had already devised at Leigh-on-Sea when asked the normal question, usually by adults I hardly knew, about what I was going to be when I grew up. I meant them to be considered as alternatives, though they merged to some extent in my own mind since they were based on closely-linked activities.

I put painting and drawing first among my hobbies (a word with condescending overtones which I disliked), often designing costumes for historical characters and painting in water-colour compositions from history or literature, with a definite bias towards drama. As I did so, I imperceptibly assumed a role in the scene, and soon I found I was writing, if seldom completing, historical plays. For all my love of Shakespeare, however, I never felt tempted to try verse. Perhaps I knew that my ear was defective. Prose was what I wanted to write, but it was highly charged, 'poetical' prose.

All these activities pleased my father, and about my drawing and painting he was proud. My mother had no objection to them as pastimes, but any implication that they could result in a career made her anxious to the point of anger. And so she encouraged them less and less.

She thought it her duty to be 'sensible', as she called it, not realising that she was swayed as much by puritanism as by any practical considerations. My painting she could not help rather liking, but she longed for me to paint something simple and truly natural, a few trees or even a sunset – which I obediently did, as birthday cards for her. And she more than once urged me to think of a career in the open air, which would be healthy, though it might not make me rich (and there were times when she spoke darkly of fearing I wanted to be rich).

'You could be a farmer,' she told me. 'That's a healthy life, and you know you're fond of animals.'

I would try to laugh. But such remarks seemed, on reflection, more hurtful than funny in their failure to comprehend me. I should be glad of a period removed from them.

How that came about I was never precisely clear. But one sad event seemed to act as a catalyst. In the autumn of 1938 Bernard's father died, aged just under fifty, and as his godfather my father took on a new responsibility. Perhaps he visited the school where Bernard was, to discuss the matter of school fees, and perhaps the school made some concession when two boys from the same family were involved. My mother stressed to me that anyway my father was paying more than he could properly afford, was making sacrifices, to give me a 'good' education. I must strive to deserve it. And in that solemn mood, she, with my father, took a suitably reticent farewell of me at Paddington Station, as I began a new life at the Oratory Preparatory School, then located at Caversham Park, near Reading.

The Oratory School had been founded by Cardinal Newman in 1859 (twenty years, in fact, before he was created a cardinal), as part of the Oratory complex in the Edgbaston district of Birmingham. He intended it to be a Catholic alternative to the Protestant public schools: for the sons of reasonably prosperous middle- or upper-class families, with an ethos devout but also enlightened. Its inspiration came from the example of the great founder of the Oratorians, Saint Philip Neri, one of the few male saints celebrated for kindness, gentleness and gaiety of spirit.

In migrating south, to Caversham Park, the school had largely lost direct association with the Oratorian Fathers but it retained many of the ideals of Saint Philip and of Newman, as well as images of them. Outside the chapel stood a statue of Newman. Inside it, we sang a hymn to the saint which praised him as essentially tolerant and undemanding. And it was very much part of the school's proud tradition that it was 'priest-free' – not run by or infested by, in particular, the Society of Jesus. Indeed, to some extent it defined itself by rivalry with a Jesuit school, Beaumont, and the great day then in the scholastic year was that of the summer cricket match with Beaumont at Lord's. About Beaumont itself the most lurid tales circulated, of 'Jays' spying nightly in the corridors, with a bias gross enough to have contented Charles Kingsley and which might have drawn a private smile from Newman.

Newman's arms as a cardinal had been adopted by the school as its own, and they were everywhere – from the cover of the school magazine to the blazers worn by us at the Prep School. The characteristically perfervid yet also cryptic motto he had chosen, '*Cor ad cor loquitur*' (Heart speaks to heart), became the school's, though a less innocent age might judge it unsuitable for an enclosed establishment exclusively of boys growing towards and beyond adolescence. But we no more gave it a thought, or even a snigger, than we did to the derivation and snobbish connotation of the term 'Brummer', originally designating lower-class people in nineteenth-century Birmingham (Brumagem).

Not long before I joined it, the Oratory Preparatory School had given up its own premises and moved to occupy the top floor of Caversham Park, bringing it and the senior school into close and economically convenient proximity. But each was run as a separate establishment, under its own headmaster, and the chief places where the two schools came together, though not into contact, were the refectory and the chapel.

Most of the intriguing implications and results of this juxtaposition I would grasp only as I became absorbed into the routine of my new existence. But I found it absurdly easy to succumb to the rhythm of that existence, so insistent and pervasive was it: relayed, as it were, through your pillow by night as regularly as it governed your actions by day.

A term for me had previously been a series of shuttlings daily between home and school. Now I had no journeys to make – nor any adjustment. School was all, for several months. And from the first I delighted in the physical atmosphere even more than in the social.

Caversham Park is a house originally built in the early eighteenth century, though subsequently burnt down, rebuilt, added to and modified, and, after another fire, rebuilt in the mid-nineteenth century. Its imposing air at first glance is not borne out on close examination, but I was content with my first glance. And whatever the peculiarities of the architecture, there could be no doubt about the charm of the grounds, said to have been laid out by Capability Brown.

The formal gardens that descended from the south front were impressive, but they appealed to me far less than the rest of the grounds, wilder in appearance though artfully planned. There was the gradually disclosed curve of the lake, lightly encircled by woodland, and slopes dotted with clumps of conifers and rhododendrons, and there was the long avenue that led to the small, ancient-seeming Doric temple.

How effectively that could be converted to Roman Catholic religious use would be revealed to me during my first summer, when it became a shrine to which the combined schools solemnly processed on the feast of Corpus Christi. The Officers Training Corps provided a guard of honour in uniform, as the chaplain carried the Host under a canopy, while younger boys scattered in its path flowers we had gathered from the rhododendron bushes.

I was to learn a lot at the OPS, though not much of what I learnt was related to the curriculum. Nor did either school seem eager to foster academic excellence – in contrast to the mystique surrounding ability at games. I never heard anything about the prospect of going on to a university. Most boys seemed destined for the City or business, in the footsteps of their fathers.

Time was one thing I learnt to regard differently. A day now seamlessly stretched from early morning getting up in the dormitory, to chapel and breakfast, through lessons and games (and an afternoon rest for the youngest of us) to the leisure of unsupervised evening activities in the common room, with chat and the playing of gramophone records.

Homework had always been a lonely task, but prep had plenty of social opportunities, if only in checking that you had the right exercise – and possibly the right answers. Thanks to the John Fisher regime, I for a while had most of those; once, by some fluke, I even gained high marks in algebra. Soon, however, I slipped from being ahead to being in the middle, if not in the rear, where mathematics was concerned.

The evenings pleasantly returned us to where the day had begun: in the dormitory, with perhaps a bout of pillow-fighting and certainly long, whispered conversations, after lights-out, as you slipped into sleep. It was much more fun than had been going to bed at home. And every so often someone would assert that he intended to remain awake all night, though we knew he was opening his eyes next morning, like the rest of us, as we started a new day.

Each day wound down to the evening, and each week wound down to the luxurious leisure of Sunday, when, after a soak, and sung Mass in chapel, the day was largely ours to dispose of. Then, regardless of the weather – unimportant in our scheme of things – we could saunter with a friend by the lake or explore the thickets behind the strangely blank temple, with its inviting porch but no interior. As we wandered or played, none of us, and least of all I, would have dared use the soppy word 'beauty'. But the spell of the surroundings was irresistible. It touched even the gardener's shed at the lakeside with mystery, while on the surface of the weed-filled water the light was always changing. There was beauty in the very way the lake lay cupped in the slope of the wooded land, and a peaceful sense of that land merging into fields and stretching away into infinity.

I should hardly need to learn to love the school grounds. Other more insistent things, I found I was learning from the first afternoon in the railway carriage with a group of fellow-pupils who seemed far from unfriendly. I had at once learnt that I was the sole 'new bug' that winter term, apart from a unique 'day bug', who did not therefore really count. I learnt, too, to see a fresh facet of the headmaster, Mr Risborough, who sat among us and wielded a light whip of ambiguous persiflage, with sufficient sting to cause boys to writhe around and cry, equally ambiguously, 'Oh, sir!', as though both amused and hurt. When he briefly left us, perhaps to smoke in the corridor, some boy whispered to me that this behaviour was typical of 'Ronnie', as he was universally known.

How diverting all this was, I thought, as characterising the wondrous new world I was poised to enter. And I should experience, without entirely comprehending, other behaviour – that of the boys – almost as soon as I found my bed in the dormitory to which I had been assigned.

My aunt Molly had mentioned to me that a very nice boy, Robin, slightly younger than myself, the son of her friend Mrs West, was already at the OPS, and she hoped we might become pals. Before I had finished unpacking, I had met the owner of the bed next to mine, a red-haired, talkative boy, and toured the otherwise empty dorm. One of the beds was labelled 'R. V. West', so I eagerly asked about him.

'The name is Pest,' my neighbour replied vehemently. 'And everybody knows that the initials stand for Rat Vermin.'

I instantly and silently denied any cognisance of West or any urge to meet him. The school had uttered its verdict, and I was the new boy who must bow to it. In later days, when I was less in thrall to the school's opinions, I recognised how weakly I had concurred, even though by then I had come to agree about the nature of someone irritating yet largely innocuous. I was never quite successful in answering my aunt's enquiries about the degree of our friendship. But something unrelated to him, and more disturbing for me, was shortly to occur.

To speed my acceptance, I was quick to let it be known that I was a cousin of (Bernard) Hoole. In fact, as usual in such matters, the information had been disseminated, but I felt I could mention it since Bernard himself had not yet arrived. He was kept at home by flu and came back a few days later, by which time I believed my newness had nearly vanished.

There was some novelty for everyone, for heavy snow had fallen. In the icy cold the lake froze over, and the grounds became an enchanted realm of almost blinding whiteness. In the afternoons, we juniors built igloos and forts, and hurled snowballs, until our gloves were sopping wet and our fingers molten scarlet. And then came Sunday, the first full day of Bernard's return.

'Keep your mouth shut,' I was told by a ring of excited, stern-looking boys. 'And swear to say nothing. Go on, swear.'

Of course, sensing some secrecy and sharing the excitement, I swore.

Then they revealed the plan, which was to ambush Bernard after lunch in the avenue leading to the temple. We should all stroll out into the snow, gradually sneaking off until he stood on his own, when he would be pelted with snowballs from all sides.

'Remember,' they warned me. 'You swore to say nothing.'

Bernard and I had hardly spoken since his return. That part was easy. But I was surprised, for I had learnt that he was generally popular. The instigators were mainly friends of his, and there seemed no motive behind the malice.

I did not enjoy lunch and I dreaded the afternoon. If I could not break my promise, I would, I decided, stand by him. Yet I was still lurking miserably behind a hedge and suddenly he was isolated and attacked, assailed by a storm of snowballs. And I remained passive, just watching.

It was horrible, even if it ended as abruptly as it had begun. And by the evening it was treated as though it had never happened. Bernard was received back into his normal, friendly circle. Nor did he ever reproach me. But I was left wondering about the world I had been so entranced to enter – very different indeed from that of my day-schools – and where I was apparently willing to do anything, or do nothing, in order to be accepted.

Something I had yet to perceive, never mind understand, was the complicated position which had arisen at Caversham

Park by bringing the two Oratory schools together under a single roof. Two worlds were thereby created, with that smaller one of the Preparatory School contained within the larger one and yet at times revolving on its own idiosyncratic axis. Anomalies existed, as also did benefits, and there were rich opportunities for us at the OPS to watch the play and potential clashes of personalities in authority, in addition to seeing a good deal of the working of the OS, the main school.

Through a peculiarity in the design of the house, we enjoyed one major physical advantage. The building had been constructed around a big central atrium, like a vast hole at its core, covered high overhead by a glass roof. Our occupancy of the uppermost floor gave us almost a god's-eye view of what might be happening on the floors below, while on our own floor no visitor to the headmaster, not even the senior school's scowling manservant, Frost, climbing the numerous flights of stairs with a tray of silver-covered dishes, or a bottle of drink, was likely to remain unobserved. We were splendidly placed to peer over the balusters, down into the central hall, where the OS would hold its regular assembly or where, more promisingly, could be detected signs of preparation for the showing of a Sunday evening film, which – with luck – we at the OPS would also attend.

Some members of staff served the two schools, and so we had our own experience of the Latin master, Mr Sempill, a sardonic, enigmatic man, with a yellowish-marble complexion, a Roman profile and a clipped manner of speech, echoed by his precise handwriting. Teaching OPS boys was probably not the task he most relished, though he brought to it typical efficiency. Sooner or later, we would hear his familiar demand from all his pupils, of 'speed and accuracy', and his tones were detectable in the briefest of his notes, neatly initialled 'F.X.S.', though that might be merely the summons to a choir practice – for he was also the highly efficient choir-master.

No personality was more vivid, important and ubiquitous in our lives than Mr Risborough. We scrutinised him and mimicked him. We admired him and we were frightened of him because of his unpredictability. His study-cum-bedroom was almost embarrassingly near at hand. We could gauge the time when he would emerge from it in the morning, elegantly clad in spotted foulard dressing-gown, on his way to a bath. For formal school occasions he wore his BA gown and its white fur hood with a panache that quite eclipsed masters wearing gowns and hoods indicative of higher or more abstruse degrees. And we saw him in other guises, in thunderous yet fragile mood demanding furiously why the bell had not rung for prayers, even if it had, and – more dangerously still – erupting into a dormitory at night, intent on beating some small boy. And then he could surprise us by coming out of his room in debonair style, smiling affably and announcing that he was going up to London for the day.

The older, bolder boys knew how to exploit such moments. Younger ones stood quietly by, admiring the sophisticated nonchalance embodied by Ronnie. Even the youngest, however, could guess that he was going to see a lady.

'Oh, sir,' a favoured prefect reproached him on one occasion, leading a chorus of teasing disapproval. 'Brown shoes with a blue suit.'

But Ronnie was ready with his answer, giving us another lesson in ways of the world. 'It's all right,' he drawled, 'when they're suede.'

For the rest of that day we kept repeating the words appreciatively. Trying to score off Ronnie seldom if ever succeeded.

Left to myself, I should have remained baffled by the man, and perturbed. As it was, I often wondered whether such and such an incident had actually occurred. Did he always pick on the youngest boy in the school, Ballantyne-Gordon, to beat at night, claiming he had or would wet his bed? It seemed the odder, since the sight of Ballantyne-Gordon's very pretty, youthful, blonde mother reduced him to a state of purring complaisance. And the kindness of the school in taking an Austrian refugee boy seemed diminished after Ronnie began declaring at lunch that if Hitler sent his planes over, we should put Weyer in a cage on the roof. By the end of the meal Weyer would be nearly in tears, but perhaps that was only because several boys had practised elementary German on him: '*Weyer, du bist ein Schwein*'.

I felt friendly towards most of the boys with whom I mixed, but I was conscious of not having a proper friend. There were moments, too, when I experienced a sudden sense of isolation and exposure, especially in the gym, where I would have performed any exercise to avoid the humiliating procedure of vaulting – in my case, not vaulting – over the dreaded 'horse'. Compared with that, it was just a minor, temporary incident when I misinterpreted a grave public announcement by Ronnie, which I heard as informing us of the death of the previous OS headmaster, Mr Hope.

Still only a few weeks into my first term, I had been surprised by the stir his announcement caused.

'Not Mr Hope, you idiot,' my neighbour in the dormitory kindly told me afterwards. 'The Pope.'

Now I understood why boys were discussing how to mark the event in their diaries. As if in reparation, I went to my locker, got out my paint-box and painted a thick purple line around the date in my own diary, with capital letters for the words: 'THE POPE DIED.' It did not matter that none of us knew which Pope it was (Pius XI). And one or two boys were impressed by my form of mournful record.

The group of boys of about my age with whom I associated, out of class as in class, included Dorneywood, himself a fairly recent comer to the school. Only slowly did I become aware of him as an individual, for he was quiet and attracted little attention during lessons or games or in the daily course of existence.

There was nothing extreme about him, unless the jut of his jaw and the intense sea-blue of his eyes. He looked friendly enough, in a reticent way, and ready to be amused. If he never appeared outstandingly brilliant, he also never appeared stupid or an abysmal failure at anything. He seemed to enter into every school activity, and to be more popular than not, yet he conveyed a strong sense of self-control and of living at a calm tempo gauged precisely to suit him alone. He was even able to part his hair neatly – which I never could.

I began to feel I wanted Dorneywood as my friend once I detected how giggly and even silly, sympathetically silly, he was capable of being. And perhaps, though the thought never occurred at the time, his character needed that vein of infectious, mischievous humour to save it from settling into the stolid and the too conventional.

Besides, as I came to know him better, I should discover other intriguing, unconventional things about him – like his preference for writing in purple ink. And then he told fascinating stories about life in Chile, where he had previously lived while his father was employed there; I was particularly taken by the civilised Chilean teatime habit of serving saucers of jam.

Undemonstratively – of course – yet firmly, Dorneywood became my friend, and with him I could discuss the ever-absorbing topic of Ronnie. We may not have been the first to do so, but both of us made long cardboard cigarette-holders in imitation of his ivory one and tried to achieve his dipping gesture and drawl when greeting an important or attractive mother. Ronnie, it was generally said, had been in the Royal Flying Corps and had been severely wounded in the head. This somehow connected with his moods and his rumoured need to relieve pain by drinking. At the age of eleven, I had not knowingly seen a gin bottle before, and I had to be nudged into comprehension of the empty bottles that stacked up for removal outside his room. 'Oh, I see,' I said, though I was not sure I did. But I saw that here was an aspect of my new life not to be communicated in letters home.

Incommunicable, for very different reasons, was the deepest impression of all made on me at Caversham Park, which can be summed up by the word 'chapel'. Like so much of school life there, it was a complex impression, beginning with the actual, austere yet satisfying, luminous shell of the building itself – and where I went to church always had a powerful effect on me. At Caversham, I more than regained my early religious enthusiasm; I became fervent in my faith, as I think most of us at the OPS, definitely including Dorneywood, tended to be.

We went to daily prayers and low Mass in our own small, subsidiary chapel, to the left of the nave. There I spent more time with head raised than bent, gazing rapt at the altarpiece, which was (unknown to me) a copy of the wonderful woodland altarpiece of the Adoration of the Child, painted by Lippo Lippi for the Medici palace chapel in Florence. And we had our own chaplain, a frail, slow, white-haired and aged-seeming Oratorian, Father Henry Tristram, in whom lived on the tradition of Saint Philip's kindness and gentleness of manner, tinged with shy humour. Rumour spoke of his being kept alive only by animal injections of some sort, and so venerable in age did he appear that I accepted the literal fact of the phrase frequently and not unfondly attributed to him: 'Cardinal Newman said to me, "Henry, my boy . . ."' I could have sworn I had heard him utter the words, and it was a shock to realise eventually that he was too young to have known Newman.

However, it was the chaplain to the senior school, Father Tomlinson, whose personality and talents gave a special, dynamic, dramatic and glamorous quality to services in the chapel for the combined schools – especially to sung Mass on Sundays and feast-days. Outside the chapel, I saw at first only glimpses of him, as perhaps he hastened along a corridor, in buckled shoes and a cloak clasped by lions' heads, a picturesque figure with a somewhat aloof expression on his high-coloured, bony, ascetic face. Occasionally, he came up to the OPS floor, to see Ronnie or visit the older boys' dormitory and read a story. Older boys generally found him more accessible, as well as hospitable, and with them he apparently relaxed more, became almost boisterously jovial and laughed his peculiar, honking laugh. He was still a young man, only in his early thirties, and everything he did seemed impelled by pent-up, nervous energy. It was easy to conceive how he could suddenly switch from tears of laughter, wiped away with a huge handkerchief, to intensely grave concentration, as in the celebration of Mass. His hospitality had its religious purposes, and he encouraged a narrow devotional group, exclusive, and to me always mysterious, whispered about as LOCK (League of Christ the King).

Tommy, as he wished to be known, had a creative if complicated history of aesthetic Anglo-Catholicism, having converted from the Anglican priesthood and then spent several years of agreeable study in Rome. The chaplaincy at the Oratory was his first post as an ordained Catholic priest, and it offered opportunities for him beyond the normal duties of a chaplain.

Time in Italy had sharpened his anyway keen visual sense and given impetus to his considerable ability as a painter. He began an art room in the school, where he pinned up postcards of great masterpieces and showed us how to manage the tricky medium of pastel. But few can be the chaplains of schools anywhere who have the talent, and confidence, to paint an altarpiece in oils for the chapel, as Tommy did at Caversham, part of the celebrations he devised when, one year, Easter occurred at the end of term. And very daring I thought it, as I realised he had depicted a risen Christ who was young and beardless, unaware that there existed at least one famous similar Italian Renaissance depiction, by Andrea del Castagno, in Florence.

Tommy's visual and dramatic sense was at work as

effectively if less obviously throughout the chapel, in the appearance of the altar, and in its appurtenances, and in the presentation of the services. If he had not positively ordered some of the most beautiful vestments, like the liturgically rare gold chasuble, he took decorous, aesthetic as well as religious pleasure in wearing it. He gilded and enamelled a plaster statue of Our Lady, and then draped over it in May, her month, a cloak of silver lamé.

I enthused about it to Dorneywood after seeing it for the first time. He grinned.

'We've seen it before,' he said. 'When we did *Hassan* last year, Wilson II was the executioner and wore it as a loincloth.'

Visual pleasure was no novelty to me. By itself perhaps, the spectacle in chapel would have assisted, without deepening, my faith. But I was unprepared for the overwhelming effect of another art, music. Other than sounds of harmonium or organ, I had never heard music in a church – certainly had no conception of a Mass completely accompanied by music. Byrd, Vittoria, Palestrina . . . the names of the composers were entirely new to me. But never did I feel that they were just decorating the Mass. For me they strengthened its shape and added tremendous, moving conviction to its implicit drama and the already sonorous words of the Latin text.

I associated all the drama of this weekly music, virtually a concert, with Father Tomlinson. Robed and remote on the altar, he would unleash a surge of sound from the choir that filled the chapel, as he melodiously intoned, '*Gloria in excelsis Deo*', and I could hardly wait for the choir's entry, with its full-throated, varied yet always jubilant response: '*et in terra pax hominibus* . . .' Then the voices soared angelically away into a musical heaven, praising God, adoring God, glorifying God, hailing Him, with epithet after epithet, as '*Domine Deus, Rex coelestis, Deus Pater omnipotens*'.

Enviously, I would glance up at the choir-loft, where

both Dorneywood and Bernard might be visible, singing intently with the trebles and the altos respectively, under Mr Sempill's stern eye and disciplined beat. Although Tommy will have heard Masses by Vittoria and Palestrina sung in St Peter's, Francis Xavier Sempill probably possessed the more expert knowledge of church music and had the advantage of being an experienced teacher. Then, the coming together of the two schools increased the range of available voices. The ambitious, unforgettable, aural beauty achieved in chapel must have been the result of complementary gifts and tastes in choir-master and chaplain. And personally they seemed to get on well.

'Why don't we have "Shoving Leopard"?' I once heard Mr Sempill tersely proposing for a hymn at Benediction, and my fierce, priggish faith was quite shocked at Tommy's guffaw of agreement when I realised the Spoonerish reference was to 'Loving Shepherd of Thy sheep'. I was due to serve that evening, and I moved around the sacristy with an excess of reverence, intended to intimate disapproval.

I now owned a Roman missal – though it was less comprehensive than Dorneywood's – and I followed obsessively the text of feast-days, as well as the changes in liturgical colours. Most of the time at sung Mass on Sundays, I had it open and knew when the choir would next come in. But nothing set out in the order of the Mass, or elsewhere in my missal, mentioned a form which became for me the mark of music in chapel, the motet. That was understandable, as the motet (in essence a sacred song) is simply a grace addition to the service.

Musically, however, there is nothing simple about the motets of most composers, and of all the motets I heard it was one by Palestrina, '*Sicut cervus*', that transported me into a pure, crystalline world of the spirit. I had no idea that, even among the huge number of his motets, this one is outstanding and famous. Nor could I have described the effect on me as I listened to the four voices singing it in the middle of Mass in the chapel at Caversham: 'As the hart panteth after the water brooks, so panteth my soul after thee, O God'. But I was worshipping something – something which I should today call human artistry.

What weeks they have been, I thought, as my first term at the OPS approached its end. And everyone around me was getting excited about the holidays.

'You what?" a fat, cheerful, usually imperturbable boy named Peters asked me incredulously when I spoke of my feelings to him in the wash-room.

'I mean it,' I said. 'I don't want to go home.'

9

Schooled in Adversity

So enchanted had my first term been at the OPS that even I was prepared for disillusionment when returning for the next one, the summer term of 1939.

There would be few novelties to experience, apart from the unwelcome one that soccer would be replaced by cricket. Whereas I enjoyed charging around the pitch playing soccer – and had actually played it one Saturday afternoon under my father's eye – I anticipated that cricket would be for me the usual blend of torpor and terror: torpor as I dozed deep in the 'field', sucking blades of grass, and terror when summoned to the wicket to face bowling that always seemed to me fast.

Yet at home, in preparation, I oiled my expensive new bat, pretending to be fond of it, and naturally I liked the prospect of wearing cricket flannels. But when it came to gathering again at Paddington Station, I somehow felt apprehensive. Nothing, I was convinced, could equal the idyllic tone of that first term, which might have been written up as a boarding-school story in one of the current boys' magazines. The sole, brief visit paid by my parents had taken its own proper place in the term's events, as they watched the game from the touch-line before taking Bernard and myself, with special permission, down to Reading for a necessarily slap-up tea.

Ideally, I should have scored the winning goal – or at least a goal – but I had certainly run around enthusiastically. And ideally, I would have wished that my parents had arrived not by bus but in a large, glossy car. That was virtually required by the length of the school drive and the grandeur of the entrance portico. But I had been privately relieved that seen in the context neither parent let me down. Presentable, if not glamorous, neither – thank goodness – seemed likely to provoke comment.

'I was pleased to see you playing at inside right,' my father had said quietly, as I came sweating off the pitch. 'It was always my position.'

Then I felt as happy as if I had scored a goal.

Tea in Reading was bound to be an exuberant affair. It was a treat, and the addition of Bernard gave it an air of family without the normal, narrow focus. And knowledge that the rest of the school would be settling to the customary teatime fare, which we represented as barely a crust of dry bread, added to my enjoyment. Our duty was to stuff ourselves, and also to swank, in a mild way, when we got back.

I could feel that I was talking too much – or revealing too much – as I began explaining that the Matron was known as 'The Hag' and that we had witnessed her encounter on the stairs with the notoriously foul-mouthed boilerman, Lingfield. Perhaps Bernard silently signalled that the incident, enthralling as it had been, should be left unreported. Yet it had been a moment to savour as she descended, with the majestic rebuke, 'Lingfield, such language in front of a lady.' But the joy lay, I could hardly convey, I realised, in his swift, unabashed response: 'I see no bloody, effing lady here.'

Anyway, to mark this outing I wanted to return with some trophy. A pot of jam seemed right, and in the general mood of the occasion my mother bought me an unusually large, two-pound pot of unusual, greengage jam. Safely away from public gaze, I kissed her goodbye with real emotion.

How could a subsequent term equal the varied delights of that first one?

I was to find that it could and did. Indeed, it was richer, I felt, and inevitably it would take on a particular quality for me retrospectively, since it was the last term of my schooling in peacetime.

The summer days softened the humiliation of cricket, although even as scorer I often failed to pay attention and spent afternoons confusedly rubbing out my pencil notations in the record-book, while runs were being made and the scoreboard failed to display them.

I was blamed for that, but nobody commented on the irony of my birthday cake – specially ordered by my mother – which was large and iced in blue and white, with the motif of a batsman at the wicket.

I had missed Dorneywood during the holidays, and missed, too, attendance in chapel. We never spoke of faith as such, but the ritual we all constantly witnessed received our tribute of imitation.

I cannot remember that anyone in particular invented a ritual we adopted at our evening bathtime which was directly inspired by the ceremony of *Asperges* which took place each Sunday before sung Mass. The celebrant, usually Tommy, solemnly entered the chapel, holding a kind of brush which he used to sprinkle both the altar and us, the congregation, with holy water, while intoning the antiphon, '*Asperges me, Domine, hyssopo* . . .' (Sprinkle me, O Lord, with hyssop . . .), immediately taken up by the choir.

The brief ceremony could have struck us as verging on the absurd, but as performed by Tommy it made an effect memorably grave and dramatic – and easily duplicated. Perfectly capturing the gesture of the acolyte carrying the water-stoup, and holding up one side of his cope as Tommy flicked the water left and right, one of us would carry a tooth-mug and hold up one fold of Dorneywood's fawn dressing-gown, as he entered the line of bath cubicles, solemnly flicking water over us with his toothbrush and singing. '*Asperges me* . . .' Perhaps we had unconsciously absorbed the meaning and the very words of the ceremony: 'I shall be cleansed: thou shalt wash me and I shall be made whiter than snow.'

When Ronnie discovered what we were doing, he seemed – wisely – more amused than censorious. He may have noticed that there was a strange reverence about our performance. We did not, or were anyway not meant to, smile. And after a while, the craze palled.

In other more private and ingenious ways, Dorneywood and I extended the influence of what we experienced in chapel. We devised badges to wear, concealed, under the lapel of our blazers, coloured to accord with the liturgical colour of the day or season. Thus they matched the colour of the chasuble worn by the priest at Mass, but gradually they tended also to reflect one's mood – as could be revealed by a quick turn of lapel. Black was far less common on the altar than on our blazers, at least on mine.

Then we had an idea of creating within our lockers a chapel-like atmosphere, to accommodate a holy object we had invented and shared. From the common slang of 'Benedaggers' for Benediction, we evolved the cult of the Holy Dagger, made out of silver paper, which could be displayed on occasion for worship.

To open the locker and allow sight of the Holy Dagger, lying on its cardboard cushion, painted crimson by me, was at first a special privilege, reserved only for a few friends. It was one more cult among many – not very different from any harmless secret society which might suddenly come into being among us simply because it was secret. Most of us felt the need to have our own rites and ceremonies of initiation, and our secrets, to keep intact our individualities within the extensive, over-arching rites of school existence that governed us by day and night.

Holy Dagger grew from a private cult into something inexplicably fashionable. More and more boys were allowed to see it, and the culmination was reached with a form of benediction by which it was publicly raised aloft, while at the sight worshippers sank to their knees.

Tommy seemed to come more frequently to the OPS floor, sometimes to pin up some religious picture or poster, and sometimes to read – with vivid impact – to the boys in the senior dormitory. One evening he even read part of Evelyn Waugh's *Decline and Fall*, and the next morning boys were still talking and laughing about Lady Circumference and Lord Tangent at the school sports (a skilfully-selected chapter).

But Tommy had not been amused to find on one visit to our floor that boys were kneeling before Holy Dagger. He spoke to Ronnie, and the whole cult of Holy Dagger was immediately abolished. Dorneywood felt no resentment and I, though shocked and resentful at the implication of blasphemous parody, had perhaps begun to tire of the whole concept.

I remained deeply devout if being devout was to be moved by the spectacle of the Mass, to be convinced of the existence of a personal God and to pray intensely for Him for help and favours. In return, I mentally abased myself each morning in chapel. I wrote into my missal my own daily 'offering' of all my words, thoughts and actions, 'for the intention of Thy Most Sacred Heart'. I might consider painting a small picture for my missal of a heart surrounded by rays of divine light. And my prayers often concluded with begging God that I should that day in the gym manage to vault the 'horse'.

Religion and the season of summer became unforgettably blended on the feast-day of Corpus Christi – a day I had not previously known celebrated. The drama of the Mass itself was enhanced by the sudden appearance in chapel of a guard of honour of the Corps, marching out of the sacristy in boots and puttees, and forming up at the altar rails, to present arms at the moment of the elevation of the Host. And then, instead of Mass ending, the ceremony seemed to merge into the sunlit, dream-like procession out of doors, with Tommy solemnly huddled under a canopy, clasping a monstrance containing the Host, flanked by the guard of honour moving stiffly at a slow march, and boys scattering rhododendron flowers in the path of the procession, as we all advanced towards the temple.

That seemed the culmination of sacred feast-days, but the school summer was celebrated by two secular feasts: the match at Lord's with Beaumont and the OPS Prize Day, at the end of term, for which Ronnie announced that we would perform scenes from *Henry IV Part II*.

If the cricket match as such held no appeal for me, I was as excited as anyone by the social prospect of a day in London and by the sense of an exclusive occasion. I already knew that for it we wore yellow carnations, while Beaumont wore the more commonplace red. Parents and friends and Old Boys would at least look in during the day. And we schoolboy spectators would be left largely unsupervised in the stands. I had heard that you could get drinks in the Tavern, and that there would be strawberries and cream for sale, so that time should pass pleasantly, quite apart from anything that occurred on the pitch, unexpectedly distant.

Some of the adults present at Lord's on that peaceful, leisurely, thoroughly English summer day may have wondered about the outcome of things more momentous than an inter-school cricket match. But my parents seemed untroubled when they arrived, and though the day seemed to me a long one, I felt exhilarated by it. And it was good to know that we eventually won the match.

The day closed with dinner at a London club and the coach journey back to Berkshire. By then most of us were tired, and tiredness soon extended to Ronnie and to the driver. It was late and dark on an empty road when we realised that we were lost. Some boys complained of feeling ill as well as sleepy. Ronnie and the driver climbed down from the coach to go to a pub, ostensibly for directions.

'Oh, sir,' somebody called out from the back on Ronnie's return. 'Ballantyne-Gordon's been sick.'

Ronnie seemed more alert now, refreshed and unfazed. His immediate solution was cigarettes, anyway for the prefects, and smoke filled the coach as we resumed our journey through the night. Occasionally, Dorneywood and I looked at each other to check the reality of this strange, exhausting yet still exciting experience.

It was very quiet at Caversham Park when finally our coach roared up the drive and stopped outside the main building. The senior school had long returned.

As we staggered out into the night air, barely awake, Ronnie issued a last order: 'Soaks all round tomorrow morning.'

He was – as we quickly learnt – reprimanded for the whole incident, though nothing in his demeanour showed it.

Prize Day was approaching, and his mind was on rehearsing the *Henry IV* scenes, of Falstaff collecting ragged recruits in Gloucestershire, and on the enjoyable aspects of prize-giving, which centred around the prize-giver, Lady Winefride Elwes. It would be a day for his speech to begin with lords as well as ladies: the chairman of governors, Lord FitzAlan, would be there, and we all knew that he was the uncle of the Duke of Norfolk. And the Duke had once been a pupil at the OS.

It was some compensation, I felt, for the fact that our scenes from *Henry IV* omitted the king and Prince Hal. Thrilled at the prospect of getting a part, I had not envisaged being just one of Falstaff's recruits, chosen chiefly because skinny, dressed only in a coarse linen tunic and required – under Ronnie's direction – to simulate fleas and scabs. Our group included Dorneywood (Mouldy), who somehow seemed less exposed, and it was with genuinely tremulous bravado that, as Francis Feeble, I delivered my best line: 'A man can die but once: we owe God a death.'

Our performance took place in the open air, on a slope where conifers provided natural wings. It was an area easily and speedily transformed into being the site of the prize-giving, with Ronnie and Lady Winefride centre-stage.

English Roman Catholicism has its notorious, deep if narrow snobberies. It clearly envisages that there will be *placement* in heaven. While God's infinite mercy extends to Italian nuns and even to Irish priests, much as does the care of an enlightened landowner to his estate workers, English county families who have held the 'faith of our fathers' down the centuries must expect preferential treatment hereafter. No less than Ronnie, who was probably the source of our information, did we savour the fact that Lady Winefride was an Earl's daughter and also the widow of the singer Gervase Elwes, another Old Boy. A *cachet* surrounded such names as Elwes and Cary-Elwes, evoking the uniquely desirable blend of true belief with good breeding.

Large, smiling, draped rather than dressed, and shaded by a picture hat, Lady Winefride embodied the lady bountiful. Graciously, untiringly, she handed out the prizes – and there seemed prizes for everyone and everything.

I was back in ordinary clothes as I went forward to receive at least one myself, for French or English or Art (the only subjects I really cared for). Never before had I received a school prize, and though we had gazed curiously at the variety of books piling up in a corner of Ronnie's room, I had not anticipated being actually handed one in public, to polite applause, with my parents looking on.

That warm summer afternoon marking the end of term, with the play and the prize-giving, and Lady Winefride, seemed to me unforgettable, but I could not know that it was unrepeatable. There stretched before me only a sense of the impending, long, tranquil weeks of holiday at home, and of home and school alternating agreeably to fill all that I discerned of my future.

I went home with particular eagerness because my father had written to say that he and my mother had news for me: a surprise about which he would reveal no more. It must await my return.

I guessed at once that my mother was to have a baby. That would be the absolute culmination of a wonderful year, and I entered the house almost expecting to find a baby in it.

'Your surprise, your surprise!' I begged, embracing my

mother tenderly and enthusiastically. 'Tell me about it.
When is it . . . ?'
She seemed puzzled by my demonstrativeness and glanced
at my father.
'It's in the kitchen,' he said.
The words subdued me. Feeling foolish, I went nervously
with them into the kitchen.
'Yes,' I said dully. 'Yes, it is nice. Very.'
I was staring at a new, extremely large and gleaming
refrigerator.

I took no account of the date, but Saturday, 2 September,
was a day of preoccupation for me, as I was preparing a
series of historical tableaux in the garden to entertain my
parents on the Sunday. I had arranged various costumes
and written out the programme, and the highlight was to
be the execution of Mary, Queen of Scots. She was a dress
stuffed with paper; the executioner would be myself.
My parents seemed uneasy, despite their usual, relaxed
weekend air and the warm weather. Poland was a country
which had meaning for us, since my aunt Florrie lived there,
and Hitler had just invaded Poland. Nothing could keep
at bay the imminent threat of Britain at war, though even
when I heard that the Prime Minister would broadcast to the
nation on Sunday morning, I secretly dreamt that he would
declare peace had been achieved.
The three of us sat in the drawing-room that morning,
listening to Chamberlain's solemn, lugubrious tones. They
seemed so incongruous and improbable in the enveloping
quiet of the day of rest, in the familiar room that appeared
slightly yet delightfully shadowy in contrast to the bright
light in the garden beyond. Out there, I had already arranged
most of my tableaux on the steps. The entertainment would
begin at two o'clock.
Chamberlain finished his speech. As we sat on, silent, the
air-raid siren sounded, and at the shock of it all I burst
into tears.

It needed no indication from my parents to tell me that they had no heart for any tableaux that afternoon. I too had none. Time hung heavily on us now, and there was nothing to do except slowly dismantle my scenes and wearily gather up the costumes. As I put them away in my dressing-up drawer, I felt I should never want them again. Just as well, for I never saw them again. Before Christmas, they – like most of our possessions – had gone into store. Six years later, with me in the Army, I suppose my parents threw them away.

I went back to school later in September 1939 in the shaken, profoundly sombre mood which pervaded my home. My mother openly dreaded every fact and implication of the war, and although my father spoke of it as likely soon to be over, he was – I could see – disturbed, untypically indecisive and unsettled. Perhaps he already knew that his Ministry would be evacuated to Harrogate and that our house must be closed, 'for', as the new phrase was, 'the duration'.

I looked forward to sharing my feelings generally, though some of the darkest I would reserve for Dorneywood alone. But when I entered the dormitory, I found everyone was at the window, talking and staring out towards London, in the direction of which were visible the grey, floating shapes of barrage balloons.

'Isn't it exciting?' was the question I heard repeated on all sides, with no waiting for a reply. 'We're at war. And we're going to smash Hitler and the rotten Germans.'

Everyone, it seemed, had a father, an uncle, a brother, who was an expert military strategist, if not an active soldier, or in the Navy, and this was the opportunity – the great game – they had been longing for.

How cowardly I must be, I felt, with my fears and worries. Soon, I was driven to make my own assertions. 'Those are some of the barrage balloons my father ordered,' I boasted. 'There are thousands of them, and they have special cables and . . .'

It was quite true that my father had been involved in the

contracts for barrage balloons (and had been given a detailed model of one in metal, fixed floating over an ashtray), but anyway nobody believed me.

When Dorneywood and I talked together by ourselves, I was amazed by his serious enthusiasm for the war – as amazed as perhaps he was by my petulant distaste for it. Even in the euphoria of its early months, he never talked of 'smashing' the Germans, but charts and maps in his locker meticulously kept track of the campaigns and its progress. And I used to watch with a sense of alienation his absorption in each issue as it arrived of the magazine *War Illustrated*, to which he subscribed.

However much I pretended, school was not the same place for me. Not everything changed, and what changed did so fitfully, almost irrationally. To me, the war was an intense and frighteningly extensive fog, what my aunts called 'a real pea-souper', with no prospect of lifting. I loathed the evidence of it that came with pats of butter and our individual jars of sugar, marking the introduction of rationing, as much as I did the period when nights had to be spent in bunks in the cellars at Caversham – part of air-raid precautions.

Of course, school existence went on – and every effort was made to suggest normality. New boys arrived, including Polish boys whose fathers were attached to the Air Force. More immediately intriguing was the arrival of a new matron, for the Prep school, Barbara Bates. She was young, dark and pretty, and her room quickly became a popular place to visit before bedtime, with no claims to be feeling ill.

Miss Bates seemed coolly amused by her popularity. If Ronnie also dropped in occasionally to see her, I for one thought nothing of it. Some shrewder boy had to give me a nudge, to wake me up to his increasingly obvious fondness for her. 'Oh, do you really think so?' I naïvely asked whoever prophesied that they would get married (which subsequently they did).

Another summer term had Ronnie rehearsing us for more

scenes from Shakespeare. This time it was *A Midsummer Night's Dream*. But at thirteen I was temporarily indifferent to its magic – and anyway, as I had guessed, we were to act the mechanicals and their play. Never was Ronnie more conscientious than in rehearsal and in previously gauging the physical suitability of each boy for his part. Wilson II had been a podgy, naturally cocky Pistol, so naturally he was cast as Bottom. And I, cast effectively opposite him, was Flute.

We acted indoors that year, and there must have been prize-giving of a sort as well. But I recall the rehearsals more vividly than any performance, and yet more vividly the irruption of grave, wartime incidents into what should have been normal school life.

It was on a day in June 1940 that Tommy came up to our floor, to declare dramatically, 'France has fallen.' Without fully understanding, we felt something cataclysmic had happened. By then, senior boys of the OS, in uniform and armed, patrolled the grounds – no longer to chase Brummers but against the threat of invasion. Their rifles held real bullets. And during some fooling around by a patrol one evening, a rifle accidentally went off and a boy of not quite seventeen was killed.

Not only a requiem Mass but his funeral followed. He was buried in the grounds, and for a time afterwards the chapel seemed haunted by the bowed yet stoic, black-clad figure of his mother. Tragic though his death was, he had not been very amiable or a very popular boy in the school. Grief alone could dictate choice of the text on his memorial card: 'Being made perfect in a short space . . .'

Then there was the incident occurring one day at lunch, in front of the two assembled schools, which happened with a sinister smoothness and speed. Officials came to take away two OS boys, brothers, who had a German name and who were presumably of German extraction. Nobody had ever thought of them as enemy aliens. The elder was, I think, an admired member of the First XV rugger team.

But suddenly they were removed from the school and sent to internment.

Enough kept happening to reinforce the truth of that common explanation for anything at the period: 'There's a war on.'

Nor was I likely to forget it, as I travelled at the end and beginning of each term between school and whatever accommodation at Harrogate constituted, for the time being, 'home'.

On the first of such journeys, for Christmas 1939, travel had its own novelty. I had no idea what awaited me in the lodgings my parents had managed to find. Still less had I any suspicion that this was a journey I should regularly be making for the next five years. And although I grew to detest the wealthy, bourgeois complacency exuded by Harrogate, I had to recognise that because of its very wealth the town possessed agreeable aspects.

In its selfish fashion, Harrogate would struggle against the depressing, engulfing atmosphere of wartime – which is probably why it so disliked the incursion into it of Civil Service 'foreigners', evacuated from the South and engaged in activities on behalf of the nation. Harrogate was proud of being a comfortable spa, with such spa amenities as an excellent public library and handsome, well-tended, municipal gardens. It also possessed a large hall which served for concerts and touring company productions. There I should see Civil Service amateurs put on a quite impressive *Othello*, though it seemed very understated compared with *King John* brought by a touring company led by Sybil Thorndike, the tones of whose wild, declamatory Constance must have reverberated beyond the hall to the nearby Pump Room and the Valley Gardens beyond.

In the White Rose Players, the town had a repertory company rightly, fondly, esteemed, though the plays it presented were often banal, conventional vehicles, barely road-worthy, yet guaranteed not to disturb the presumed sensibility of Harrogate playgoers. But when the two juvenile principals appeared next on stage, after their marriage and short honeymoon, the whole audience burst into applause. In fact, the company itself might have served as subject for a play – perhaps by J. B. Priestley, whose works featured, along with some by Barrie, among the more 'advanced' productions. Above all, Harrogate had its shops. They managed somehow to preserve an allure of prosperity throughout the war. The grandest of the grocery shops never looked denuded. As I should delightedly discover, resourceful tailors were able to produce a roll of fine, speckled tweed when you wanted made a sports jacket. And always attractive to me was the tree-lined row of antique and fine-art shops, where competently-painted, gold-framed pictures – the equivalent of old-fashioned, well-made plays – were prominently displayed.

They were painted in a convention I never questioned. Many a morning I mooched past the windows, absorbed in studying the shiny, painted interiors, where mirrors and parquet floors competed in gloss, forming interiors for groups of figures no less glossy. A few women costumed in vaguely eighteenth-century-style dress lounged among potted palms and behind fans: 'Douceur de Vivre'. More intriguing were similar settings for two or three cardinals, with perhaps the odd bishop, usually seated at a lavish, lace-covered table (the lace exquisitely rendered), sharing a joke or raising their wine-glasses: 'The Grateful Toast'.

Not even to myself did I admit it, but those pictures were for me ways of forgetting the war. It was not hardship, as hardship was meant during the war years, but I saw it as such to spend every holiday from school in lodgings at Harrogate. No longer, I felt, was I growing up freely. It was as if the physical and atmospheric cramping also cramped my development, and below lay a deeper fear, one barely expressed, that as I grew into my teens so I was approaching 'military age' – with all that that implied.

I hated life in other people's houses, whether we were sharing the spacious one of a rich though uncouth Yorkshire

widow, or lodged with two pleasant, unmarried sisters in a
house too small for what became five inhabitants when I
turned up. Only our very first stay, with a grandmother and
grand-niece, had any novelty. The girl, Ann, was about my
age, and she took the initiative in a surreptitious exchange of
notes (left under the stair-carpet) which led to our meeting
secretly in my bedroom. It was all absurdly innocent. We
barely cuddled but we chattered a lot – and we were 'discovered', with inevitable consequences of being forbidden
to meet or speak.

Ann's grandmother had taken against me from early on in
that Christmas holiday period. Gnome-like and hook-nosed,
she had been standing one morning in the over-furnished
parlour lent to us by her, talking to my mother while I
sat quietly at the table. Suddenly she stopped and looked
indignantly at me.

'Why,' she exclaimed. 'He's been drawing my face!'

Quick though I tried to be in scrunching the paper up,
she had seen sufficient.

I was doubly in disgrace before the holidays were over.
And in our subsequent lodgings I never encountered any
children.

School at least provided company. But the school itself
was changing and rapidly declining as an institution. That
too was perhaps a part-consequence of the war. After the
summer of 1941, just as Dorneywood and I were due to go
on to the senior school, it gave up Caversham Park. Where
it would eventually go was then uncertain, and so must have
been the chances of its survival.

I was worried on hearing that to enter the Oratory School
proper I should have to sit an examination. I had assumed
that we all went painlessly on from prep school to senior
school. And had I known the real state of things, I ought to
have worried more about whether there would be a school
to enter.

Talk of 'Common Entrance' and of the possibilities of

winning a scholarship (and thus saving my parents money) made the exams seem an ordeal. I felt I would do badly, although Dorneywood, also sitting them, had intimated that nobody ever failed to get a place.

By the time I confronted the Latin paper, I was convinced that I would prove the exception. Without much thought or attention, I had usually managed in class to serve up sentences about Labienus and his monotonous demand for cohorts, Caesar having left the camp; and sometimes I had looked ahead in the grammar book to more interesting exercises when we should be able to use Latin idioms such as 'I care not a straw' (for it). But my brain seized up on suddenly being required to define and illustrate the use of the gerund. The gerund? What had I been doing, I wondered, when we were meant to be studying the gerund? Probably the answer was that I had been thinking pleasurably of the next period being English or Art. On one occasion, when we were set an essay to write, I had written something which got commended as original – even as imaginative. I had been rather pleased with myself when on the theme 'Once in a blue moon', I fantasised about moons of other colours too, pink and green. And the theme blended with a postcard Tommy had pinned up in the Art Room, of a mysterious moonlit scene where stood the dark silhouette of a single figure by a river-bank, playing the flute amid lush, cactus-like vegetation, out of which giant snakes slithered at its sound. I never noticed the name of the painter, Henri, Le Douanier, Rousseau. Sadly, less dreamily exotic was the light of common day in the examination-room, and more urgently demanding the requirements of 'Common Entrance'.

Somehow, I suppose, I passed, or I was scrambled in. Without a scholarship, I should yet be going to the Oratory School. As for the school itself, we all learnt – with shock – that it was going to be taken in for a period as a lodger by the much larger, Benedictine establishment of Downside. There, in Somerset, every Oratory boy would effectively become a new boy.

Far away in their lodgings in Harrogate, my parents hardly understood what was happening – except, of course, that there was a war on. Nor was anyone in a position to explain. What life would be like for the Oratory as an entity within Downside would emerge only as it was experienced. And, in its undoubtedly peculiar way, it emerged as rather enjoyable for us, the boys.

We had our own refectory, our own common room and dormitories, but otherwise we shared Downside's impressively organised though lively, enlightened existence. Perhaps because of the change of regime or because I was older, I sensed in the teaching a keen, committed professionalism. Some of the monks who taught us had incisive, amusing, unconventional personalities; and they seemed unafraid of exhibiting in class intellects no less incisive.

At Downside I began a new subject, Greek. I had always believed I should find it more stimulating than Latin, though we were not to remain at Downside long enough for me to gain more than the rudiments. Still, there was a welcome change of emphasis from Caesar and his camps and cohorts in even the simplest of Greek sentences that we translated. The limits imposed by the necessity at that stage to use only the verb λύω(to loose) actually made for effects more poetic than prosaic: 'The sailor is loosing the horses on the island.'

Something always seemed to be happening, in or out of school-hours. And in most of those happenings, we were free to take part – whether it was a debate, a concert or, less conventionally, the slaughter and dismemberment of a cow (watched by most of us with fascination and some repugnance, yet no pity). We were more isolated in Somerset than we had been in Berkshire. The nearest city, Bath, was out of bounds, and anyway transport was largely non-existent, but in the surrounding countryside were delightful villages which could be visited on 'days of obligation', feast-days on which we had hours of leisure after morning attendance at Mass. The charm of the villages for us was not in their water-colour picturesqueness but in their provision of draught cider – cider of a potency which often, and speedily, reduced us to lying comatose on the verge or even in the middle of a tranquil, traffic-free lane.

The core of Downside was not the school but the abbey. Visually, its bulk dominated the site and, whether or not attended by us, it remained always present at the heart of the community, sensed if not consciously heard, and kept forever beating in the regular chant of the monks in the choir, as they celebrated the office of each day.

As pupils of the Oratory, we were not under direct supervision of the monks who ran Downside, but the Benedictines appeared to lack all the creepy associations we liked to make with the 'Jays' of priest-ridden Beaumont. It was a new experience, however, to be within a monastic environment and to have 'chapel' replaced by ceremonies in the abbey which could be tremendously resplendent on a great occasion or modest and ascetic – in no less extreme and stirring degree – within the daily routine.

I had never worshipped in a church as vast as Downside abbey, and its size impressed me more than its style of decoration, which I recall as anyway plain, with huge windows of clear glass and little obvious ornament, apart from the box-like gilt shrine containing the body of Blessed Oliver Plunket (his head being preserved at Drogheda).

The building seemed to adapt to varying moods. Essentially and diurnally, it was the private devotional church of the monks in their stalls. On a major feast-day it accommodated and heightened pageantry when the abbot, in splendid vestments (blue, in honour of Our Lady, on one occasion) and firmly clasping his crozier in a gloved hand, advanced in procession down the thronged nave. But never did I feel its spell more intensely than very early on a winter morning, as I entered that dark, cold, silent space on my way to the sacristy, having volunteered to serve at Mass on some small side-altar.

My shivering state was half-physical and half-emotional. Perhaps it was the hour which prompted thoughts of the Early Church, but there was something movingly simple and austere in gravely bowing to the cowled priest before accompanying him in darkness to the designated altar. Familiar though they were, every murmured response and every action seemed charged with fresh meaning. This was the monk's personal Mass, unattended by anyone except the server, and there was nobody to note as I barely shook the bell, to give a thin tinkle signalling the *Sanctus*. The whole ritual was brief and almost devoid of human contact, but the experience seemed strangely to reinforce the opening words of dialogue between celebrant and server: '*Ad Deum qui laetificat juventutem meam*' (To God who giveth joy to my youth). Somehow, after serving at such a Mass, I enjoyed my breakfast more.

However, the days of the Oratory at Downside were ending. We – those of us who still belonged to the school – were moving on, to further novelty: a new site for the school, technically in Oxfordshire but not far from Reading, at Woodcote House.

It was May 1942, and soon I should be fifteen. The Battle of Britain was over but the war had become more complex and more global, with the entry of Japan and the United States, and with Germany's invasion of Russia. There was no longer any talk of when the war would end. It was simply an inescapable fact governing everyone's existence.

So dominant and pervasive was the war that it had helped perhaps to disguise or modify the abnormal, shrunken condition of the Oratory School. At Downside the reality had been partly camouflaged, but now at Woodcote we were on our own. Rather like survivors from a disaster, we could look around and see who and what had vanished, and count how many of us still adhered to the school.

The OPS had ceased to exist. From the OS nearly all the

masters had gone, possibly into forms of war work. Several boys had left, some staying on at Downside, while older ones disappeared inevitably into the Forces.

Woodcote House looked what it was: a pleasant, unpretentious, typically English country house on a small scale, set down by itself in a pleasant, typically English landscape, half-arable and half-wooded. It was the sort of house that appears modestly in the background of many eighteenth-century portraits, and in fact it had been lived in as a family home until the outbreak of war.

No drastic conversion or additions were needed to turn it into ideal accommodation for a school whose pupils then numbered less than thirty. From the first, we accepted it as 'school' in the fullest sense; yet I think most of us were conscious, if only dimly, of how delightfully free the building was of any ugly, utilitarian, institutional associations. There were no long, tiled corridors or iron staircases. Our common room had the air of a handsome drawing-room. Although its panelling was painted, unconventionally, black, the result was far from sombre, for long windows filled the garden side of it. And the black panelling made an effective background for a portrait of Cardinal Newman – still with us in effigy. Outside one classroom an ancient wistaria writhed, thickly dripping with mauve blossom and seemingly absorbed into the brickwork of the wall. On the lawn beyond, a yew tree had grown luxuriant, and when it shed the red jelly of its berries the odd pheasant could not resist alighting to eat them.

With the loss of my own home, and with the break-up of 'Homeleigh', I looked on Woodcote as a substitute home – which did not mean that I was always happy there. But it was where, in wartime conditions, I would live the last years of my schooling, with no clear vision of any life ahead.

Some continuity with Caversham days was given by the headmaster, Gerald Headlam, who had remained as head during the interregnum at Downside and who would remain a dryly benevolent, distinguished presence at Woodcote after his retirement. An acute schoolboy wit had once dubbed him 'Bones', and rightly the nickname stuck. It summed up his tall, skeletal figure, usually clad in suits of Prince of Wales' check, and his bony, bespectacled face, where a glint of humour was conveyed as discreetly as was the hint of *eau-de-Cologne* on his person.

'Bones' might have passed as a judge out of robes, so omniscient and urbane, yet distant, did he seem. He loved music, and his room was dominated by a gramophone with colossal horn. In the evenings he often offered us the opportunity to listen to music there, but I cannot recollect going. He not only hovered, in discreet manner, over school activities but he would involve himself in some of them, as when producing *The Taming of the Shrew*, the rehearsing of which was to be so dramatically interrupted by the news that the chapel was on fire. But even in those rehearsals, I never felt any personal contact with him nor could be quite sure that he knew my name.

It was not unexpected that he, already in his mid-sixties, should retire at the end of 1942. It was unexpected, however, that another personality from Caversham should re-appear, to take over the headmastership: Tommy. The school had also acquired a Second Master, Bernard Webb, who came from Beaumont – of all schools. He was an experienced, middle-aged bachelor teacher, determined to give the war-time Oratory (where, many years before, he had taught) tough and unremittingly disciplined standards in every area he touched – and they ranged from the playing-field to the Corps, via classes in English and Latin.

The contrast between him and the new headmaster began with their physiques, though it extended very much further. Yet, for all the patent strain between them, the 'creative tension', as we would now say, they were united in commitment to keep the frail ship of the school afloat.

Up on the bridge stood Tommy as captain, a tall, stylish, debonair-seeming figure, very consciously, if tensely, in command. More cultured than deeply erudite, and lacking any teaching experience, he yet exuded a sense of superiority to all around and of being a natural 'Head'. By his very manner, he denied that the vessel he commanded was tiny or liable to sink. There might be a touch of fantasy in his conviction that it was (or would soon become) a mighty ocean liner, laden with passengers, but some denial of oppressive reality was necessary for the enterprise to survive in grim times. Fortuitously or not, a similar spirit then invested Britain too – and he and the country would see that attitude miraculously vindicated.

Down in the engine room, out of public gaze, Webb ('Barney' as he wished to be known) laboured away, squat and graceless, often with a scowl on his pudgy features, angrily blowing a whistle or waving in menacing disapproval his crab-like hand. Self-knowledge had probably whispered to him long ago not to attempt suavity or stylishness. His was the unglamorous but vital task of making things work – especially of making boys work. If being a good, conscientious schoolmaster, as he was, meant unpopularity, he accepted it. He never presumed that he would be much liked by anybody, or be much thanked.

At once utterly disparate though ideally matched for the purpose, this pair had a crew that was indeed motley, often changing and sometimes mutinous. Young masters were – unless ill or conscientious objectors – uncommon in wartime. Some older and gifted ones came, galvanised a subject for a term and then abruptly departed. A bushy-eyebrowed, highly eccentric but essentially kind and donnishly-learned man, Mr Hoare, remained, to give the school the untypical *cachet* of an author on the staff (he had written a book on *Papacy and the Modern State*). And there was a youthful, enthusiastic chaplain, Father Tombs, whose unvarying good humour verged on the inane.

Jokes about his name signalled our growing lack of respect. But we and he enjoyed crowded visits to his small room as a way of delaying having to go to bed, and he cheerfully dealt with our pseudo-theological questions and even submitted to horse-play that often became uproarious.

'That is heresy,' he declared once, when asked about the statement 'Nothing can come in this world but what God wills.' 'Oh, Father,' we reproached him. 'Those are the words of St Thomas More.' And before he could explain further, somebody dived at his crotch, tugging at his fly-buttons and shouting – as was untrue but customary to claim – that they were open.

It was the epitome of all school tableaux that amid the uproar one evening Tommy should suddenly manifest himself in the doorway. We froze, and Father Tombs tried to pull himself and his clothing together. Tommy's expression marvellously mingled disdain and reproof. After a weighty pause, he said with withering sweetness, 'I had been hoping, Father, that you might be free to hear my confession.'

Father Tombs knew Greek and was therefore deputed to teach the sole boy studying it – myself. But our one-to-one classes dwindled into gossipy sessions, through my ability to side-track him, and on a hot afternoon he would gradually slip into a doze as I wrestled ineffectually with translating a play by Sophocles for which I had neither grammar nor vocabulary.

Few female presences mitigated the all-male atmosphere of the school – just flitting, nervously grimacing, 'backward' maids, who came from some mental institution, and the contrasting pair of Miss Cox, the Bursar's secretary, and Miss Pearson, a mild, grey-haired, truly maternal matron. Miss Cox had her room in the centre of the school and emerged from it in an odour of flaunting femininity, her cardigan draped around her shoulders and her face boldly made-up, adding a wisp of black lace, *à la* Carmen, when devoutly on her way to chapel.

Girls – women generally – were increasingly our preoccupation. They represented the pleasure of growing up, though also, for several of us, a challenge. When we talked intimately among ourselves, it was remarkable how little many of us knew about them. Seldom could anyone claim to have a real girl-friend. In the dormitory, after lights-out, things were different. Sexual boasting then became almost obligatory, though often it sounded suspiciously vague or patently pornographic.

However, it was easy to believe in the sexual successes of Sutton, an impudently good-looking boy, with much of Errol Flynn about his appearance and manner. I felt it would be impossible for me to emulate his careless confidence over girls of every kind. Yet, as I lay there, listening to his exploits recounted in the freedom of the twilight, I comforted myself with the hope that shy, artistic, 'different' though I might be, I should one day meet and marry a girl of similar character.

Since adolescence, I had never confronted girls *en masse*. It appeared a promising prospect when Tommy sent a group of us over to some nearby wartime establishment staffed by girls, to play table-tennis and have supper. Its female principal had telephoned in desperation, seeking male company, and he was sufficiently amused and sensible to agree. It proved all very entertaining, for even the least mature of us was welcome – and Sutton scored a deserved success – yet I cycled away distinctly daunted by the skills needed for conversational ping-pong between the sexes.

Some older boys had often talked of their chances with Miss Cox – or implied her attraction towards them. But, ungallantly, I saw her as having reached a certain age and without any allure for me. And from all the talk of sex around, I suspected that it would – rather like an exam – have its difficulties in practice.

Firm friends as we still were, Edward Dorneywood and I (advanced to private use of Christian names) talked only occasionally and fleetingly of such serious matters. He hinted at some point that there was a girl living near him at home whom he planned to marry. But we were shy of being explicit, much as we felt shy in the showers, where it was obvious that other boys were hairier and altogether more physically developed. Yet we were growing older too. Almost anxiously, we took up surreptitious smoking and – when cycling around the local countryside – risked going into pubs. It seemed daring, if expensive, to order not beer but a gin and orange.

Sex could mean only girls or women. Any attraction any of us felt towards each other lacked conscious sexuality, and we would all have recoiled from the suggestion that an element of that coloured our friendships. I was certainly aware of which boys seemed to me good-looking, and good looks added to the charm of the company of Nusselbacher, a slightly younger boy of partly German descent who made up a trio of friendship with Dorneywood and myself.

Peter Nusselbacher excelled at games. Blond, blue-eyed and lithe, he could have modelled for a Hitler Youth poster. He looked rather arrogant, though in fact he was shyly gentle and affectionate, and utterly without aggression. A general, genuine innocence of atmosphere invested occasions such as those afternoons when Dorneywood and I might drop in on him as he took a bath after some game, to sit chatting unhurriedly about how to spend the remainder of the day. When I responded to his request to chuck him a towel, I simply admired his glowing skin and felt how good it was to have him, as well as Dorneywood, as a friend of mine.

Timelessness descended on a bathroom full of steam but free from all tension. There was luxury in the des-ultory discussion about whether to take our bikes and go down to the local village shop. Regardless of purchases, we could be sure of a friendly welcome there. In its tiny, crammed space, the fat woman proprietor would emerge behind the counter seeming even fatter but always buoyant, healthy and jovial. And it was with affection that we had adopted the nickname first given her by Barney Webb, of 'Blossom'. School-life had some charm about it on those afternoon occasions. Had I formulated a wish, it would have been to prolong the moment, just as it was, and for there to be no tomorrow. But while we chatted or were silent, the light would be perceptibly fading, even in summer. Nusselbacher had dressed, and the three of us could not sit forever in the bathroom at the top of the house, with its window that looked down the drive to the school-gates.

Life outside made its demands. If this was Saturday then tomorrow would be Sunday, when Dorneywood and I would be serving at sung Mass, and Tommy would probably be officiating. And then would come Monday and the regular demands of the week, with the khaki routine of the Corps, which I loathed, and organised, compulsory games, at which I was so bad. Most boys liked to complain of the classes, on any subject, but to me they were always preferable.

Although the view from the bathroom window showed a countryside apparently steeped in peace, beyond it was the continuing reality of war.

One visible reminder of it were the sad-eyed Italian prisoners-of-war whom we saw working in the fields. Italy had surrendered, but the Germans were stubbornly resisting the Allied advance up the peninsula, while war was raging more fiercely still in the Far East.

Dorneywood and I were now among the senior boys. We had taken the places of those just ahead of us who had left to join the Forces, and unless the war abruptly ceased it would soon be our turn – incredible though it seemed – to join the fighting. Already, Dorneywood was, calmly and characteristically, prepared. He would enter the Rifle Brigade, in which his elder brother was serving as an officer. I was a few months younger – which was excuse enough, I thought, to delay any decision. That we would all be commissioned was not in doubt, and over a choice of regiment Tommy had several times pronounced that boys with brawn should enter the Guards, boys with brain the Rifle regiments.

United though we might be in friendship, Dorneywood and I were divided not only by temperament but by currents of authority within the school, under the very different influences of Tommy and of Barney Webb. In Dorneywood Tommy rightly saw a boy who deserved to become Captain of the school, and who would have deserved such promotion in an establishment far larger. Ambivalent about me, not least in the very area of the visual arts where we ought to have had something in common, Tommy only reluctantly made me a prefect. The contrast he felt between us could be detected in the relative positions assigned to us as altar-servers: Dorneywood as the master of ceremonies, reliable and assiduous in attendance on the celebrant throughout the Mass, and I in the secondary yet showy role of thurifer.

It surprised me when I realised that Tommy had become a close friend of the whole Dorneywood family. But perhaps Dorneywood was surprised that I, while unable really to like Webb, grew to welcome his academic guidance and to be grateful for what he gave me in uneffusive, unexpected yet very positive encouragement.

'Art' was the sole subject Tommy taught. He made his art-books accessible and he talked stimulatingly about painting. Casually propped in his gracefully-arranged room was his own small pastel-souvenir of Italy, of a storm over the Alban Hills. But when he stood by my desk and commented on my work, my scene, say, from *The Duchess of Malfi*, he could never hide his innate disdain. And when he found I had pinned up colour reproductions of Pre-Raphaelite paintings in the prefects' study, his shudder was at once humorously exaggerated but intentionally stinging. With an exclamation equivalent to 'Ugh!', he declared, 'They remind me of the decoration of the parlour in a seaside boarding-house.' I did not know at the time that his widowed mother had, during his childhood, taken paying guests in their house at St Leonards-on-Sea.

Classes with Webb I tended not to enjoy, until the day he threw back at us our English essays, most of which he called dreadful. One boy in particular had failed to write an essay at all – but what he had written was highly original, unusually imaginative prose. The subject was 'Martyrs', and he would read some of what this boy – sit up at the back and pay attention – conveyed in evoking a scene of Christian martyrdom in a Roman amphitheatre.

He asked me to stay behind after class. Then he reiterated dourly that those paragraphs were no essay. But had I written comparable pieces before? I had. For my own pleasure, I often composed evocations of episodes and scenes from history and literature.

'Come and read one of them to me some evening,' he said. 'I'll give you a cup of cocoa.' So, carrying my black book of essays (as I still thought of them), I went for a first evening in his room. It was large and well-lit, and it could have been handsome, but Webb had turned it into a virtual critique of Tommy's. The sparse furniture – even the bookcase – shouted out in ugliness. Each item seemed selected for its drabness, its refusal to be comfortable or even personal. Only a few photographs on the walls suggested an inhabitant, and I noticed a small one of a rather vacuous-looking boy awkwardly dressed up in Tudor costume, holding a white horse. Later, Webb would tersely answer my enquiry by saying it was of the youthful Duke of Norfolk, who had been his pupil.

To senior boys, on semi-official occasions, Tommy would offer a half-glass of sherry and – with a snort of laughter – throw himself into a pose consciously relaxed yet attentive.

Seated away from me across the inhospitable room, in a thinly-padded, wooden-slatted chair, pair to the one I sat in, Webb listened impassively to my reading. Readings they would become, because I was often to return with a freshly-written piece and to drink a mug of cocoa.

Seldom did he say much, and rarely did he openly praise what I had read. But he warned me against over-writing and similar sins of indulgence with colourful adjectives and unnecessary adverbs. He spoke of discipline, of my need generally to work at English, to think about the language and to read – above all to read widely in and far beyond the syllabus for the then statutory School Certificate and Higher Certificate.

'You might try for a university scholarship,' he remarked one evening, in an off-hand tone. 'But you would have to work very much harder, and throughout the holidays.'

'And not go into the Army,' had been my immediate though unspoken thought.

In class, Webb never alluded in any way to my writing as such. Nor did he single me out – unless for objurgation. And, turning purplish-red in the face, he could let his temper rip with us all, perhaps for deliberate though frightening effect, just as he did on the playing-field or, in bulging uniform, as 'Captain Webb', during some exercise of the Corps.

Favouritism was not a charge he could be accused of with anyone; and an academic goal hardly appealed to most boys in the school. Dorneywood was typical in envisaging, after the Forces, a career in the City, while other boys planned to enter some family firm. And if my evening visits to Webb's room were noticed at all, it was with the sentiment 'better you than me'.

As he proposed, I read widely in the holidays. I had, in fact, little else to do to pass the time in Harrogate, and it was an advantage that the public library there was so good. I read fiction of all sorts, and yet remained laughably ignorant of contemporary novelists. Devoted to the historical novels of Marjorie Bowen (later celebrated in an essay by Graham Greene), I was profoundly chagrined one morning to find on 'her' shelf only a book or two by one Elizabeth Bowen. A glance inside them deepened my disappointment.

Yet, encouraged by Webb, I read a mass of eighteenth- and nineteenth-century English fiction, some of it digested with difficulty though largely with enjoyment – and without much critical sense. Jumbled up in my mind were Fielding, Hardy, Meredith, George Eliot, Jane Austen, Mrs Gaskell, Wilkie Collins, Trollope and the Brontës. I never got to the best of Trollope, away from Barchester, and of course I was too young to savour fully the fierce, disciplined power of Jane Austen – as an artist more akin perhaps to Racine than to Shakespeare.

Dickens failed then to do more than disturb me. I was reminded – not wrongly – of the baleful, hateful atmosphere of those fairy stories thrust on me in early childhood. His humour seemed constantly to border on hysteria, and I am glad now that I never attempted the later books, with their superbly black, murderous moods, for which one needs to be thoroughly adult and mature.

But one novel, above all others, I found myself not so much reading as entering, from the day I opened it and began the first, magically beguiling paragraph. Thackeray's *Vanity Fair* drew me in before I realised it, and so it goes on doing at each of many re-readings. It ought to be recognised as one of the finest novels ever written, for its scope, its sophisticated tone and its unbridled zest. Like its heroine, Becky, it aspires to wear spangles and trousers and dance through our literature with sparklingly stylish, life-enhancing effect. No remorse or suicidal ending for that errant woman, whose impudent, enduring vitality can – even today – shock as well as delight.

One summer day in 1944, as if to provide me with both visual and intellectual stimulus, Barney Webb took me to Oxford. He gave me lunch at the Union and let me gaze at the exterior of Balliol, where he believed I should go, before we visited his own old college of Pembroke. And he introduced me to Blackwell's bookshop. With some money saved, I bought a copy of Chaucer's *Canterbury Tales*. Partly, that was tribute to him, for he had imbued me with a fondness for Chaucer which would ultimately be incomparably enhanced by studying under Nevill Coghill.

All I experienced of Oxford on that first occasion enchanted me, though I am sure I gracelessly failed in adequately thanking Webb for the day's revelation. I returned determined to go to Oxford but, in another, more serious failure I must have disappointed him by not gaining a scholarship. Yet he implied that after the Army, after the war, I should try again for a place.

After the Army . . .

It was in the civilised atmosphere of Tommy's room that I should next find myself, seeking his advice and aid over which regiment to enter. He thought a Rifle regiment would be suitable, and nodded at my choice of the King's Royal Rifle Corps (the 60th Rifles), which attracted me by its élite status and elegant uniform.

He arranged for me to have an interview in London, where a trio of courteous old colonels seemed friendly. One of them recalled being impressed by the war memorial in the chapel at Caversham – jolly dignified in design. It was good to know of my enthusiasm for the 60th Rifles, though at that stage in the war no more direct commissions into it were being made. Still, by volunteering, I could ensure that I entered the regiment, and in time would no doubt become an officer.

I volunteered. It was a prosaic but quite unreal little ceremony in the shabby recruiting office at Reading when I swore to serve with the Colours for five years (and seven on the Reserve) and actually received the King's shilling.

What it meant I had perhaps not fully comprehended until I got off my bicycle again at the school-gates. I needed a commission to cancel the length of service to which I had committed myself. The alternative would be that I was bought out – by, of course, my father.

All such prospects were dim and slight, compared with the immediate fact that I was leaving school. An epoch in my life was about to end. At the top of the rising drive, Woodcote House stood warm-seeming, unpretentious and welcoming, still looking more like a country seat than a school. I did not ask whether I had been happy there, and a retrospect would have included days that were wearisome, days that were miserable, along with many that were merely humdrum. I could not claim that I should miss any of the masters and few indeed of the boys. But the school had constituted a base for my existence, and it would no longer be there for me.

At the left was the chapel, converted out of the squash-court, where I had privately prayed and publicly served as thurifer. On the altar another boy would be deputed to serve.

There would be no more opportunities to be amused and yet admiring on entering the chapel and discovering Tommy's latest ingenious improvement of its stark interior. His effect of oranges glowing among dark foliage, contrived by yew sprays from which hung dyed tennis balls, had brought to it a breath of Italy (though I failed to detect the debt to the bushes in Uccello's painting of the 'Rout of San Romano'). God would still be available to me in the Army, I had to suppose, but I should miss the make-shift chapel.

Fit, cheerful and unchanged, Edward Dorneywood had come down one day to school on leave. When we were alone, I pestered him with urgent questions about Army life, about surviving the parade-ground and drill, uniform and fatigues, and the whole ethos of the barrack-room. Was it all absolute hell?

Perhaps my vehemence made him smile. He was, as ever, reticent and moderate. He said life in the Army was hard to convey: it had its good aspects, and he was now used to it. But I pressed for a more explicit answer. Whatever he had undergone, I knew I should undergo far more painfully.

'Well,' he said at last, lightly and dismissively. 'At times it can be quite tough.'

10

Parading as Men

Winchester station had nothing out of the ordinary about it, as far as I could see, arriving there one day at the beginning of May 1945. The war was still on. Although I had a travel warrant and not a ticket, and was about to 'proceed', in military idiom, to the barracks, I felt myself to be very much the civilian my clothes suggested.

Barely had I stepped outside, however, than the extraordinary happened. My status vanished, and with it went temporarily my individuality as well. I had not merely joined the Army, I had been absorbed into it.

For the next two and three-quarter years it was my home, my parent, my God, my school, my life. I should find it demanding, constricting, restless, capricious, coarse, absurd, but also responsible, never wantonly cruel or oppressive, strangely caring though quite unimaginative, and accidentally fecund in almost daily provision of bizarre situations and of a gallery of no less bizarre human characters. Thus, with alternating cuffs and licks (many more of the former) it thrust on me a form of education – one approximating to the kind an animal mother in the wild gives its young.

Very speedily on that May day did it strip me, literally, of all my civilian clothes and dress me, down to 'drawers cellular', in its regulation uniform. But then, on demobilisation, it would come forward with the issue of a new civilian suit and shirt, a choice of shoes (brown or black) and even – most touching of all – a soft, trilby hat. The Army could not conceive of letting soldiers leave it and return to 'Civvy Street' with heads naked.

I had intended to stroll lazily from Winchester station and take my time in reaching the barracks. Opposite me in the carriage I had noticed a bullet-headed, shiny-faced boy of about my own age – a cockney butcher's boy, I opined – who seemed likely also to be joining up, though as one of nature's 'other ranks'. But we might walk together to the barracks.

We left the station together, only to halt outside. Somehow, in the bustle and noise of the platform, we had received our instructions and were already obeying them. Out in the station yard other boys in civilian clothes stood, grinning at each addition to their group, yet sheepish and subdued.

A non-commissioned officer, sergeant or corporal, appeared. Without barking, he gave his orders, and as he did so we silently coalesced into two files. Stumbling rather than marching, yet trying to keep in step, we set off through the streets, vaguely aware that here and there people gazed uninterestedly at us, the latest batch of recruits on its way to the barracks.

Already, we were separate from those people. It was they who were now alien. Even before we reached our destination, before we changed into uniform, we had altered. A simple word of command had been sufficient. The several disparate teenagers descending from the train had gone. In their place was a single entity, one welded into what it was addressed as: men.

On my knees in my bedroom at home, I had frequently prayed to God for an accident that should prevent the arrival of the day I joined the Army. It could be fatal, for all I cared – indeed, I bargained for that. Even on the train journey to Winchester, though with diminishing conviction, I believed He might yet intervene.

In any real sense, it could not be the I whom I knew myself to be who was shuffling along some road, entering the gates of a huge, brick-red barracks, crossing the expanse of parade-ground and climbing the stone staircase in the allotted block ('Talavera', or some other battle honour) to the allotted barrack-room, to find the allotted bunk. But I entered a room which proved to be full of individuals, united only by the fact that this was their first day in the Army. Some were shouting, whistling, jostling each other and joking. Others sat on their bunks bewildered, while one or two walked up and down as if to work off a desperate misery.

The corner in which I found myself, and recovered some of my own individuality, was itself a cross-section of the room's cross-section of social class. I met a reserved but friendly Glaswegian, who said his name was Booth, and somebody taller and older-looking, called Saunders, for whom the experience was not entirely novel, since he had been in the Fleet Air Arm in Canada. And there was a dark-haired boy from Marlborough, Meadows, who spoke and behaved in a superior, aggrieved fashion. He was disconcerted to be among ordinary, General Service Corps privates (not as yet even riflemen) when he had expected to go from public school straight to a commission. He disclaimed any knowledge of the Oratory School and showed scepticism when I spoke of also being marked out for a commission.

Nobody seemed more intensely unhappy than a very tall boy, with a narrow, sculpted face, who sat with clasped hands and whose thin body was contorted in quiet agony. He looked much as I felt.

'His father's a judge,' Saunders told me authoritatively.

Under the outward uniformity which the Army imposed on us that evening, step by step, as we drew our palliasses and were issued with our identity tags, our kit-bags, our mess-tins, and razor, comb, lather-brush, toothbrush and hairbrush, social divisions were becoming almost physically apparent. Most voices betrayed their origins – none more incongruously than those rapidly detected and derided as 'Effing OCTU' (Officer Cadet Training Unit), whose presence in the barrack-room seemed an insult if not a provocation to decent, working-class lads called up to serve unambitiously in the Army and then get out as rapidly as possible.

I had not been to Eton, nor did I live in the Old Kent Road, and I would be slow to realise that my chosen regiment preferred one extreme or the other. It took me a while to see how uncompromisingly the barrack-room divided, and how Booth, Saunders and I associated together as beings awkwardly stranded in the middle.

It took me a while longer to see that in my new existence it was best not to ask questions. Much of Army life became tolerable only by unquestioning obedience – though that did not mean a failure to pass comment on any given situation. Despite never serving in the Army, Tennyson had famously caught the gist of the basic premise for every soldier: 'Their's not to reason why . . .' But it was every soldier's right to comment, privately and forcefully, on what was about to happen and on the orders that led up to it. Regardless of your place in the hierarchy, orders always appeared to originate at one remove above, at a level where it was natural to suppose there reigned pervasive irrationality.

'Seems daft to me,' a platoon commander might comment aside to his sergeant, having been briefed by the company commander, who had thought the colonel's order as received a total nonsense. He had not heard what the colonel had said to the adjutant after getting instructions from brigade.

'All balls, sir, if you'll pardon the expression,' the sergeant would agree. 'Shall I fall the men in for your orders?'

But on that first evening in the barracks at Winchester, I was still a cross between Candide and Alice in Wonderland.

'Funny they give us two identity discs,' I said questioningly to Saunders. Mine already had 'R.C.' stamped on them, I observed.

'One remains on your body when they bury you,' he explained.

'Oh, really?' I responded faintly.

I had just noticed that for my bunk I had 'drawn' blankets, of a dusty grey and mud colour, but I must have missed the issue of sheets. I looked at Booth and at the grey and mud-coloured blankets on his bunk.

'We don't get sheets,' he answered when I asked, kindly keeping his voice down.

I shall never sleep – or never wake, I thought, at the raucous shout of 'Lights Out!' Yet my own light went out as quickly as anyone's, and the next thing I knew was a comparable shout of 'Wakey, wakey!' It was morning again. The reality of where I was and what I had become hit me only when I entered the infernal area, jammed with half-naked bodies, designated 'Ablutions'.

We marched to breakfast, and we marched back. Already it seemed quite normal that daily existence was defined by 'falling in' or 'falling out'. The earliest parades on the barrack-square were ordeals, but ones for which the Corps at school had been some preparation, and at least parading in battle-dress was marginally more agreeable than the antiquated discomfort of wearing tunic, breeches and puttees.

It was on the square that I heard, or heard of, a first Etonian encounter with the Army. Perhaps it was improved in the barrack-room subsequently but it delighted me, though some earnest people like Meadows frowned their disapproval when it was recounted.

'You 'orrible man,' a sergeant had suddenly roared, on detecting a discrepancy about one figure in the ranks. 'You're improperly dressed. Why aren't you wearing gaiters?'

'I don't approve of gaiters, sergeant.'

The silence and sensation were tremendous. And though the sergeant tried to rally with heavy sarcasm, and bluster about a charge, and the other NCOs looked suitably scandalised, he had been worsted.

'Absolutely typical of Angus,' said another Etonian afterwards, calmly amused without being impressed.

I longed to meet someone who could behave like that – in the Army. And so, in time, I should.

When we were not on parade during those first few days, we carried out obscure duties, 'fatigues', such as sweeping out the gym or peeling potatoes, 'spud-bashing'. It was while some of us quietly spud-bashed one afternoon, that I learnt the news that the war in Europe was over. I asked my last but most urgent question:

'Will we all go home now?'

'Laddie, laddie,' said the corporal who was supervising us, reproachfully. 'We've still got to beat the bloody Japs.'

Before that would occur, the Army moved me from Winchester. I had begun to wonder whether it had forgotten that I was meant to be in the 60th Rifles – much as I wondered sometimes whether I had been forgotten by God. Not that the Army allowed Him to be forgotten by me, for it dutifully ensured that I paraded every Sunday morning for Mass, along with 'other Denoms' attending non-Church of England services.

I had my first experience of entraining in the Army. Squads of us lined up at the station by night, before being crushed into dirty, ill-lit, increasingly smelly compartments, travelling far north, to a destination undisclosed, and apparently under wartime conditions. Strict security precautions prevailed throughout our journey, though it seemed unlikely that either the Japanese or the defeated Germans would or could bomb our train – still less inflict on it a gas attack. And even when I learnt that we were about to arrive at camp near a place called Barnard Castle, County Durham, I (having never heard of it) scarcely understood what arrival implied.

To start with, Booth and Saunders had receded from my life. It was not in their company that I should in future drink that suspiciously yellow lemonade and eat those slightly stale but delicious ginger biscuits – comfort food – which the NAAFI provided everywhere. It had seemed

absurd to say that we would keep in touch. We knew
we wouldn't, though I had been grateful to them both for
crumbs of culture, as well as company. Booth had confided
in me that his father collected the water-colours of Russell
Flint (an artist whose work I then greatly esteemed), and
Saunders had lent me a book, *Scum of the Earth*, by Arthur
Koestler. Books of any kind were very seldom seen in the
army – least of all, I should discover, in officers' messes.
Koestler's book, dealing vividly with the appalling plight of
refugees and displaced persons in Hitler's Europe, made me
unexpectedly glad to have my three blankets and my bunk
in the British Army.

The camp near Barnard Castle was a base for the two
'Greenjacket' regiments, the Rifle Brigade and the 60th
Rifles. It represented, in its way, military paradise after
the purgatory of Winchester. In sending me there the Army
had heard my prayer. No longer a mere private, I was now
a rifleman, wearing the distinctive 60th cap-badge in black.
Another distinction was the fact that riflemen never slope
arms on parade but carry their rifles at the trail – a relief
to me who had always failed to keep my head still when
sloping the heavy Lee Enfield rifle of the period.

'Thank God,' everyone in my hut kept saying, 'for decent
Greenjacket officers at last.'

'And,' an Etonian pointed out, 'Raby Castle isn't far. I
bet the dowager asks us over one evening for cards.'

'Giles is in the mess here, but so is that frightful twerp
Simon Stoye-Jones. Who on earth gave him a commission?'

'All right, you lot,' the corporal in charge of the hut
called out, feeling a need to assert some authority. 'Cut
the effing chat. Stand by your beds in twenty minutes for
hut inspection.'

'Oh, but corporal . . .'

'What?'

'I've lost my lather-brush, and anyway I prefer brushless
shaving cream.'

'You should know regulations by now. Every man's kit

includes razor, comb, toothbrush, hairbrush and lather-brush. Doesn't matter a blind bit if you're bald and toothless and don't shave.'

'Actually,' the rifleman on the bunk above mine said loudly, 'I think Corporal Sweetman lives up to his name.' 'Effing Octu types.' The corporal swore automatically, but could not prevent himself blushing.

It was true that ours was a hut where every rifleman, regardless of which school he had been at, seemed to expect a commission – and fairly promptly – into one of the two regiments. Etonians might be sufficiently confident to take such matters lightly, but others worked zealously and constantly – from obsessive nightly polishing of their boots to reading up in pamphlets on weapons-training and man-management. And all the time, roughly and toughly, we were being managed ourselves, and tested. And all the time, I sensed that I was falling behind, if not failing.

Physical failure – over, say, assembling the Bren gun – might sting, but it was only a temporary humiliation. Anyway, we were partly there to be humiliated, to be shouted at and verbally abused, not praised. It was an aspect of the routine which not even the ardent boot-polisher could escape.

However, my sense of failing, of floundering, of not meeting some standard, was much more extensive. It was odd to feel that the exclusive ethos represented by our hut suited me little better than the crude barrack-room at Winchester. And, ironically, the very association with the people whom I found most sympathetic, and who were friendly enough to me, drove home – often by chance – the gulf between us.

'Home' was the apt word on the evening when for a diversion my bunk-mate, John Challinor, proposed that we wrote each other's addresses on the envelopes of our Sunday letters to our parents. At his dictation, I wrote down simply: The Great House, Grantley, Herts. And then I had to give him, with an inner struggle, the number and the street of mine, Leatherhead, near Epsom, Surrey. He wrote it simply too, without any sign whatsoever that it was not Leatherhead Hall. But even his good manners – and a visit to the NAAFI for lemonade – could not soothe away my feelings of inferiority.

Challinor was too civilised, and too nervously intelligent, to bear military life. His aim was not a commission but a discharge. He insisted on wearing pyjamas at night, which was probably against King's Regulations, and displayed every eccentricity to achieve his aim, until – sadly for me – a board of psychiatrists pronounced him unfitted to remain in the Army.

My unfittedness was more subtle, and my sense of it increased as I listened to knowledgeable talk of the stages leading up to a commission: first the interview in camp with the Colonel commanding; next, and crucially, a War Office Selection Board (WOSB); then pre-Octu training, and eventually an Officer Cadet Training Unit itself.

Had I not carried the secret, self-inflicted burden of having volunteered, with its promise to serve for five years, I might have been content to stay uncommissioned. The routine of Army life at the lowest level could be strangely lulling, requiring, as it did, minimum thought. Somebody was constantly taking responsibility for you, from the moment you were awakened until the moment you were told to go to bed.

Lulling too, if one were honest, was the simple, half-innocent tide of obscenity that flowed through daily existence. The filthy songs we sang – or learnt to sing – were robbed of the truly perverse or 'dirty-minded', for which the Army had no tolerance, by a certain charm and sometimes wit. Who could fail to join in, as we sat rocking back and forth, tired and grubby, returning to camp in the back of a three-ton lorry, and somebody started to sing of Mary who lived in a mountain glen? Time has turned old-fashioned the outcome of her manoeuvres with a fountain-pen, which led to the birth of a blue-black child:

'And they called the bastard Stephen, For that was the name of the ink.'

Then, at the end of long, exhausting marches and elaborate twenty-four-hour exercises, complete with packs and rations and the hated burden of the mortar, there came solicitous, near-maternal care for the state of each man's feet. They must be paraded, after washing, and inspected.

Easier, I sometimes thought, to be the inspected rather than the officer inspecting – especially if you were Lieutenant Stoye-Jones, trying to retain some dignity while under a sergeant's stern eye, going through the motions of inspecting the bare toes of fellow-Etonians.

'Er, um, good,' he would say hastily, eager to pass on and obviously biting back somebody's first name.

'Socks in very poor shape, sir,' the sergeant interjected, detaining him. 'Should report to the QMS for issue of a new pair.'

'Oh, yes. Yes, good idea. Thank you, sergeant.'

'Sir.'

In the very tone of the delivery, and in the terrific salute which seemed to dismiss Stoye-Jones as ostensibly as it honoured him at the end of the inspection, there was a perceptible hint of contempt. And Stoye-Jones had succeeded no better in the hut.

Even those who had not known him at school agreed with the general sentiment: 'God forbid one should ever have to inspect Stoye-Jones's foul feet.'

It was nice to join in the laughter, and it was nice on Saturday afternoons when groups of us could go by truck into Barnard Castle and – despite wearing battle-dress – cease for a few hours to belong to the Army.

The town was small, rural and tranquil, which we savoured rather than tried to disturb. It had its cinema, its bookshop and an attractive, old-fashioned hotel where the richer and more sophisticated of us would go and dine. And it had the colossal surprise of the Bowes Museum, a vast nineteenth-century re-creation of a French château in the Durham countryside, packed with an assortment of treasures and trivia, shawls and silver, chairs, plant-stands, and possibly ferns too, as well as porcelain and paintings. In that crammed, unarranged state there was the fun of exploration, only increased by the sense of being from Saturday to Saturday the sole visitors to its echoing, empty galleries.

Then it was time for another interview, with another courteous colonel. I was starting to formulate what experience would bear out: colonels, having achieved the plateau of responsible command, could afford to be confident and were therefore courteous, whereas majors tended to be tetchy, under the stress of seniority without full responsibility. Even as they murmured, 'Yes, Colonel, I entirely agree,' they were wondering how soon they would replace the old boy.

My interview covered school and games, and also sports like shooting, which, even when encouraged to talk about, I could hardly pretend to have done. And although it was a point in my favour that I had volunteered, it was largely cancelled out by the admission that I had no intention of making the Army my career. And so, as I had foreseen, I failed to be judged suitable for commissioning in the 60th, though worth consideration for the infantry.

Most of the people in my hut emerged more successfully. They seemed to be on their speedy way to commissions in their chosen regiments. But soon the whole unit would be on its way, moving for a period to a large camp in the West of England, then shifting elsewhere, back North, and I became as disoriented physically as mentally. I remained a rifleman very much in the ranks, deprived now of much of the aura of 'Effing Octu', and often doubting whether I should ever be sent to a WOSB, the testing gateway needing to be passed through before officer-training began. And among the host of initials which dominated Army life, none seemed more ominous than those that marked failure following a WOSB: RTU (returned to unit).

Congenial or not, my immediate set of acquaintances in Barnard Castle days had disappeared. There were long periods when I thought that my personality too had disappeared. Never mind my future, had I really had a past? Time in terms of weeks and months had lost its meaning. I often asked myself quite seriously: how old am I? It was strange to realise that I was still only eighteen.

After a day's training in the art of grenade-throwing, or in the refinements of bayonet-stabbing, it was impossible for a while to recover a sense of individuality. 'Fix bayonets,' was simply one more order among many. I had become as inanimate as those straw dummies we attacked with such induced ferocity, shouting, 'In, out, on guard!' as we trampled on them before plunging our bayonets into their dry, sack-like bodies, our minds carefully suspended from giving any imaginative reality to the exercise.

There were occasions when, abruptly and briefly, my earlier life would come into focus. One night when I was doing guard duty in Wiltshire, the orderly officer proved to be a senior boy from the Oratory. I had barely known him, but he paused for a few moments to talk in a friendly way in the darkness, before we reverted to our separate ranks. And then the eddying currents of Army existence brought me face to face, in the same camp, by daylight, with Wilson II, now a Lieutenant, whom I was prompt to salute.

After that, it seemed almost inevitable that Edward Dorneywood and I should have our brief encounter. I think he must have first sought me out in my hut, where the incursion of an officer brought everyone to attention. Obviously we could not talk there, nor in fact could we be seen talking anywhere. So we arranged that, after nightfall, I should risk punishment by entering the officers' lines (strictly forbidden) and that we should talk at the window of his individual room.

Our conversation may have been banal, as we tried in haste, and in whispers, to join together bits of our differing experiences, but the episode had its edge of danger and farce, and the patent overtones of Romeo and Juliet made us giggle.

He had been sent to the camp on some course. I reported that I still awaited a WOSB.

'But I'm sure you'll get through,' he said cheerfully.

'I'm sure I'll fail,' I said gloomily.

I had no time to recite my list of Army failures so far, notably my failure as a driver of trucks – or to describe the bitter-sweet day of my driving test. Then, a languid, elegantly casual 60th officer, Captain Lord Tay, had been my examiner, sitting calmly beside me as, tense yet pleased, I let the vehicle meander gently along. Some mild word from him prompted me to accelerate. My boot pressed down on the pedal. We shot forward violently, swerved at a corner and his clip-board slipped from his thin, elegant hand.

'Perhaps,' he had suggested, not looking at me, when finally we halted, 'you'd like to try reversing.'

Wrenching at the gear lever, more than usually stubborn, of course, on this occasion, I managed grimly to reverse. The back of the truck left the verge, crossed a ditch and mounted the bank, before the engine stalled.

Captain Lord Tay made a pencilled note or two, while I sweated in my battle-dress, which had never felt more suffocating.

'Well,' he said at last, with a flicker of apologetic smile, 'I'm afraid I can't give you very high marks.' A pause, in which I felt dissolved in sweat. 'But I expect it was just nerves. And it seems a shame to fail you completely.'

Even had there been time, I don't think I could have explained to Edward Dorneywood that my waiting and my wanderings as a rifleman had been made more than tolerable by being shared. I had met the Angus of the early gaiters incident, Angus Heriot. He too had been politely rejected as officer material for the 60th Rifles, but was due to go at some indeterminate date to a WOSB. Meanwhile, the Army seemed to find it convenient to bracket us together, perhaps as two oddities.

Angus Heriot was not so much odd as totally, content-
edly, idiosyncratic. With his freckled face and upturned
nose, and eyes of a cat-like green, and his habit of making
stylised, 'Egyptian' gestures with his hands, he gave off an
air of idiosyncrasy which no amount of khaki uniform
could stifle. And, similarly, all outward circumstances,
discipline, barrack-room ways, barely impinged on the
life he conducted within his own mind. It was an interior
furnished with a cultural richness that both oppressed and
intrigued me. Glad though I was that he permitted me some
limited access, I often felt clumsy there, blushing at each
fresh revelation of my ignorance: of Glyndebourne, Mozart
in general, Ida Rubinstein, Cocteau, Anatole France, and
Flaubert's *Salammbô* (I desperately hoping to regain some
cultural credit by raving about *Madame Bovary*).

While the rest of the barrack-room lay on their bunks,
smoked and snoozed, leaving us largely alone, Heriot would
declare that we must design costumes, with an extravagantly
Egyptian emphasis, for *The Magic Flute*.

Perhaps I drew better, but his designs were bolder and he
knew far more about ancient Egypt. He was scornful in his
attitude to conventional religious beliefs, yet believed fixedly
in theories of reincarnation within an Egyptian context.

'Oh, balls,' I said, as rudely as I dared, when he first
asserted that he had lived in the time of Akhnaton.

He shut his eyes and crossed his arms and became as
rigid as a mummy. It was a retreat to the luxury of his
mind, slamming the door on any further contact with me
that evening.

'I may have lived once before, in the Italian Renaissance,'
I proposed on a later occasion, partly in reparation and
partly to advance my own knowledge and my claim to
interest.

'No,' he replied firmly. 'You never did.'

Together, Heriot and I were moved from camp to camp,
and as we queued up for meals or fresh bedding, he
transformed our dingy surroundings by expatiating on the

Pharaohs or singing a chorus from Walton's *Belshazzar's Feast*.

It was together that we eventually received our orders to proceed to a WOSB, at 'Orchards', near Godalming in Surrey.

'I wonder what it'll be like,' I said anxiously, as we sat in an otherwise empty carriage in the train. I was thinking of all I had heard of the combination of physical testing by day – with literal climbing through hoops – and psychological testing subsequently.

'It's one of Lutyens' earliest country houses,' Heriot replied.

And after the three days, which had indeed combined the physical and the psychological, he commented only that at the interview with the psychiatrist, which I had found brief and tepid, he had provided lots of deeply fascinating misinformation.

Together, back in camp, we waited to hear the results. Heriot had a friend in the orderly office, and before we were officially notified he got wind of them. Heriot's was the awkward task of breaking it to me one evening that he had passed and that I had failed. Awkwardness sharpened his brusqueness, and I felt first anger at him and then an engulfing, suicidal despair. I had to rush out of our hut, out into the darkness of the camp and just stand there alone in my misery.

A day or two later, we were marched in to receive the notification officially. Heriot's friend had made a muddle. It was Heriot who had failed; I had passed.

So the Army, which had brought us together, decisively separated us. To the *bouleversement*, Heriot professed indifference – perhaps quite truthfully.

'I never really wanted to be an officer,' he said, shrugging. 'I'm perfectly happy in the ranks.'

The awkwardness was now on my side, and I might ask myself whether I also, as the process began, really wanted to be an officer. And although Heriot and I had never established a proper friendship (in my mind he would forever remain 'Heriot'), I already felt that I should miss him. I never presumed that he would miss me. I knew he would hate any conventional words at parting – most of all talk of keeping in touch. Nor did we meet again, though we did keep in touch by occasional letters as the Army disposed of us each in the world beyond England: I to Egypt and he to Athens, whence he wrote of enjoying his life as a corporal in Welfare.

By then I was able to report comparably of finding life in the Army more enjoyable than it had been before, though I was impatient for demobilisation to come and for my conventional education to resume.

In the meantime, the Army had been doing its best with me and for me. After a slight tussle, in which I surprised myself by seizing the initiative, it had decided to attach me to the Education Corps in Egypt. For a few marvellous months I actually lived a semi-civilian-style existence in Cairo, working at GHQ and lodged in a pensione so ridiculously rich in atmosphere – with its tatty ethnic hangings and gimcrack ormolu furniture – that it might have served for a film-set. And its proprietor, Madame Lubenka, went with the atmosphere, holding chuckling audiences with us 'boys' in her bedroom after dinner, while she lay mountainous under the bedclothes, every so often helping herself to a heaped plate of cream tarts – we having been allowed just one each previously at dessert.

However, before I could savour such Egyptian flesh-pots, I had to be turned from 'officer material' into officer. It never occurred to me when – as it seemed, in the far-off past – I sat in Tommy's warm, well-appointed study at Woodcote, balancing my half-glass of sherry and idly considering with him which regiment to be commissioned into, that the business would be taken so strenuously by the Army.

I never foresaw the rigours of pre-Octu training in the

harsh conditions of a camp at Wrotham, in Kent, during a winter so excessively cold that one weekend the Army summarily sent us home on leave. But for the rest of the time there, we learnt to blanco our belts nightly, with frozen fingers, in a crude lean-to, and to wake each icy early morning, as both doors of the hut blew open, to a sergeant bellowing, 'Out of those wanking pits!' Officer-cadets as we may have become, we had not yet reached the stage where the yelling of such orders was followed by the word 'gentlemen'.

That was reserved, I think, for the final period of training, at an Octu. And for that a less crude environment was required, usually one created by some country house. For all its severity, Wrotham had brought me into contact with a few friendly, pleasant companions, and even in the relief of escaping from it – eventually – I was sorry to find that none of them would be proceeding to the Octu designated for me, Alton Towers.

The Army kept widening my knowledge of our English counties, and it now added Staffordshire and that picturesque, extravagantly neo-Gothic house, which had richly-wrought interiors to match its romantic, baronial exterior. We, however, lived less romantically in Nissen huts in what had perhaps been the kitchen-garden of the grounds. And I felt much more response to the grounds, especially to the secluded, fantastically-scaped valley with a lake, encircled by winding paths and thick shrubbery, and interspersed by artificial islands on which pagodas were perched. It formed a miniature Xanadu where I liked sometimes to wander alone.

Although Alton Towers was a novelty in terms of experience, it strangely brought me back in terms of acquaintance to my earliest days in the Army. As officer-cadets, we were all equal; and equally the unit lacked the familiar military dimension of actual 'men'. While one by one we would take turns at being an officer, drilling and giving orders, the remainder of us played at being them. But for me the unexpected element was discovering Greenjacket people I had known, and who had apparently long ago sped past me in the Army's game of snakes and ladders, among the same intake and due to be commissioned on the same date. As that goal drew close, though before it was assured for any of us, tailors descended from London and the question of uniform became agreeably topical. We all had our personal choices still of regiment, and the tailors were expert in illustrating the niceties of tunic, belts and buckles which separated one regiment from another, as well as giving us tantalising glimpses of refinements in the way of mess-dress and forage caps, leather-covered canes and other accessories. Yet, even as they dutifully measured and fitted each of us on their visits, they were careful not to finish the uniform beyond alteration. Even when commissioning in itself had become a virtual certainty, the matter of regiment was yet to be resolved.

For most if not all of us, euphoria swallowed up any disappointment at our final postings. Few of our wishes were realised, since in peacetime several regiments, including the rifle regiments, had no use for temporary-commissioned officers.

'What have you got?' we asked each other, with more politeness than interest, and treating it as a form of lucky dip.

Looking back, I realised how little I should miss the hut-full of my fellow cadets, though I was relieved that one friend from Winchester days was also to be posted with me to the King's Shropshire Light Infantry, in Shrewsbury. It was not the moment to say that I had never heard of the regiment. Fortunately, the tailors knew more. And Shropshire would be yet one further county to experience. But I felt I could understand how my mother, never given to malapropism, proudly referred at first to my having been commissioned into the King's Scottish Light Infantry.

The KSLI did not retain me long at Shrewsbury. Within a few weeks, in which the stuffy, port-laden atmosphere of the officers' mess threatened to suffocate me, it sent me off to the vague destination of the Middle East, with an unsympathetic fellow-lieutenant and a contingent of men who included, for obscure military reasons, a group of Danes. Young, non-regular officers were not popular at the barracks, and he and I were even more unpopular after we had neglected to march our men through Shrewsbury with their arms at the slope.

I could not call it punishment to cross the Channel for the first time in my life and to be in France. I forgot about our men, who had become officially absorbed into some much larger group, as I sat watching the French countryside unfolding and changing in a day's train journey – as it was – from Calais to Toulon. Two or more days of delightful delay occurred, allowing me to visit places like Le Lavandou and Bandol out of season, before we sailed for Alexandria. A small group of us even succeeded in meeting some French girls – which revealed how rudimentary was my knowledge of the language. I had only one last, slightly awkward contact with the men who had been under my joint command. I miscalculated the rate when changing their money into Egyptian piastres, and it was necessary to parade them specially for refunds before we parted.

I was to proceed to Heliopolis, on the outskirts of Cairo, and await posting. I thought of Heriot as I arrived, though there was none of the glamour of an ancient civilisation about the modern blocks of apartments and the rows of small, commonplace shops. But there was the sun – dry, exhilarating, steady sunshine of a kind I had never known. And at Heliopolis I was interviewed, along with other young, unplaced officers, and asked to choose between a job in Welfare (in Suez) or one in Signals (in Turkey). Neither appealed to me. Somehow, I had heard of the Education Corps, and I stubbornly went on insisting that I was suited for it, even after being informed that there were no vacancies.

'Oh, go and see Captain Oakley at GHQ,' the interviewing

officer said finally, in exasperation, as though consigning me to the devil. 'He'll tell you the position himself.'

'There is nothing in the field,' Captain Oakley told me in his office that afternoon, smiling coolly and balancing a pencil as he talked. 'However . . .'

I had not expected Captain Oakley to look so young and so unmilitary – like a frail, very pale curate – and to be so patently efficient and commanding. He seemed to epitomise GHQ. I could believe that he knew off-hand the disposition of all the Education Corps personnel indicated on the zones of the maps hanging behind him.

'However, I could do with a junior assistant here,' he said musingly. 'Yes, I think that might be a possibility. I'll have a word with the Brigadier. Of course, it's up to him.'

I was effusive if not incoherent in my gratitude – which he at once cut short. Callow as I might be, I was capable of realising that when Captain Oakley decided something, it was unlikely to be altered.

By that evening I was living in Cairo. It was Captain Oakley who had mentioned in an off-hand manner that we could see, if I cared, whether the pensione where he lodged could also accommodate me.

The winter was coming, and soon I should be experiencing my first Christmas abroad – in Cairo. I was nineteen. After post-war England, the shops seemed glowing and bulging with luxury items, iced cakes, dates and crystallised fruit, and I excitedly ordered exotic parcels to be sent home to my parents. And, no sooner had I recovered from the impact of seeing the treasures of Tutankhamun's tomb in the normally empty Museum, where the attendants might have been mummified, as they slumped on chairs while flies crawled over their faces, than it was Christmas Eve.

I sought out the cathedral, away from the mosques and the Coptic churches, and attended a packed Midnight Mass. I hardly knew what country I was in – or at what rite I was assisting – by the time the archbishop made his entrance, preceded by page boys wearing white plumes in their dark velvet hats.

Before I could tire of Cairo, assuming I ever should have, GHQ moved out of it, and then I too was moved – to a post as Education Officer at District Headquarters in Canal North. After the eternal, usually noisy and often dusty bustle of Cairo, where a few boulevards of extreme sophistication barely masked the teeming, myriad alleyways of ordinary humanity, I was to encounter something no less eternal and even more fascinating: the silence and emptiness of the desert.

Apart from the presence of two Army camps, nothing gave character to the place named Quassasin. But it remains memorable to me for many reasons. I was lucky to be quartered in a medical mess, with highly congenial colleagues, under the command of one more kindly, civilised, courteous colonel. I was luckier still that an orchestra had been formed in Canal North, from German prisoners-of-war (still *de facto* prisoners in 1947). I often walked back to my tent, through the shifting yet buoyant sand, like quicksilver under the feet, in the thrilling cold of a desert night, the stars corruscating overhead, and my mind filled with music never heard before, by Weber, Tchaikovsky, Mahler and Bruckner. Even before the horns sound, at the very words, '*Overture: Oberon*', I am transported back to nocturnal Quassasin.

I exulted in the unvarying alternation of hot days and icy nights, and in the long drives down straight mud roads, lined by sparse vegetation shimmering in the sunlight. Goat-like sheep would be grazing by the roadside, guarded by a night-shirted boy, and here and there would be inviting, elusive hints of shade and water. To me, there was appeal even in the smelly villages – through which native drivers loved to speed in superior, show-off fashion. And always there was the infinite, calming, alluring expanse of the desert.

Writing home to my father, I had the urge once to ask him for a favour. My thoughts were on life after the Army

– not at all on any career but on fresh travel, to Italy and to see paintings in Italy. I asked him therefore to go to the National Gallery and buy an illustrated book of its Italian paintings.

With some difficulty, he obtained and sent me a pre-war volume of illustrations in strictly utilitarian format and black and white reproduction. And I lounged in my tent at Quassasin, not actually pining but growing impatient for release, turning the pages and dreaming over the pictures.

Epilogue

Bells in Trafalgar Square

'But where exactly is it?' I could hear myself asking with increasing plaintiveness, while the well-bred, plummy voice at the other end of the telephone grew increasingly remote. I detected distinct though urbanely-controlled irritation at the need to repeat the instruction yet once more. And this time the tones were booming and final:

'You will find the office entrance to the left of the main entrance, standing with your back to Trafalgar Square.'

I put down the receiver still not absolutely certain that I should locate the office entrance and bemused by that unusual pronunciation of 'Trafalgar', with the accent on the first syllable, which added to my sense of disorientation.

Although I had under my hand while we talked the tersely-worded form-letter from the Civil Service Commission, which had come in the smallest possible buff envelope, suggestive of call-up papers or some other summons, I kept finding it hard to give credence and reality to the news it contained. Could it actually be a fact that – as it was 'pleased' to inform me – I had obtained a job as Assistant Keeper, Grade II, at the National Gallery in London? After all, as my mother swiftly pointed out, there was a two-year period of probation to serve. She had begun to wonder aloud, and would often wonder comparably in the following decades, whether they would want to retain me.

Yet I had not only the piece of paper but the evidence of my telephone call. I had obediently been in touch with the Keeper of the Gallery, Mr William Pettigrew Gibson, who showed no surprise at hearing my name. He gave me my directions and the date I should present myself at the office entrance.

'Oh, but I could come long before that,' I said eagerly. 'I'm quite free.'

'Thank you,' he replied. 'But we must adhere to the date that has been specified by the Commission.'

I was prompt on that Monday morning, more apprehensive than excited.

I thought the public face of the National Gallery was fairly familiar to me. I could even claim to have visited the Gallery more than once during my years at Oxford, though I had never conceived of people working there, apart from the uniformed men invigilating in each of the exhibition rooms. Only half-jokingly were friends asking whether I would become one of them. Or was my job, perhaps, at the Zoo?

Easily enough could I visualise the dome, the portico and the flights of steps of the main entrance, but no indication of offices or an office entrance. Yet, as I dutifully stood with my back to Trafalgar Square, on that morning, confronting the façade, I saw at the left a concrete path leading from a few steps up to a tall doorway and two brightly-polished bells. One was marked 'Visitors'; the other, 'Staff'.

Barely hesitating, and with a sudden impulse of pride, I pressed the second, nearer bell. The door immediately opened, and I stepped inside.

After the Army, Oxford had provided me with delirious liberty – yet I was glad of the rough education in life which had preceded the academic one. Oxford may have been primarily a matter of hard work but it included a good deal of living – and loving – in addition to study. I enormously enjoyed my years there, and I had the lasting benefit, for which I shall never cease to be grateful, of a great teacher and tutor in Nevill Coghill. He was humane in spirit, generous, cultivated, kindly and also shrewd, a man on a physically generous scale too – often seeming larger, brighter and more expansive than suited the dim confines of Exeter College. Fortunately, you forgot its inherent dreariness as you entered the highly personal atmosphere of his elegant, artfully casual rooms. But strong though my love for Oxford was, I remained intensely conscious of being in transit there. While I sometimes longed to stay forever, I guessed that I should not. When I accidentally left and lost my B.Litt. thesis (unfinished) in a café in Oxford, I gave myself my marching orders. It was only unfortunate that I was devoid of ideas of where to go.

In the months that followed, my mother often doubted despairingly – and audibly – whether I would ever be employed by anyone, despite my First in English from Oxford. As usual, my father was confident that something would eventually turn up.

A girl I had known at Oxford was similarly placed. I went to stay with her in London, and she asked for my help in giving credibility to her application for a vacancy advertised for an Assistant Keeper at the National Gallery. We had gone and looked at paintings together in Italy, both attracted particularly to the work of Giovanni Bellini – looking purely for pleasure. And the more I studied the application form, the more I thought I too might apply for the job.

'Oh, don't,' she exclaimed. 'You'll get it instead of me.'

'Actually,' I said, 'neither of us is qualified, and neither of us will get it.'

It was on a day that she and I had agreed to meet in Brighton and visit the Royal Pavilion that I learnt of my appointment. Although I had thought my interview went strangely well, with much laughter from the interviewing board at some of my answers ('Had I considered going to the Courtauld Institute to study?' 'I've only just heard of the Courtauld Institute.'), I had never dared to expect this outcome.

Not until we were having lunch did Susan refer to the National Gallery, and I felt it was not for me to initiate the subject.

'You remember that job,' she remarked. 'Well, I had a letter this morning, telling me I hadn't got it.'

'I received one too,' I said. 'Telling me I had got it.'

Everybody looked round as she shrieked in the genteel hotel dining-room. But she forgave me, even for my previous silence. She generously said that I deserved it more than she did and that she had never really seen herself working in an art gallery or museum.

On that first Monday morning in December 1951, the attendant at the door asked me to wait while he notified the Chief Clerk. There was no waiting-room in those days so I stood nervously in the high stone vestibule until the Chief Clerk came to greet me, which he did with great, condescending suavity. Only much later would he mention that in his youth he had sometimes greeted and ushered into the Board Room Lord Curzon, then Chairman of the Trustees.

'Very affable he always was, the Marquess,' he told me. And I could sense that something of the manner lingered on.

He showed me into an austere, cell-like room that would be my office, and asked me to wait there. The Keeper, Mr Gibson, travelling up from the country, would arrive as usual in about an hour's time, at 11 a.m.

I sat at my small, empty desk and looked at the empty bookcase and listened to the silence. There was a telephone on the desk but it never rang and I could not think of anyone to ring.

When a big, burly man in a blue suit bustled amiably into the room, I was quite startled. I had begun to think my presence forgotten. He introduced himself and shook

hands heartily, and I heard again those agreeably plummy
tones of voice.

'Now,' he said, 'you must meet your colleagues.'

My colleagues: almost irrationally, though presciently,
I felt stirred by the words. As yet, I had no inkling of
what three of them would mean to me over the next
twenty or more years, of how they would teach me,
guide me, shape me and – best of all – give me their
friendship.

Nobody could have had inklings of any kind on that first
morning. Even the Keeper's voice, confidently discoursing
of this and that Gallery matter, very much as man to man,
faltered somewhat as we went from one office to another
– only to find them vacant.

That the Director was abroad, he had already explained.
Then there was a Deputy Keeper, Neil MacLaren, whose
handsome, spacious room I saw. But he himself, Mr Gibson
suddenly recalled, was absent on long leave, preparing a
catalogue of the Gallery's Spanish paintings. Adjoining my
office was that of Cecil Gould, the other Assistant Keeper.
He would normally be there by now but tended to come in
later on Monday mornings.

'Ah, Martin.' The Keeper seemed as relieved as I was to
encounter a living person as we approached another office.
'We were hoping to find you.'

Smiling sweetly, the slight, pale, elfin figure of Martin Davies, the other Deputy Keeper, greeted me with
touching friendliness, while gently murmuring, 'It *is* my
research day.'

His was a name I already knew, and I was in awe
of his scholarly reputation. I had read a long, respectful
review of his recently-published catalogue of the Earlier Italian Paintings – but not the catalogue. In fact,
I was none too clear what was meant by a catalogue.
And I had difficulty in equating massive scholarship with
his airy, scrupulously polite manner, as he took over
the task of showing me around the non-public parts of

the building. He assumed without quite enquiring that I had read a certain amount about, for instance, Italian painting.

'Oh, yes,' I responded. 'Yes, lots.'

His glance implied interest.

'Well, I've read all Berenson's books.'

'I trust you found them enlightening.'

Some nuance in his voice checked my enthusiasm – for the first but not the last time.

The gradual, subtle process of learning from him, and also about him, had begun. Before the day was over, I should have met Cecil Gould, who seemed at first acquaintance as aloof in manner as he was physically tall, with good looks to enhance his superior air. And a few weeks later the door of my room was thrown open and a plumpish, bald-headed man whirled in energetically, declaring loudly, 'I'm Neil MacLaren'.

So the trio, then constituting the complete curatorial staff of the Gallery, received their new colleague – each in his own characteristic way. Of course, it would take them and me time to establish *rapport*. But once established, it could only deepen, and now that I alone survive I see the actual, carefully-chosen gifts each of them gave me when I got married as symbolic of all they were to give me intangibly but unfailingly during the decades ahead. Nor shall I ever forget what I owe them.

When I first rang the bell and stepped across the threshold of the office entrance of the National Gallery, I was entering on my life proper. It was too soon for me to comprehend the full extent of my good fortune: that I had entered an environment privileged yet not rarefied, one demanding and consistently practical, where close daily contact with personalities who were intellectually able, aesthetically acute, to me kind and ever-hospitable, was intimately linked to close daily contact with and responsibility for supreme works of visual art.

I should find useful, on occasion, such lore as I had

acquired during all the years of Roman Catholic immersion. But the system had never engaged my intelligence, and probably its hold was slipping imperceptibly before I confronted the facts. Possession of a real life, a real occupation – and real love – combined to give impetus to the activity my whole upbringing and education had been intended to suppress: thinking for myself.

Once more, this time only metaphorically but with permanent effect, the chapel was on fire.